ALFREDO CASELLA - VIRGILIO MORTARI

THE TECHNIQUE OF CONTEMPORARY ORCHESTRATION

(Second revised edition)

English Translation with Contemporary Applications
by
Thomas V. Fraschillo

RICORDI

E. R. 2935

Title of the original italian edition:
La tecnica dell'orchestra contemporanea
Casa Ricordi - BMG RICORDI (Milano)

Produced and distributed by:
BMG PUBLICATIONS S.r.l.
via Liguria 4
Frazione Sesto Ulteriano
20098 San Giuliano Milanese (Milano) - IT

with permission of:
Casa Ricordi - BMG RICORDI S.p.A.

© Copyright 1950 by BMG Ricordi S.p.A. for the original italian edition
Tutti i diritti riservati - All rights reserved
2004 - Printed in Italy

© Copyright 2004 by BMG Ricordi S.p.A. for the English translation
Tutti i diritti riservati - All rights reserved
2004 - Printed in Italy

ISBN 88-7592-771-5

E.R. 2935

To my good friends and mentors
William J. Moody and Luigi Zaninelli
on whose shoulders I have leaned for many years

"Siamo nani," ammise Guglielmo, "ma nani che stanno sulle spalle di quei giganti, e nella nostra pochezza riusciamo talora a vedere più lontano di loro sull'orizzonte."

Umberto Eco - *Il nome della rosa*

"We are dwarfs," admitted Guglielmo, "but dwarfs who stand on the shoulders of those giants, and in our insignificance we are able then to see further than they over the horizon."

Umberto Eco - *The Name of the Rose*

Foreword to the Translation

No effort of this magnitude is ever undertaken alone. In that light, I would like to thank Brad Snow, Doctoral Candidate in Conducting, for his untiring efforts with the placing of the examples in the text. I am likewise indebted to my associates in Italy, namely Fulvio Creux, conductor, *La Banda dell'Esercito*, the Italian Army Band, in Rome; Angelo Bolciaghi, one of my graduate students and a great colleague; and my teacher Anna Chiarenza without whose never ending advice in the wonderful Italian language I could not function.

Finally, I would like to thank those at BMG Ricordi, Milan, Dr. Ilaria Narici, Editor Classical Repertoire & Special Projects, for the opportunity to explore the wonderful work of Casella-Mortari.

Thomas V. Fraschillo

This translation was made possible through the assitance of the
Ministry of Foreign Affairs of the Italian Government
with a grant to the translator, Thomas V. Fraschillo.

Preface

The present work is designed to be a practical and up-to-date manual that concentrates on the technical and expressive possibilities of the instruments in the contemporary orchestra. The text does not enter in-depth into the art of true orchestration, for that requires diligent work, knowledge, and the study of the scores of great composers, all assisted by an expert teacher.

By relying on personal experiences and on the experiences of colleagues, Alfredo Casella and I drafted the work in close collaboration during 1945-46. Casella, unfortunately, died before being able to see the volume published; therefore, it was left to me to execute the scrupulous and careful examination of the final proof.

The text was supposed to have been dedicated to a teacher of orchestration; however, since nothing had been definitely proposed, I took the liberty of dedicating my efforts in creating the work to the memory of my great friend.

Being also mindful of our collaboration, I provided for the recognition of the valuable specialists, whose names are listed, for their advice that strengthened and guaranteed our effort.

Rome, July 1948   V. M.

CONSULTANTS

FLUTE AND PICCOLO – Professor Renato Paci, first flute in the Orchestra dell'Accademia di S. Cecilia, Rome; Arrigo Tassinari, teacher in the Conservatorio di S. Cecilia, Rome; Gastone Tassinari, Milan.

OBOE – Professor Sidney Gallesi, first oboe in the Orchestra della Radio, Rome; Riccardo Scozzi, first oboe in the Orchestra dell'Accademia di S. Cecilia, Rome, and teacher in the Conservatorio di S. Cecilia, Rome.

ENGLISH HORN – Professor Enrico Wolf-Ferrari, English horn in the Orchestra dell'Accademia di S. Cecilia, Rome.

CLARINET – Professor Fernando Gambacurta, first clarinet in the Orchestra dell'Accademia di S. Cecilia, Rome; Giacomo Gandini, first clarinet in the Orchestra della Radio, Rome; Carlo Luberti, teacher in the Conservatorio di S. Cecilia, Rome.

BASSOON AND CONTRABASSOON – Professor Rosario Gioffreda, first bassoon in the Orchestra dell'Accademia di S. Cecilia, Rome; Aldo Montanari, first bassoon in the Orchestra del Teatro alla Scala and teacher in the Conservatorio G. Verdi, Milan; Carlo Tentoni, first bassoon in the Orchestra dell Radio and teacher in the Conservatorio di S. Cecilia, Rome.

HORN – Professor Domenico Ceccarossi, first horn in the Orchestra della Radio, Rome; Antonio Marchi, first horn in the Orchestra dell'Accademia di S. Cecilia, Rome.

TRUMPET, TROMBONE, FLICORNO, AND TUBA – Professor Pietro Muzzi, teacher in the Conservatorio di S. Cecilia, Rome.

SAXOPHONE – Professor Baldo Maestri, Rome; Alfredo Mari, Rome.

TIMPANI AND PERCUSSION – Professor Luigi Pellegrini, timpanist in the Orchestra della Radio, Rome.

HARP – Professor Clelia Aldrovandi, Rome.

HARPSICHORD – Professor Ruggero Gerlin, teacher in the Conservatorio di S. Pietro in Majella, Naples.

VIOLIN – Professor Vittorio Emanuele, first violin in the Orchestra della Radio, Rome.

VIOLA AND VIOLA D'AMORE – Professor Renzo Sabatini, teacher in the Conservatorio di San Pietro in Majella, Naples.

VIOLONCELLO – Professor Massimo Anfitheatrof, Rome; Antonio Janigro, teacher in the Conservatorio di Zagabria, Yugoslavia; Giuseppe Selmi, first violoncello in the Orchestra della Radio, Rome.

CONTRABASSO – Professor Tito Bartoli, teacher in the Conservatorio di S. Cecilia, Rome; Domenico Mancini, first contrabass in the Orchestra di S. Cecilia, Rome.

ACOUSTICS – Dr. Ginestra Amaldi, Rome.

JAZZ – Maestro Luigi Colacicchi, music critic.

THE SOUND

All of the sounds and all of the noises that we hear always come from some source that produces them. This source is called the sound source (*sorgente sonora*). Because the sound is transmitted, it is necessary that the source vibrate quite rapidly, completing at least 16 oscillations per second.

The sound spreads through air, any solid, or liquid body. In the air the sound moves with a velocity of 340 meters per second.

When a body vibrates, it does so in oscillatory motion around a position of equilibrium occupied when the body does not vibrate. The particles of air that are found in the immediate vicinity of the source are subjected to an alternated succession of rarefaction and compression and are transmitted one to the other by going away in all directions with the velocity of the propagation of the sound, i.e., with a velocity of 340 meters per second. It is a spherical wave, subdivided in alternative compressed and rarefacted layers that always continue in space.

Figure 1

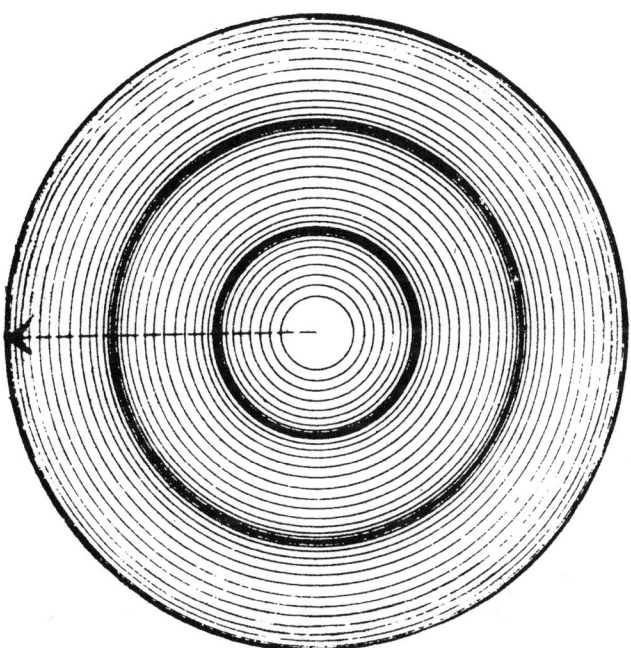

Characteristics of sounds

The characteristics that distinguish one sound from another can be reduced to three; intensity, i.e., that characteristic for which one sound is strong or weak according to the amplitude of the vibration; the height, that distinguishes the low sounds from those high ones according to the length of the wave; and timbre, for which sounds of the same height and intensity can be of diverse color.

Vibrating strings

A common sound source to many musical instruments is the string. For example, a violin string is placed between two points A and B (fig. 2). If it is plucked or excited with a bow, it begins to vibrate and one hears a sound: below in the form of a spindle. Points A and B of the string that remain in place are called nodes. he middle point, M, in which the vibration has the greatest width is called the loop.

F. 2

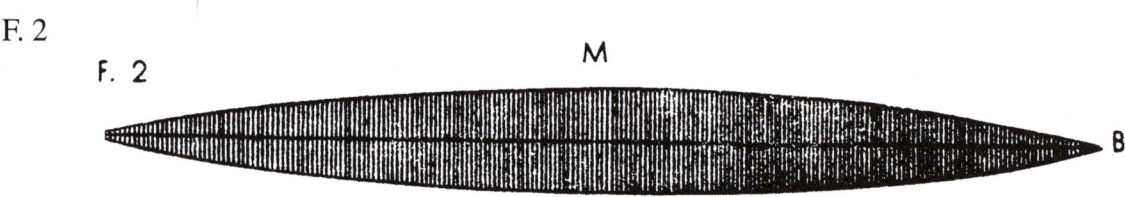

Harmonic sounds

When a string vibrates as in figure 2, with two lateral nodes and a loop, one says that it renders the fundamental sound. If, therefore, one lightly places a finger at the mid point, C (fig. 3), one sees that the string, if it is put in vibration, forms two spindles and point C remains still. Three nodes appear (in points A, C, B) and two loops in the midpoints of the segments AC and CB.

F. 3

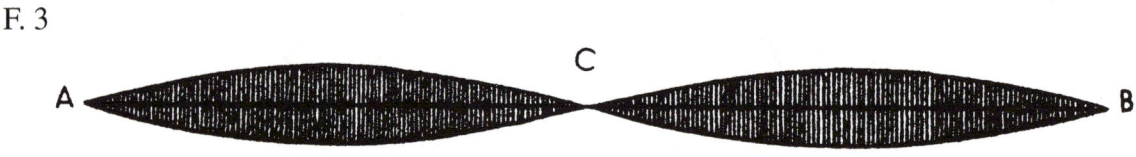

If, instead, one lightly places a finger at point D (fig. 4), a third of the length appears, the vibrating string breaks into three equal spindles, and then possesses four nodes A, B, C, D. ith the preceding analogies one can realize that the string divides in more than three equal segments that vibrate. The sound that vibrates as in figure 2 is called the fundamental sound. The produced sounds when the string divides in two or more segments are called the harmonics.

F. 4

The produced harmonic in the case in which the vibrating string divides itself into two spindles, has a wave length equal to one half of the wave length of the fundamental. The produced harmonic in the case in which the string divides in three spindles has a wave length equal to one third of that of the fundamental sound; and so forth.

Assuming the low C of the fourth string of the violoncello as the fundamental sound (that is referred to as the first sound [Note: or fundamental as it is generally referred to today]) the following is the harmonic series (called sounds [partial] 2, sounds 3, etc.) based on C.

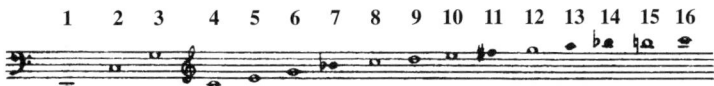

N.B. - The sounds 7, 11, 13, 14 are of imprecise intonation. The sounds 7 and 14 are flat, the sound 11 occurs between F and F♯, the sound 13 occurs between G and A.

In general, therefore, a vibrating string never assumes only one of the corresponding forms to the fundamental sound or to its harmonic sounds. Assuming that it vibrates the fundamental sound, the string also produces the harmonics. Its vibration, therefore, is a superimposition of various vibrations: that of the fundamental sound and those of its harmonics. Naturally the fundamental sound predominates.

It is interesting to note that the timbre depends on the quantity and the intensity of the harmonics that accompany the fundamental sound. By being able to equalize the order number and the quantity of the harmonics, a light variation in the intensity of any one of these suffices in order to determine sensitive timbral differences in the sound. The more the sound is lacking in harmonics, the more the timbre will be inexpressive and empty (a typical example is the diapason sound, absolutely pure and without harmonics). Yet an adequate number of harmonics, especially if consonant, will provide a full and vigorous timbre.

Sounding tubes

If one blows through a thin aperture into a tube, setting in vibration the air inside the tube, one hears a sound the highness of which depends on the length of the tube.

All the wind instruments are sonorous tubes. In them the air is put in vibration by the breath of the player. As with a string, the tube can produce either the fundamental sound or its harmonics.

A tube, therefore, behaves in a way essentially different according to whether it has both the ends opened or a closed end and an opened end. In fact in the first case (the opened end), the air is free to vibrate, in these two points therefore one finds two loops; in the second case, however, the closed end must for strength find a node. Because the air at that point is stopped, it must form a loop at the open end.

A conventional figure represents the state of vibration of the air in the inside of a tube. The point in which the dotted lines meet represents a node, i.e., a point in which the particles of air are stopped while the points in which the dotted lines reach their maximum distance represent a loop in which the air is put in sensitive agitation. This is referred to as "consonance" (that space in the spindle comprised between two nodes).

Open tubes. At the two extremes of the tube there will always be two loops. When the air contained in the tube vibrates with the correct wave length of the fundamental sound, one node forms in the inside of the tube. The vibrating state of the air is represented as in figure 5.

F. 5

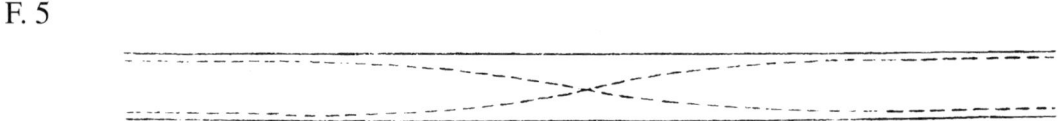

We then have two half consonances with a loop at each extremity of the tube and a node in the middle; in truth, therefore, we have one complete consonance.

But if instead, with a different pressure of the lip, one produces the first harmonic that corresponds to a wave length equal to half of that of the fundamental sound, the state of vibration of the air in the inside of the tube cannot be that which is represented by fig. 6. Since, as was pointed out previously, at the two extremes of the tube, two loops must be present.

F. 6

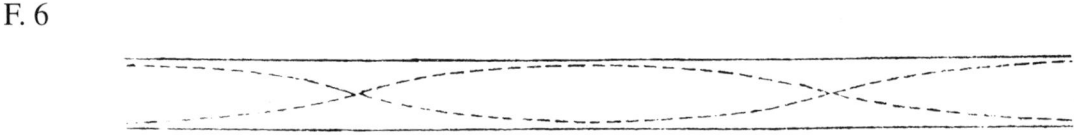

An internal consonance in the center of the tube and two half consonances at the sides result, therefore, in two complete consonances.

For the second harmonic there will be three nodes and, as usual, two loops at the extremes. (fig. 7);

F. 7

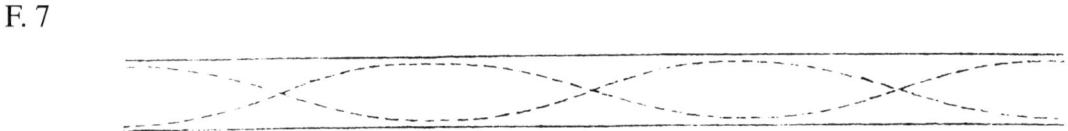

Three entire consonances appear, and so forth in following.

Therefore, in an open tube we can have either one consonance, two, three, or four. The tube can emit either the fundamental note or its harmonics.

Closed tubes, i.e., that are closed at an extremity. Since at the closed extremity there cannot be any movement of the air, a node appears. The open extremity then is usually a loop. The air in the inside of the tube will be able to vibrate only as is represented in fig. 8, and for the fundamental sound one will have only a half consonance.

F. 8

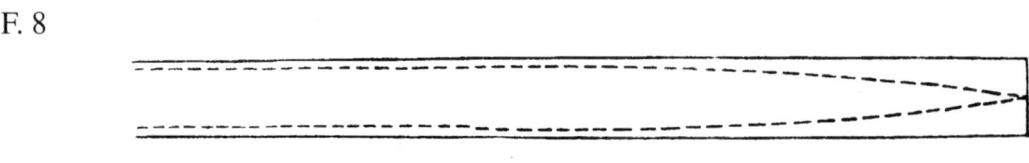

With a different pressure of the lip the tube produces harmonics. It, however, cannot produce, as an open tube, all the harmonics of the fundamental sound, but only the third, the fifth, etc., i.e., only the odd harmonics. Since the gradual pressures of the lip produce successively three half consonances (fig. 9),

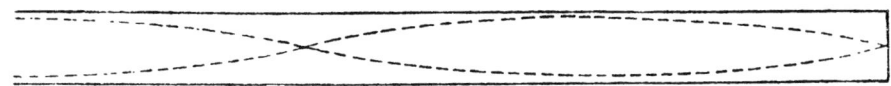

the sound of the wave length equals to one third of that of the fundamental sound. With the five half consonances, as shown in fig. 10, the sound of the wave length equals to one fifth of that of the fundamental sound, etc.

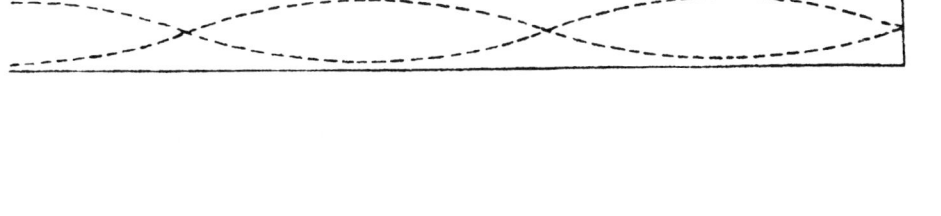

Harmonics of open tubes:

Harmonics of closed tubes:

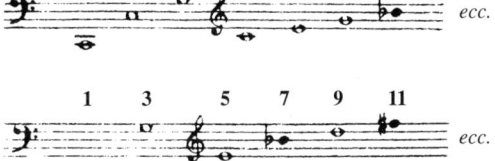

So that the column of air can begin vibrating, it must be broken or, in some way, excited when it enters the tube. Ways of putting the column of air in vibration are different.

In the instruments at the mouth, e.g. the flute, (*istrumenti a bocca*), the breath of the player excites the column of air breaking it against the edge of a small circular and longitudinal aperture, called the mouth plate (*appunto bocca*). In the reed instruments (*istrumenti ad ancia*) (oboe, clarinet, etc.) the column of air vibrates by means of the oscillatory movement of the single or double reed (*ancia semplice o ancia doppia*), excited by the breath of the player. In the instruments with mouthpieces (*istrumenti a bocchino*) (horn, trumpet, etc.) the lips of the player by vibrating under the influence of the air, function as a double reed.

The wind instruments are all open tubes (and produce, therefore, the harmonics in their normal order), but the clarinet, although an open tube, functions as a closed tube and gives only the odd harmonics (1, 3, 5, 7. . .). The reasons for this are complex, but, undoubtedly, they result in the concurrences that interact between the reed and the internal form of the tube, that, for most of its length, is cylindrical.

THE FLUTE

The old transverse flute, heir to a lengthy bucolic and Hellenic heritage that recalls a certain pastoral feeling, has, after a period of relative disfavor with Wagner and his disciples, suddenly experienced notable developments. These developments are found not only in the area of its expressive possibilities as it functions in the orchestra, but also in its newly discovered technical virtuosity.

The system of holes and keys is that of the German, Theobald Böhm (1794-1881). It is this principal and cylindrical tube construction that provide good intonation, according to equal temperament, for all of the tone holes. To this system, however, even more modifications have been made in the last half century. Today the flute offers few difficulties that can be attributed to the construction of the instrument.

Range

Within these limits today the performer knows how to find the correct fingerings, so that all of the notes give an expressive and uned result with sufficient exactness, either at the *piano* or *forte* level. Only the highest two notes ( ) are very difficult at the dynamic of *piano*.

Some flutes descend to the see Respighi: *Pini di Roma*, p. 56, or Schönberg: *Pierrot lunaire*, p. 72.

More frequently, the highest limit of range is exceeded. It is not rare now to see the and in Stravinsky's *Jeu de cartes*, p. 101, there is often an . These notes render violent and inexpressive sounds especially above the "D♯". Their use, therefore, must be carefully controlled.

Timbre

On the flute one is able to distinguish the following registers: the low, that produces all of the fundamental sounds; the middle, formed from the first harmonic of the tones in the low register; and the high, formed by the second harmonic of the fundamental tones comprised in the range ; and the very high register formed by the corresponding harmonics to tones 3, 4, and 5 (see the opening chapter on the sound).

example of the registers:

The flute has a timbre quite homogeneous, so that the characteristics of one register merge themselves with those of the next register if the passage between one register and the other happens gradually. More noticeable, instead, is the difference when one goes from the lowest to the highest, or vice versa, by means of a large interval (an octave or more). The flute has a clear and transparent timbre. While from the medium register one ascends toward the highest, the sonority always becomes more brilliant, until it is forced and quite "whistling" in the three notes of the extreme range.

The low register has a warmer timbre than the others and its mysterious intensity has been much exploited by modern composers.

I. Pizzetti: *La sacra rappresentazione di Abramo e d'Isacco*, p. 74. Ed: Ricordi

Cl. Debussy: *Iberia*, p. 68. Ed: Durand

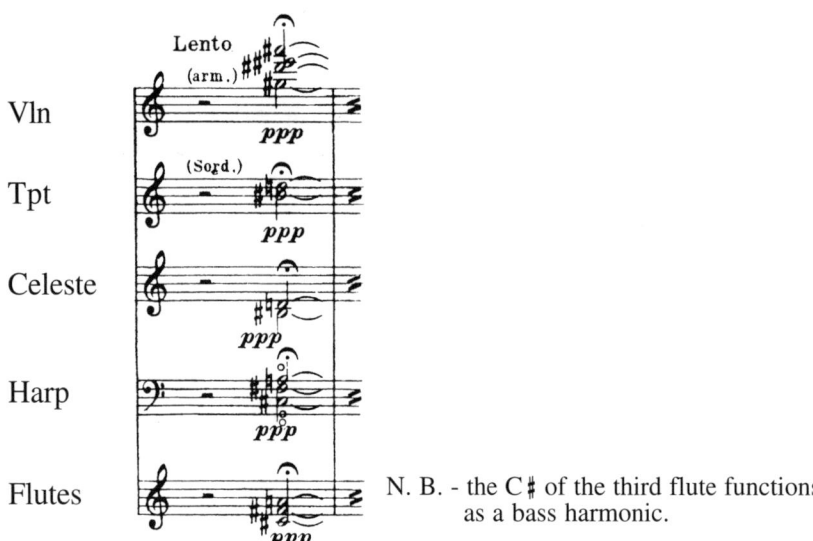

A. Casella: *A notte alta*, p. 61. Ed: Ricordi

A. Tansman: *Quatre danses polonaises*, p. 12. Ed: Max Eschig

A. Casella: *Il convento veneziano*, "Notturno", p. 73. Ed: Ricordi.

The orchestrator has often directed particular attention to the flute, and among the many examples, here are two of the most famous.

Cl. Debussy: *Prelude à "L'après-midi d'un faune"*, p. 5 and following. Ed: Jobert

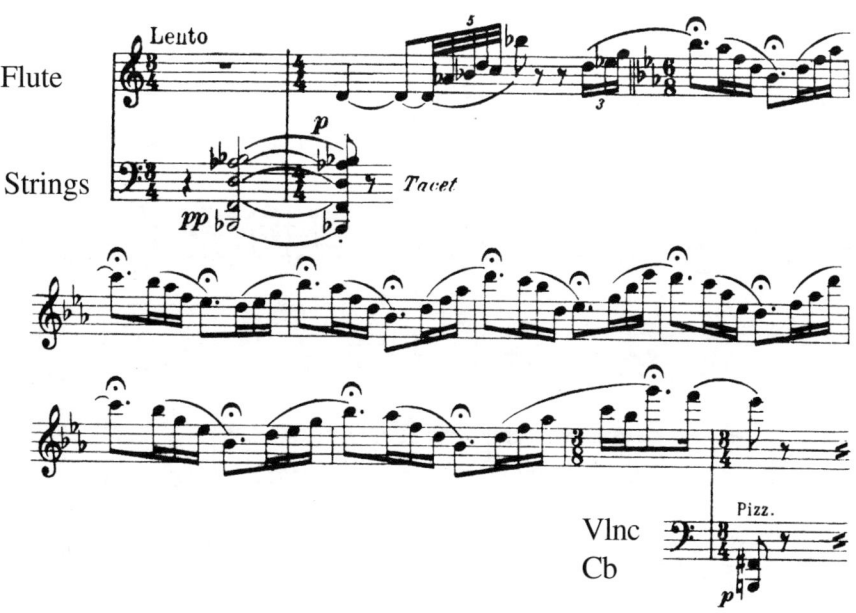

I. Stravinsky: *Petrouchka*, p. 41. Ed: Russe de Musique

Trills

Today all major and minor trills are possible with good result in the following range:  but these major trills are produced imperfectly (the second is quite harsh) and these other two are difficult: all four are not advised at a *piano* dynamic and are better if used in a passage in which more quantity than quality of sound is required. Some exceptional performers, however, know how to perform the following trill softly:

This trill , impossible not many years ago, today is done by the use of a special key found on many instruments. This key, however, makes the following tremolo quite difficult and almost impossible: . For this tremolo it would be necessary to add another special key, but such a key would make the following trill almost impossible: . Some flutes, then, are equipped with a mechanical device so as to be able to produce both the above examples, but such devices create other problems.

Tremolos

(x) complicated and tedious, a little difficult
(xx) "lazy," very tedious, difficult
(xxx) of poor effect, quite difficult

(1) see preceding paragraph
(2) the E tends to be flat

(3) the G♯ tends to be flat
(4) the A♭ tends to be flat
(5) it is better played *forte*

N. B. The abnormalities of the defective tremolos are more evident at *forte*, but are negligible if not exposed, i.e., in orchestral playing if they do not play an important role.

As the interval widens, the tremolo will tend to become less rapid. Octave tremolos cannot be rapid, for they are not true tremolos. The flautist performs them by tying the notes as indicated in this example.

In tremolos with notes above the [staff figure], i.e., that use harmonics, the fundamental harmonic can also often be heard. This defect is often more evident the wider the interval.

The high tremolos are possible with special harmonic fingerings.

Harmonics

Since the use of harmonics is a normal part of the technique of the instrument, the indication *suoni armonici* (harmonics) for the flute is not always clear. In truth, the player, when reading such indications only will produce different harmonics from the usual ones; e.g., sounds found in the following range [staff figure] if they are indicated as *suoni armonici*, harmonics, are played with the third harmonic rather than, as we know, with the second. The result is detrimental to intonation, i.e., the so called "harmonics" will be flat. Maybe it is exactly for their slight defect of intonation that they produce a special sweet, almost ethereal and transparent color. Stravinsky in *Le Sacre du printemps* discovered a cold and almost enchanted sonority by combining a chord of flute harmonics with another chord given to the harmonics of the divided contrabasses, and placed above the contrabasses in a different key. [In the following example the notes indicated with an "o" in the flute are sounding. Ideally the composer should write the fundamental note to be fingered in order to produce the harmonic.]

I. Stravinsky: *Le Sacre du printemps*, p. 77. Ed: Russe de Musique

Slurring

The flute is among the most agile instruments. All scales, arpeggios, and many wide intervals are possible, and often easily executed. There is no difficulty, at least until the middle register, performing rapid passages of alternating octaves. There are, therefore, infinite possibilities, that the following examples display.

I. Stravinsky: *Le Sacre du printemps*, p. 139. Ed: Russe de Musique

A. Schönberg: *Fünf Orchesterstücke*, p. 51. Ed: Universal Edition

Fünf Orchesterstücke, p. 42

A. Schönberg: *Pierrot lunaire*, p. 71. Ed: Universal Edition

Pierrot lunaire, pp. 16-17

One notes that with the flute, as with the rest of the wind instruments in general, it is easier to slur ascending intervals than descending ones.

The following notes: are quite difficult to slur, either ascending or descending, and above all in rapid passages. Some instruments, however, are equipped with the means to perform such slurs easily.

Tonguing

Tonguing on the flute can reach almost the level of agility of bowing on the violin. It is possible to use three types of tonguing: single, double, and triple.

The single tongue that is obtained by pronouncing the consonant "t" produces a robust and energetic sound. It, however, cannot be very rapid.

From ♩=112 one can reach starting from up to 16th notes at a quarter note ♩ = 120.

From the and higher the articulation is less agile.

Double tonguing, instead, permits adding a tempo up to 16th notes at a quarter note ♩ = 140, in the first 4 notes above, and in the middle and high register up to 16th notes at a quarter note ♩ = 160 and more. Above the agility diminishes. Double tonguing is accomplished by pronouncing alternately the two consonants "t" and "k", and it is extremely useful for rapid passages, above all for repeated notes. One should note that it does not have the same clarity of the single tongue.

The triple tongue is accomplished by pronouncing successively this group of three consonants: "tkt, tkt, etc." It is suitable for very fast groups of three, but it is less equal to the preceding articulations. There is a tendency to lean on the first note of each group. It can reach tempos up to: = circa triplets at 138.

It is difficult, above all at the *piano*, the rapid tonguing of the notes included in the following range: and above the .

M. Ravel: *Alborado del gracioso*, p. 10. Ed: Eschig

Easily performed octave leaps on the flute.

M. Ravel: *Daphnis et Chloè*, "Pantomine". Ed: Durand

E.R. 2935

Double tongued notes with an airy character

Cl. Debussy: *Pelléas et Mélisande*, p. 141. Ed: Durand

I. Stravinsky: *Dumbarton Oaks*, p. 24. Ed: Schott

Note: The short slur that one frequently finds in this work, other than having an expressive function, serves to let the lip rest since the passage contains rapidly tongued notes for many measures. One notes, then, the interesting short rests for the musical dialogue and their usefulness as breathing points for the player.

Flutter tonguing *(suoni frullati, flatterzunge, tremolo dental)*

One produces this technique by fluttering the tongue in a certain way that results in notes of undetermined value and tempo as in a dense and rapid tremolo. For the most part it is for special effect, but at times it has been also used in expressive passages.

The flutter tongue in the low register is easier at *piano*, while in the upper registers it is easier at *forte*.

M. Ravel: *L'Enfant et les sortilèges*, p. 67. Ed: Durand

A. Schönberg: *Pierrot lunaire*, p. 72. Ed: Universal Edition

V. Mortari: *L'allegra piazzetta*. Ed: Carisch S. A.

Breathing

The flute demands a great amount of air. It is necessary, therefore, that the composer not impose on the performer passages of lengthy notes and phrases without the possibility of taking frequent and adequate breaths.

The greatest length of a low C (the low register demands far more air) is around 8 seconds at *forte* and around 15 seconds at *piano*. As one ascends, the possibilities of length of the note become greater and above the  they reach 12 seconds at *forte* and 20 seconds at *piano*. In the extremes, the lip strain makes it difficult to sustain the sounds at great length, above all at *piano*.

Some uses of the flute:

1. Flutes in the low register balanced with a soft sound of the muted trumpet in the low register.

Flute

Trumpet (with mute)

M. Ravel: *L'heure espagnole*, p. 125. Ed: Durand

2. A curious mixing of the flutes with the muted trumpet.

Flute

Trumpet (with mute)

Cl. Debussy: *Pelléas et Mélisande*, p. 409. Ed: Durand

E.R. 2935

3. Flutes as trumpets in the distance.

G. Petrassi: *Concerto per orchestra.* Ed: Ricordi

4. The sweet pizzicato of the harp accompanies well the timbre of the flute.

Cl. Debussy: *Nuages*, p. 12. Ed: Jobert

The flute in the low register adds a particular softness to the bassoon in the following example of Ravel.

Note the different written nuances (flute *ff*, bassoon *f*) so that the timbre of the bassoon in a sonorous register would not overpower that of the flute, quite soft in the low register.

M. Ravel: *Concerto in G major for piano and orchestra*, p. 72. Ed: Durand

THE PICCOLO
(Ottavino or flauto piccolo)

As with the flute, the piccolo's mechanism is that of the Böhm system.

Range

The useful range begins with the low D. The low C, therefore, is possible only on some instruments.

Generally on the piccolo the highest B is difficult to execute, and on some instruments it lacks credibility.

The piccolo sounds one octave higher than the written note.

Timbre

The piccolo continues the range of the flute in its extreme register, but it does not have the same expressive tone quality as the flute.

The low register is weak and difficult, and it would be advisable to substitute it with the corresponding much more warm register of the flute. The medium and high registers, instead, are brilliant and the last octave can be extremely sonorous.

Once limited to the purely mechanical functions of doubling an octave above more expressive instruments, the piccolo has grown in esteem in the last twenty years among composers who have given it a greater autonomy and importance. Ravel did not hesitate to give to it the principal theme of the first movement of his *Concerto per pianoforte e orchestra* by highlighting its thin sonorous quality in an orchestration of the greatest lightness and transparency.

M. Ravel: *Concerto in G major for piano and orchestra*, pp. 30-31. Ed: Durand

All that was said about the flute as to trills, tremolos, slurs, tonguing, etc. is the same for the piccolo. It has the same mechanism except in smaller proportions.

The following example will demonstrate the level of virtuosity that can be achieved today by this instrument.

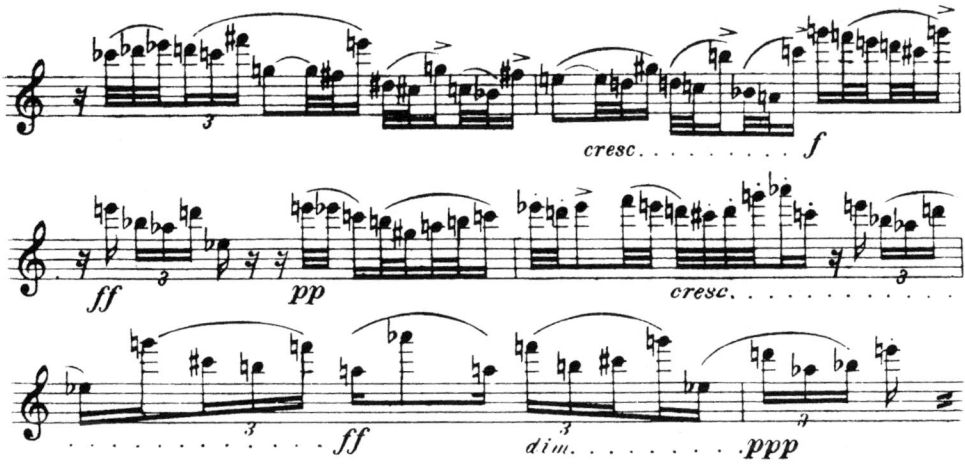

A. Schönberg: *Pierrot lunaire*, pp. 61-63. Ed: Universal

Flutter tonguing, as on the flute, is no longer limited to only decorative effects. Ravel, in the example below from the previous *Concerto*, used it in an expressive phrase.

An abundant use and abuse has been made of the piccolo by using it to double the melody at two or more octaves above.

Cl. Debussy: *Iberia*, p. 49. Ed: Durand

Note that the lower octave of the melody is given to two performers in order to strengthen the sound of the flute in the low register in a way that its timbre can have sufficient strength to balance the second clarinet sounding in the same tessitura.

E.R. 2935

This icy quality is quite effective for the dramatic situation:

A. Catalani: *La Wally*, preludio del IV atto. Ed: Ricordi

Debussy, in the Spanish atmosphere colored and illuminated by rhythmic and sonorous play, obtained an effect with the bassoon, and the piccolo playing two octaves above.

Cl. Debussy: *Iberia*, p. 6. Ed: Durand

THE ALTO FLUTE

(flauto d'amore) (flute in F or flute in G)

The alto flute is a valuable instrument that still is not normally used (Note: in Casella's time). It is tuned in F or in G so that its sounding pitch is a fifth or a fourth below the written note.

Range

(1) The most effective register

Range in G:

Range in F:

The most useful register is the lowest because it adds an expressive quality to the lowest register of the normal flute. No instrument can be more effective than the alto flute for the following cantilena:

I. Stravinsky: *Le Sacre du printemps*, p. 81. Ed: Russe de Musique

And more noticeably in *Le Sacre du printemps* is the beautiful sonority of the alto flute in G in the low register and in the same tessitura of the English Horn, with the chordal background of horns *punzecchiati* (teased) by pizzicato strings and by the percussion.

Also in the same work, the following is a wonderful example of the alto flute in G with the E♭ clarinet two octaves above.

An example follows of the flute in G that continues a descending scale of the piccolo and of the ordinary flute.

M. Ravel: *Daphnis et Chloé*, "Pantomime", pp. 60-61. Ed: Durand

The same techniques that have been described for the flute apply as well to the alto flute.

BASS FLUTE (OR BASS FLUTE IN C) [1]

The bass flute is tuned an octave below the ordinary flute. The most useful sounds are those of the lowest register, but are not very effective. Its production is not easy and requires much air, therefore, tiring the performer after only a few measures.

The use of the bass flute is quite rare, and it is still more rare to locate an instrument and moreover a player who can and has the desire to play it.

R. Zandonai: *Francesca da Rimini*, p. 27. Ed: Ricordi

---
(1) Called the *Albisiphon* since it was created by the previously mentioned Prof. Albisi.

OBOE

In the last forty years the characteristics of the oboe have not changed significantly. While its fundamental qualities reached a strong development for new means of expression during this time, its essential physical features remain almost unaltered and it continues to be the principal means for expression in the woodwinds. This fact is in part due to the oboe's having been influenced for only a short time period by jazz, and, therefore, did not undergo – from that most powerful forceful alteration – the evolution, for example, of the clarinet and the trumpet.

The holes, the keys, and the chamber of the modern oboe are arranged according to two principal systems: the Italian system and the French Lorèe system. The most used is the French system, which however – as all other wind instruments – has undergone technical modifications according to the countries and the needs of the performer. Each performer is also part of the technique of his instrument. An oboist, above all in Italy, would find it difficult to play on reeds different from those that he made or adapted to his taste (the excitation of the air column depends on the reed, and therefore, the quality of the sound is sensitive to the means by which it is produced).

Worthy of great interest is the oboe invented by Professor Riccardo Scozzi of the Conservatory in Rome and by the instrument maker (technician) Spartaco Incagnoli. It is an oboe that unites in one instrument the Italian and French systems; however, its use has not been widespread and largely accepted.

The most used system in the world is the Lorèe and on this system all of the following is based.

Range

The low B♭ is quite difficult to attack at *piano*: The robust sound is one that is not easily manipulated. The low D♭ has about the same characteristics as the low B♭. In general, all the notes in this tessitura  are difficult to attack and sustain at *piano*.

Above one loses the characteristics of the oboe, the timbre is modified, and the sound becomes poor. In all practicality the F♯ is considered the normal high limit.

The G♯ above is a non-timbral sound and most difficult to attack.

Above the notes are difficult to reach from an interval greater than a minor second and always more difficult the greater the interval. For this reason the following passage is not advised.

I. Stravinsky: *Jeu de cartes*, p. 45. Ed: Schott

All the other sounds can be considered of homogeneous timbre and of satisfactory intonation. The performer knows how to correct, with the lip or special fingerings, eventual defects of the instrument.

Timbre

The oboe has a very soft timbre that is a somewhat nasal in quality, related to that of the bagpipe. It is sweet, almost effeminate, a kind of "melancholy soprano" of the orchestra. The nasal quality augments as much as it strengthens the sound.

According to the physical nature of the sounds we can distinguish a low register (registro grave), formed by the fundamental sounds, a middle register (registro medio), formed by the second sounds of the low register, and a high register (registro acuto), built by the higher harmonics.[1]

The first major sixth of the low register is coarse, intense, and penetrating. As it ascends from to the high register, the timbre becomes continuously sweeter and softer.

Above the sound becomes thinner and loses some of the oboe's characteristic timbre, as well as its expressive quality.

Movement from one register to another is not noticeable, unless the lowest notes that have special characteristics are in use. The color of the oboe is so ingratiating that it acquires importance easily; therefore, it is necessary to take into careful consideration timbral relationships. Not having great varieties of color nor technical resources, the oboe has not been exploited as much as, for example, the flute or the clarinet. It is, however, in its roles, such that no instrument could equally be as effective. Nothing is more appropriate, in the opera *Fra Gherardo* by Pizzetti, than the oboes that sing sadly coupled with a sonority of strings.

(1) In order to facilitate playing the harmonics, the oboe is equipped with a mechanism called the "*portavoce*" or octave key mechanism. The first octave key serves the notes between , the second, the notes between . For the very highest notes one must use different fingerings that may or may not use the octave keys.

In the past the oboe has not deviated from its function as an expressive instrument. Nevertheless, in recent years, its agility has been greatly extended, almost competing with the flute and the clarinet. This is due in part to technical advancements in its construction and in part due to the extraordinary virtuosity reached by the performers.

M. Ravel: *Concerto in G major for piano and orchestra*, p. 33. Ed: Durand

M. Ravel: *Daphnis et Chloé*, p. 7. Ed: Durand

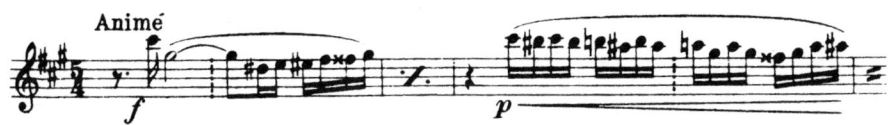

Daphnis et Chloé, pp. 81-82

M. Ravel: *Rapsodie espagnole*, p. 55. Ed: Durand

The top note, G, reached by a great leap and at a rapid tempo is very difficult. The passage is doubled in the flute that compensates, in part, for the eventual uncertainty of the oboe.

Trills

Trills are possible and effective either at *piano* or at *forte*. All of the major and minor trills are possible in the following range:

The trills using the lowest notes are less easy, and their execution depends much on the kind (quality) of the instrument and certainly on the ability of the performer.

Tremolos

(x) difficult (xx) very difficult, complicated, of poor quality
N.B. - Tremolos omitted are impossible or inadvisable due to their poor quality.

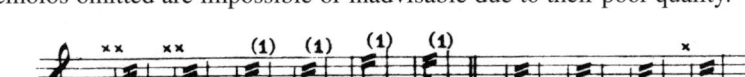

(1) harsh; (2) poor effect; (3) possible with special devices not always available; (4) D♯ out of tune (5) good at *piano* (6) these tremolos are facilitated – or in the case of the most difficult, remain possible – on oboes provided with the so called "automatic octave key"; (7) with special harmonic fingerings. As for the rest, for the highest tremolos one must employ special fingerings. In general, the possibilities or the ease of performance of the tremolos depends much, besides the kind and quality of the instrument, on the commitment of the performer to know how to find suitable fingerings. It is not improbable, therefore, that some performers have different possibilities from those indicated in the above table.

The tremolos with notes above the , i.e., those that employ harmonics, sometimes also produce the fundamental sound, but the result, usually, is less evident than on the flute.

For the oboe, as for the flute, the anomaly of defective trills, is more evident at *forte* than at the *piano*, but such anomalies are overcome when the oboe does not have an exposed passage to perform.

As the interval grows larger, the tremolo tends to become less rapid. At times the rapid repetition of slurred notes two by two is possible; therefore, tremolos indicated previously as difficult or unplayable can become accessible. Here is an example:

Harmonics

That which was said about harmonics on the flute is applicable to the oboe. The various harmonics in practical use produce excellent results, and often due to their inaccurate intonation, are used for special effects. That such harmonics are ever indicated by composers is unsure; however, by knowing how to benefit from their qualities, one can obtain sweet and effeminate as well as cold and enchanting effects. The best tessitura for these is the following:

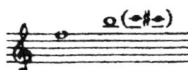

Slurring

The oboe is generally more adapted to expressive and *cantabile* passages than to those that demand technique. In rapid passages, movement on the instrument is made easier by writing in a scale-wise manner and/or arpeggios in simple melodic structures. It is always better if the tempo is moderate and if one does not move into the highest register. All of the intervals can be slurred, but – as with the flute – it is easier to slur ascending intervals than to slur descending ones, especially if there are large leaps in the passage (greater than a perfect 4th). An octave passage such as that from the *Concerto* by Ravel is possible, even though not easy at the requested tempo. It would be much easier if written as follows:

Tonguing

Tonguing on the oboe is precise, pungent, and of excellent effect, but it cannot be as rapid as that of the flute due to the flute's ability to execute double and triple tonguing. Tonguing also cannot be performed *fortissimo*. Here are the maximum recommended tempos for tonguing.

      low octave - sixteenth notes at a quarter = around 120
      middle and high octaves - sixteenth notes at a quarter = around 132

If two or more notes are slurred and if the lip and the tongue have time to rest, one can often tongue much faster. Therefore, it is suggested that lengthy passages be avoided, slurred or tongued, since the performer has frequent need to rest.

Flutter tonguing

Some performers are successful at executing the flutter tongue, although for a short duration, but the result is not spontaneous and effective as on the flute. In general it is not effective with instruments that employ the use of a reed or mouthpiece in the mouth.

Stravinsky: *Le Sacre du printemps*, p. 8. Ed: Russe de Musique

Muting

The use of the mute has had scarce practical application and is, for the most part unknown to performers. Here is an example:

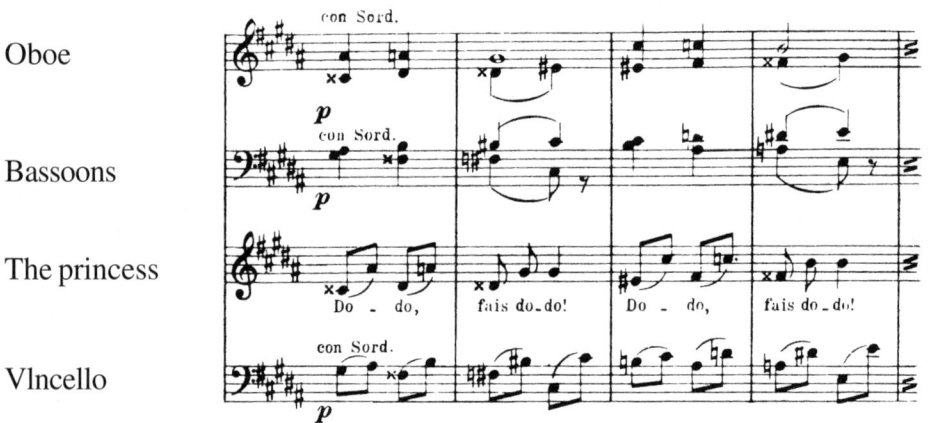

N. Rimsky-Korsakov: *Kachtchei l'Immortale*, p. 119. Ed: Belajeff

Portamenti

In jazz, the oboe has also been used. It has adopted the use of the portamento; however, the technique is generally unknown and rarely accepted by the normal orchestral oboist. The portamento should be limited to small intervals and not go beyond . It is more easily approached from below than above.

Breathing

The length of the breath on the oboe, while difficult and tiring, has such possibilities that no wind instrument can compete with it in this regard. In the low octave: around 12 seconds at *forte*; around 20 seconds at *piano*. In the middle and highest octaves: around 20 seconds at *forte*; around 35-40 seconds at *piano*. As to the relativeness of this data to other winds, one should refer to the section on the flute.

Some uses of the oboe:

Note the "fat" and heavy sonority of the oboe in the low octave; the bassoons (supported by the English horn and the first bassoon tongued) that accompany the melody in the third oboe; the doubling two octaves above by the first oboe that will display a typical soft and quite amorphous color; and the celli and double basses, very dry and short, articulating the rhythm.

I. Stravinsky: *Symphonie de Psaumes*, p. 6. Ed: Russe de Musique

The oboe accompanies muted brasses well.

A. Honegger: *Sinfonia N. 1 in do*, p. 59. Ed: Senart

Following is a passage nearly unplayable at the desired tempo, one that is extremely difficult. Fortunately the passage also involves the flutes and clarinets that help compensate for the difficulty and poor effect that the oboe will render.

P. Dukas: *L'apprenti sorcier*, p. 16 and following. Ed: Durand

M. Ravel: *Daphnis et Chloé*, first suite, p. 63. Ed: Durand

The high Gs on the third and fourth beat above can be reached, but the successive D♯s are sacrificed, so that the performance will result as follows:

In the following solo passage of Zandonai, the oboist is given a true task. (In general the instrument is not adapted to such virtuosic agility.)

This interval  is difficult. If used in continous rapid passages, its results are poor.

Although an arpeggio is feasible, one should not insist on such passages.

On tremolos, however, the oboe is quite agile. (See the table of trills.)

It is useless to write, at a fast tempo, passages such as the following, for they are unplayable.

ENGLISH HORN

Considered the alto oboe, the English horn is tuned a fifth below the ordinary oboe. Although the instrument has an ancestry from the *Oboe da caccia*, found often in the *Cantatas* of Bach, its exact heritage is not clear. While the English sometimes call it the French-horn, it is thought that the origin of the name is French and that *anglais* is a misinterpretation of the term *anglè* (angle). This is substantiated by its early construction in a decided curved form, like a horn, therefore, the evolution of the term, *anglé* or angle.

Range   sounding

[1] The low B♭ is in parentheses since it is often not used. Note, however, that there are examples of its use. (Mussorgsky: *Pictures at an Exhibition*, orch. Ravel, p. 100, Ed. Boosey & Hawkes).

Timbre

With the exception of the lowest note (B♭) with a strong and particular timbre and the highest five notes that somewhat lose the timbre of the instrument, all of the tones are homogeneous and are easily played.

As to the technical possibilities of the instrument that which was said for the oboe holds true, keeping in mind that the oboe is more agile with a tighter hand position. The ease of the attack is less than on the oboe, therefore, hindering rapid tonguing especially the lower one plays.

Trills

All of the major and minor trills are possible in the following range:

The low trills below those indicated are difficult and if used should be of short duration above all at *piano*. The following trills are difficult if not impossible and should be avoided.

Tremolos

(x) difficult (xx) very difficult, complicated, render a poor result
N.B. - The tremolos omitted are impossible and unadvised

(1) poor result

(2) possible with special devices.

N. B. – Other tremolos are also possible with the use of the automatic octave key.

Flutter tonguing

Examples of flutter tonguing for the English horn at this writing are non-existent.

Portamenti

As on the oboe, the portamento is possible, but generally is not used.

Breathing

Although one can sustain lengthy phrases on the English horn, it does not have the same capabilities for sustaining as on the oboe. The instrument also, even more than the oboe, has enjoyed enormous strides in timbral uses in the last thirty years. One special use of the low notes demonstrates a harsh and fierce effect.

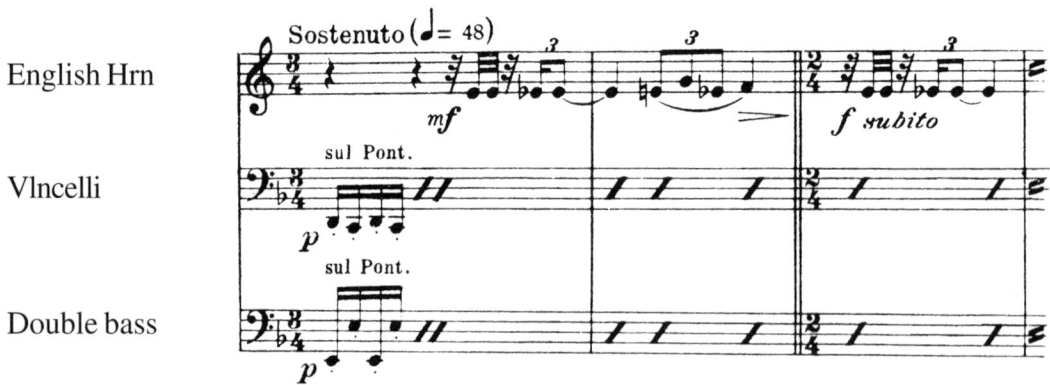

I. Stravinsky: *Petrouchka*, p. 80. Ed: Russe de Musique

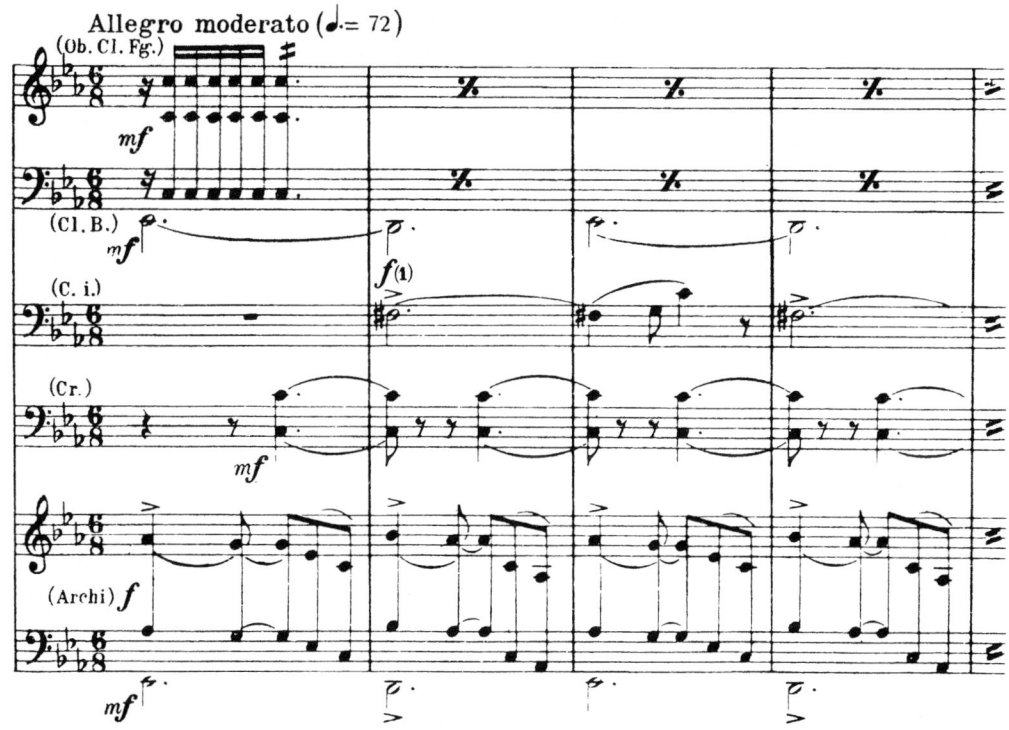

(The example is written in sounding pitch.) C. Saint-Saëns: *Sinfonia in do min*, pp. 13-14. Ed: Durand
(1) The third of the chord is given to the solo English horn.

One solo in the *Sombrero de tres picos* of de Falla (*The Three Cornered Hat*) approaches the rough and harsh sound of the *copla catalana*, a type of large mountain pipe (bag pipe). The passage is difficult especially for the rapid staccato tonguing in the low octave.

M. de Falla: *El sombrero de tres picos*, p. 25. Ed: J. and W. Chester

Mute

Rimsky-Korsakov indicated muting the English horn (*The Legend of the Invisible City of Kitèj* No 355, *Pan il Voievode* No 1). Today's performers are unfamiliar with this application with the exception of the use of a small light cloth placed in the bell of the instrument that serves to deaden the lowest notes to 🎵. In this case, however, 🎵 cannot be played and 🎵 is almost impossible.

Very often the English horn is given to the same performer assigned to the second or third oboe part; however, today's performer generally prefers to avoid passing between the two instruments. In the best orchestras, the English horn is generally played by a specialist.

OTHER OBOES

The *oboe d'amore* is tuned a major third lower than the oboe. It has a spherical bell (while the oboe has a conical one) giving it a soft, homogeneous sonority that other similar instruments do not have.

The technique is that of the ordinary oboe. The *oboe d'amore* is above all adapted to soft and singable passages. Among the modern composers who have used this instrument are Strauss, *Sinfonia domestica*, and Ravel, *Bolero*.

Another important instrument to note that has a penetrating and aggressive quality in its upper range is the *Soprano Oboe in E♭*.

The soprano oboe has not yet been used in contemporary orchestrations.

The *Heckelphon*, so called by the inventor, W. Heckel di Biebrich in 1904, is close to a *Baritone Oboe in D*, that sounds an octave lower than the typical oboe, but is written an octave higher in the treble clef.

 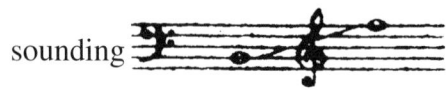

The timbre of the instrument is powerful and often aggressive, and finds great use in *Salome*, *Elektra*, and in the *Alpine Symphony* of Strauss, as well as in the *Mona Lisa* and in the *Moloch* of Max Schillings. In Germany a small *Heckelphon in F* is used for the playful call that announces the arrival of the ship in the third act of Wagner's *Tristan*.

* * *

In recent research compiled on the vast work of Antonio Vivaldi, an instrument called the *Salmò* (or *Salmoè*) is often noted. This term, however, was nothing other than the corruption of the French word *chalumeau* and the instrument used was really a type of bass oboe that extends in the low region of the Heckelphon. One finds an important part for the *salmò* in the *Concerto in C major* of Vivaldi (Ed. Carisch S. A. Milano, 1943. Revision by Alfredo Casella). The part is normally performed on the Heckelphon.

CLARINET

Since Buffet, the French manufacturer, applied a system of rings to the clarinet, like those used by Böhm on the flute, no fundamental changes have occurred to the instrument. Modifications to the instrument, however, that usually vary from instrument to instrument and from performer to performer have been made.

Today clarinets in B♭ and A are in general use.

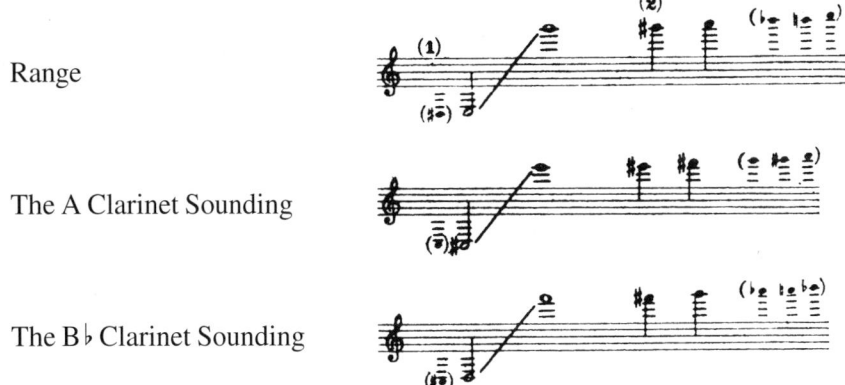

Range

The A Clarinet Sounding

The B♭ Clarinet Sounding

(1) The clarinet in B♭ has, at least in Italy, almost always a special key in order to produce the note in parenthesis. This key can also be found on the clarinet in A.

(2) The highest G and the A are in the extended range; however, most performers now are used to reaching them. Above these notes playing becomes continuously more difficult and perilous, with uncertain intonation.

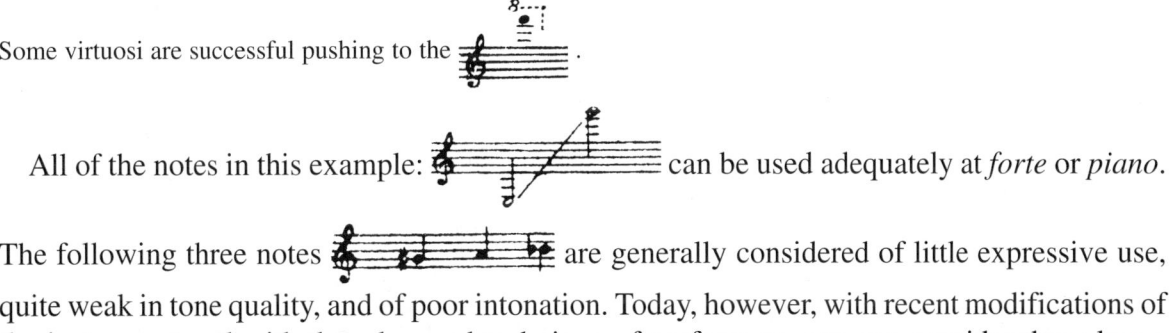

Some virtuosi are successful pushing to the

All of the notes in this example: can be used adequately at *forte* or *piano*.

The following three notes are generally considered of little expressive use, quite weak in tone quality, and of poor intonation. Today, however, with recent modifications of the instrument and with the advanced technique of performers, one can consider these less a problem.

Timbre

The clarinet has a fluid and mobile timbre that lends itself to many types of expression. It is capable of an almost imperceptible *pianissimo* as well as an intense *fortissimo*. There are two principal registers: the low register, called *chalumeau*, is that of the primitive instrument and that which produces the so called fundamental (1st harmonic); and the high register, called *clarino* (clarion), that produces an interval of a 12th (3rd harmonic) above the fundamental sound. These harmonics are obtained by means of a key, the register key, that covers a small hole that makes a node in the column of air that is broken in three equal parts. It is thought that this key was invented in the seventeenth-century by Cristoforo Denner. The register of the harmonics was called *clarino* for the clear and open sound of the piccolo trumpet (clarino was the old name for the trumpet);

therefore, the name gave origin to the name of the entire instrument.

(1) The highest pitches are obtained by means of the 5th, 7th, and 9th harmonics (the 7th harmonic is very flat).

The lowest register is menacing, dramatic, and dark while the highest is brilliant and incisive.

The notes above are forced and often difficult to maintain in a homogeneous timbre.

Since its appearance in the orchestra, the clarinet has demonstrated itself as a significant instrument either for effects of color or for expressive melodies. Nothing could be more beautiful than the clarinet in the following melody of the third movement of *Summer Concerto* of Pizzetti (*Concerto dell'estate*).

I. Pizzetti: *Concerto dell'estate*, pp. 98-99. Ed: Ricordi

This instrument, a favorite of Mozart, Weber, and also of so many great composers of the twentieth century, has revealed unsuspected expressive resources. At first used as means for expressive melodic content, the clarinet has assumed new roles. Since its adoption by the unspoiled genius of the black North-Africans, it has acquired a comic, grotesque aspect. This aspect reflects the art of the clown with a shrill, chattering, and petulant voice.

These grotesque capabilities, generally limited to jazz, are exceptional cases in symphonic music. Today, however, the limits between learned and light art are not always easy to define, and in the rapid evolution of events, predictions are difficult to make.

For example, harmony like that of Debussy, once frighteningly revolutionary, has gradually fallen to its lowest level in contemporary dance music.

Therefore, the clarinet of today, like no other, is an instrument of various and opposite resources. If one appreciates contemporary art and its new esthetic elements, one will welcome the clarinet's audacious and unprejudiced conquests of the highest register.

Trills

All the major and minor trills contained in the following tessitura are possible.

Likewise these two trills are easily playable if the instrument possesses a special key that exits on almost all clarinets used in Italy.

Tremolos

The tremolos under the  are not playable rapidly; therefore, they are not true tremolos.

(x) difficult with poor result
(xx) inadvisable, therefore, very difficult and perilous with poor result

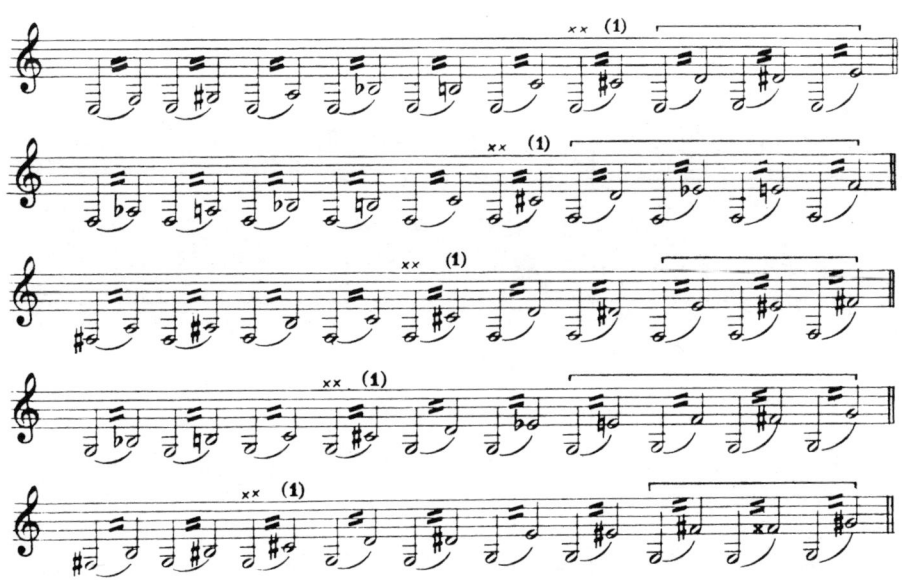

(1) Best with the bridge key, however, this key is still limited in its use [Translator's Note: at this writing (1945-46) the key was in limited use.]
(2) Best with the forked E♭ key.
(3) Better if the key that produces the low note is added.
(4) Possible with special fingerings not necessarily known by all performers.

As indicated in the preceding table, one is reminded that the tremolos, especially those under the bracket, are less rapid the greater the interval.

Some of the tremolos cited as good are slightly defective or out of tune (especially those played with awkward fingerings). By taking into account these small deficiencies, one should not discount the effect of a tremolo.

Some tremolos, although not shown in the table, are still found in scores. It is then a question of masking the tremolo with the other instruments of the orchestra at a *forte* dynamic level, when the composer uses a tremolo that may be ineffective. Diligent care is advised.

The student will do well to maintain a close relationship with players and to ask their practical advice, for the technique and construction of the modern clarinet change every day.

Slurring

The clarinet is one of the most agile instruments. Scales and arpeggios of every type and speed can be played as easily as on the flute. Every composer has made use of the agile qualities of the clarinet from its inception as a normal practice. The following are contemporary examples.

W. Walton: *Sinfonia Concertante*, p. 65. Ed: Oxford University Press

A. Schönberg: *Erwartung*, p. 20. Ed: Universal

N. Rimsky-Korsakov: *Il gallo d'oro*, "Introduction". Ed: Rob. Forberg

Tonguing

Single tonguing is the only articulation used on the clarinet. The most rapid tempo generally achievable is a quarter note at 120, but for brief passages the tempo may be increased. Above the articulation becomes more difficult. In passages that are not rearticulated tonguing is easier and can be used at a faster tempo, approximately a quarter note at 132.

As for reiterated notes one finds rapid passages as indicated, but these are unusual examples in which there are no demands of precision and cleanliness. The rapid tempo is also possible if a passage is very brief and can be played *con bravura*.

M. Castelnuovo-Tedesco: *Ouverture per "La dodicesima notte" di Shakespeare*. p. 12. Ed: Ricordi

Double tonguing is possible and there are some virtuosi who know how to double tongue with excellent results.

Flutter tonguing

As with the oboe flutter tonguing is difficult, inexpressive, and for a special effect. It is called for as in the following example:

M. Ravel: *Alborado del Gracioso*, p. 31. Ed: Eschig.

Mute

A mute is used in Mascagni's *Iris* and occasionally one finds its use in jazz. The apparatus consists of a cover of cardboard inside which the instrument is placed and that has two holes through for the hands. The result is a dark, veiled, and quite beautiful sound.

Portamento

The portamento is an effect used in the jazz style and serves above all comic or grotesque purposes. These aspects reach their apex in the African-American virtuoso. The orchestral performer is still generally against the effect and considers it damaging to the instrument's legitimate technique and sound.

[Translator's note: Although this text was published after the second world war and long after the effects of Gershwin's *Rhapsody in Blue*, the authors still held a certain prejudice against special effects.]

The length of a single breath on the clarinet is formidable: around 40 seconds at *piano* and 25 at *forte* for all of the notes between 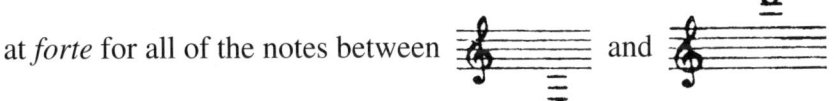 .

For the higher tones more air is needed and therefore the duration will be less.

Key

In ordinary modern practice one uses only the clarinets in B♭ and A. One more than the other may be used in order to avoid passages in awkward keys or those with many accidentals. A work in E♭ major, for example, probably could be performed much more easily with the clarinet in B♭. Therefore by using one, then the other, of the two instruments it is no longer a question of the key. Today's performers are conditioned to virtuosic playing on both regardless of key.

In order to change the A clarinet from B♭ or vice versa, little time is required (around one count in a moderate **4/4** time), but it is advised that the performer be given enough time to warm the new instrument. Twenty or thirty seconds of playing before an expressive passage should be given to the performer before the actual passage.

I. Stravinsky: *Petrouchka*, p. 64, Ed: Russe de Musique

A. Schönberg: *Pierrot lunaire*, p. 13 and p. 32. Ed: Universal

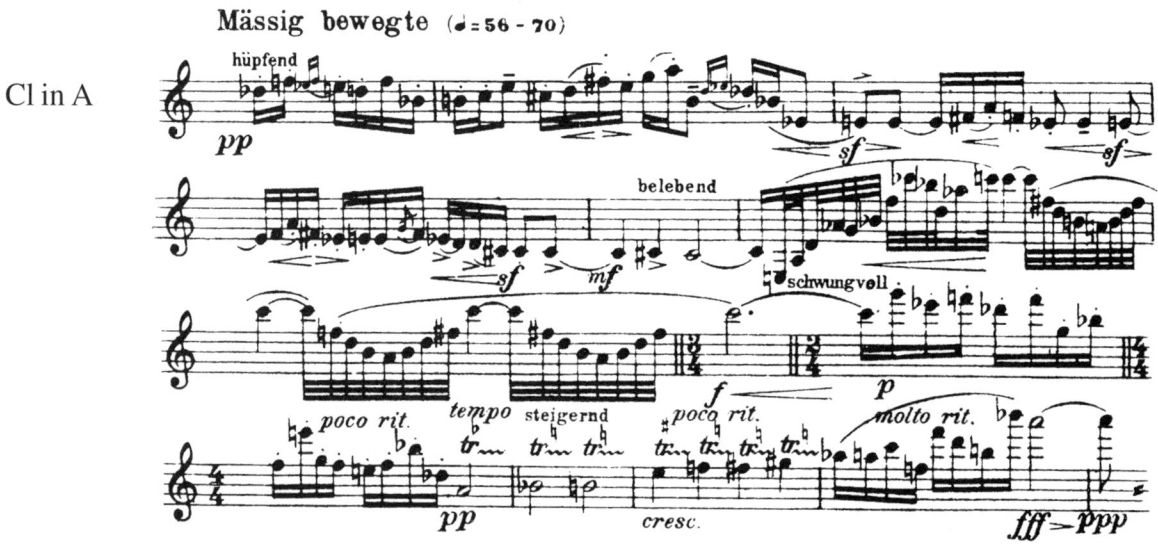

A. Schönberg: *Pierrot lunaire*, p. 50 and following. Ed: Universal

I. Stravinsky: *L'historie du soldat*, p. 4. Ed: J. e W. Chester

G. Mahler: *Sinfonia VII*, "Finale". N. 252. Ed: Peters

E♭ CLARINET
(small clarinet)

The same technique is required for the small clarinet as for its counterparts. Most often it is given to the same performer who plays the second or third part. Today's clarinetist, however, prefers to avoid passages using both instruments in rapid succession due to the difference in reeds. On the small clarinet the reed is such that the upper tones are easily played by imposing a sudden adjustment of the lip. This agility is not always achievable without damage to the purity of the characteristic sound. In most of today's large orchestras the small clarinet is played by a specialist.

In general the only small clarinet used is the E♭. Its range is as follows:

Range:

Sounding:

Small clarinets also exist in D. Wagner used them in his *Incantesimo del fuoco* from *Walkiria*. Others exist in F and in A♭. These last two, however, do not seem to have been accepted by ensembles other than the band.

The passing of the small clarinet from the band to the orchestra is a relatively recent event. The celebrated paradoxical use by Berlioz in his *Symphonie fantastique* has remained isolated; it possibly discredited the use of the instrument for many years.

H. Berlioz: *Symphonie fantastique*, p. 93.

It has only been since the end of the 19th century that the small clarinet has reappeared in the orchestra, first in the symphonic poems of Strauss, and then taking an almost normal position through the French, by means of, and above all the works of Ravel. His use was almost exclusively as reinforcement for the flutes in order to give them strength and brilliance. But in his most recent works, examples exist of independence that are a long way from the sinister treatment of Berlioz.

In jazz the small clarinet is wonderful for those grotesque effects indicated previously.

M. Ravel: *L'enfant et les sortilèges*, pp. 178-179. Ed: Durand

Stravinsky, by placing the bass and small clarinet two octaves apart among the trills of the flutes in three octaves, obtained an almost make believe effect.

I. Stravinsky: *Le Sacre du printemps*, p. 38. Ed: Russe de Musique

CONTRALTO CLARINET [ALTO CLARINET]

There are two types of contralto clarinet: the contralto, appropriately called, that is E♭, and the contralto in F. The first is still used, for the most part, in bands, the second, although it is a better instrument is no longer used.

Range

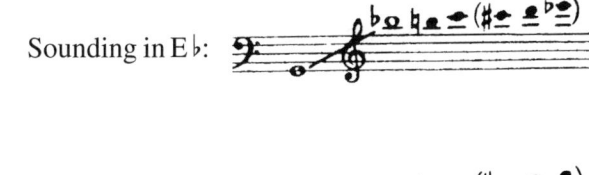

BASSETT HORN

A type of contralto clarinet in F, the bassett horn has a different shape and has its own characteristic qualities.

As for the technique of the instrument there are no substantial differences from the ordinary clarinet. Its most useful register is the lowest which offers a soft and velvet kind of sonority that is full of charm. It has not found favor with modern composers, however. Examples of its use are limited to Mozart, Beethoven, and certain minor composers. Today in order to perform those works the instrument is usually substituted by the alto clarinet in E♭. Strauss, however, experimented with the instrument.

BASS CLARINET

The bass clarinet is tuned an octave lower than the ordinary clarinet. Bass clarinets exist in B♭ and in A. Generally both are not owned by one performer; therefore, use has usually become limited to that of the one in B♭.

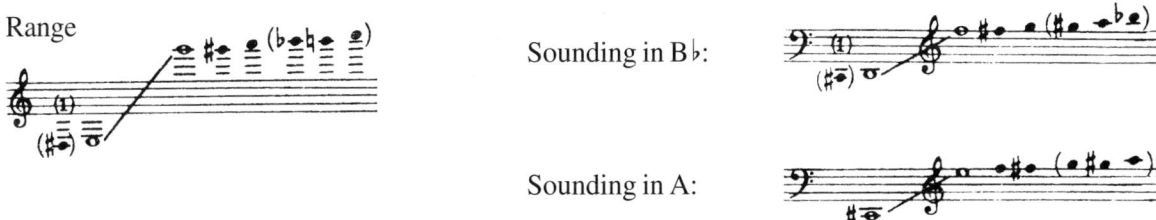

(1) The bass clarinet in B♭ almost always possesses the added keys for descending to the lowest notes in parentheses.

From *Lohengrin* (1848) and after, Wagner gave the instrument a regular place in the orchestra. He wrote in his scores where it sounds in the bass clef, a most logical approach. This is a technique that one is advised to use without hesitation.

E.R. 2935

This method, however, alters the system of writing that unifies all of the transposing instruments. That is why opinions on the notating of the instrument according to Wagnerian reforms are still not agreed upon. In every case one cannot adhere to the practice as above, e.g., changing the clef when the melody moves between the extremes, for this writing must undergo an octave displacement as in the following example:

I. Stravinsky: *Le Sacre du printemps*, p. 5. Ed: Russe de Musique

The low register is that of greatest use, for it is that which continues the timbre of the ordinary clarinet into the lowest regions of the family. In the lowest register are the instrument's most beautiful notes. These notes have a tremendous singing quality that has attracted the attention of many composers since Meyerbeer who introduced the bass clarinet in the orchestra for the first time (*Gli Ugonotti*, 1836). Later then came Wagner, Liszt, and subsequent composers.

By now almost all contemporary scores contain the bass clarinet. Often it is treated in passages of importance and above all in the low register. It acquires curious meanings at times as in the example cited by Stravinsky or in the following passage from *Le Sacre du printemps*:

I. Stravinsky: *Le Sacre du printemps*, p. 111. Ed: Russe de musique

Examples of flutter tonguing also exist, e.g., A. Schönberg: *Pierrot lunaire*, p. 27; I. Stravinsky: *Le Sacre du printemps*, p. 24. For these cases, however, the same considerations made for the oboe should apply.

Also the bass clarinet, as on the ordinary clarinet, has numerous possibilities of nuance as no other instrument has.

A. Schönberg: *Pierrot lunaire*, pp. 21-22. Ed: Universal

A very beautiful example of flutter tonguing follows from *Pierrot Lunaire*. Note the doubling of the instrument with tremolo in the cello.

A. Schönberg: *Pierrot Lunaire*, p. 27. Ed: Universal

CONTRABASS CLARINET

This instrument was created from the fantasy and initiative of the great builder of instruments, Adolph Sax. It is tuned in F and E♭, an octave below the alto clarinet.

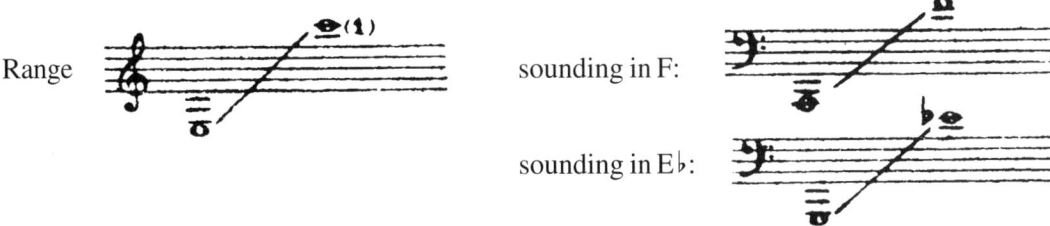

(1) Higher sounds are possible (as on the ordinary clarinet), but they are of little practical use.

There is also the contrabass clarinet in B♭, at the octave below the bass clarinet, and the effect is quite beautiful. They are rare, and also are the performers who are trained in their use. Their employment is now quite limited. However, one is able to see some use of them in the opera, *Fervaal* of V. D'Indy, in the opera, *Hélène* of Saint-Saëns, and in the *Orchesterstücke* of Arnold Schönberg.

BASSOON

The bassoon today is constructed according to two systems: the Buffet French system and the German Heckel system. Substantial improvements have not been made to the Buffet system in the last half of this century; however, the Heckel system, previously preferred by Wagner in the nineteenth century, has had notable changes in its mechanism and has had positive acceptance. The Heckel has a larger chamber with some holes shifted so that the sound of the different registers proves to be more homogeneous. The combination of harmonics offers a greater equalization and ease in the highest register. In this register, however, the sound is more pleasing on the Buffet. The Heckel, used greatly in North America and, above all, in Germany, has two systems of keys: the English, that is similar to the Buffet, and the German, that offers technical advantages in the low register 𝄢 so as to make possible in this tessitura some trills that are impossible on other systems. These trills, however, remain sluggish due to the thumb's not being an agile finger.

The bassoon, unexplored in the jazz idiom, has not had the immediate revolutionary jazz influence that other instruments have experienced, e.g., the clarinet and the trumpet. But the bassoon with its affable and homely appearance still today has endless resources that come to it from its fundamental character as handyman of the orchestra.

Range

(1) These notes were introduced by Alban Berg: *Lulù*, p. 35. Ed: Universal
(2) This F♯ can be obtained only by slurring it with the F natural before it.

The last six highest notes are difficult to play and are easier if reached by adjacent notes or by small interval. Likewise, they are less of a problem if they are approached in a legato passage. Tongued, these notes are perilous. At *forte* all of the tones are equally good. At *piano* these three notes 𝄢 are difficult to attack. Of the rest it is impossible to obtain a true *piano* below the D natural. The *pianissimo* is not possible below the low G. The 𝄢 is the ugliest note on the instrument.[(1)] At one time these three notes were also defective 𝄢 , especially the F♯, but today, either through improvements in the mechanism, or improvement in the technique of the performers, these three notes are usable without worry. As for the rest, today's performers are adept at correcting them, with alternate fingerings or tricks; therefore, all of the defects on the instrument can be performed imperceptibly.

Some composers have written for the bassoon to the 𝄢 (Wagner: *Walkiria*, act I, scene 3; Mahler: *Symphonies II and IV*).

The Heckel system will produce the note, but in general, the builders of bassoons remain faithful to 𝄢 as the lowest note.

---

(1) Today with the use of a special key, one can reach this note easily.

Timbre

As a double reed instrument, the bassoon belongs to the same family as the oboe and like the rest of this family has certain characteristics. Its timbre according to Rimsky-Korsakov is "senile and clever in the major mode and suffering and sad in the minor." In tongued passages in the low register it easily assumes a comic role. One can distinguish three registers corresponding to the physical nature of its sound: the low register, formed by twenty fundamental tones; the middle register; and the highest register that is the result of harmonics.

The low register has a perfect fifth that is superb, vibrant and of sonorous potency, especially the lowest note . It can balance with the horns and often with the trombones, however, naturally not at *forte*; as it ascends, the sonority little by little loses the consistency of the lowest tones. The middle register is veiled, and in the last notes fuses itself with the highest register in a tense expression, almost like the violoncello, without having the sensuality of the string instrument.

V. Mortari: *Rapsodia*, p. 1. Ed: Ricordi

Trills

The most effective trills are those found in the range:
Below the lower note other trills are possible, but they are very sluggish and, for the most part, are of poor quality. One should consider the following notations:

(x) usable if not overbalanced
(xx) difficult and of poor effect (sluggish and heavy)
(xxx) impossible
(1) possible on the Heckel
(2) some virtuosi are able to attempt this trill, but it will probably be always tentative. Likewise it is very dangerous to adventure above the highest limits indicated above in the range, at least with the Buffet system.

Tremolos

Possible tremolos:

x - difficult
xx - very difficult
xxx - impossible or almost so

(1) Easy on the Heckel
(2) Good on the Heckel
(3) Possible on the Heckel, but harsh

Slurring

The bassoon is possibly the only woodwind instrument that offers such difficulty in the slurring of descending intervals of a certain width (other than a 3rd). The performer is always concerned at the beginning of the *Sigfrido* due to a slur of a seventh.

It is advised, therefore, that slurring descending intervals of a certain width take place only in a slow passage, and it is probably advisable to double the slur with other instruments. The greater the descending interval, the greater the difficulty of the slur, especially at *piano*. The ascending slur, instead, is not difficult for intervals.

Tonguing

Not withstanding its most used role in its lowest register, the bassoon is an agile instrument capable of making rapid leaps between registers. That agility, coupled with its timbral characteristics, gives it great importance for comic possibilities and other special effects. It is prudent, especially with repeated notes, to not go beyond, especially in ensemble playing, the following tempi for staccato passages:

Low register: 16ths at a quarter note = 116.
Middle register: 16ths at a quarter note = 138.

Rapid articulations should not be lengthy, unless the lip can reposition itself on two or three slurred notes. Tonguing, then, can be achieved at greater tempos.

The following is an example of rapid, but very brief, articulation:

M. Castelnuovo-Tedesco: *Ouverture per "La dodicesima notte" di Shakespeare*, p. 12. Ed: Ricordi

Flutter tonguing

No significant examples of flutter tonguing existed at the writing of this text.

Vibrato

Vibrato is a natural and expressive sound technique on the instrument. The "tremolo sound" is an exaggeration of vibrato, but the "trick" is too evident and the resulting timbre quite impure.

Mutes

There are some examples of the application of a mute on the bassoon. (Rimsky-Korsakov: *Kachtchei l'Immortale*, p. 119.) Performers generally prefer not to use it, since it offers little effect and corrupts the softness of the sound.

Breathing

As one descends into the lower register a greater quantity of air is always necessary. These are approximate medium limits for the player:
  Low register: 15 seconds at *piano*, 6 at *forte*.
  Medium and high registers: 30 seconds at *piano*, 15 at *forte*.

Tchaikowsky in his time had already attempted new avenues for the bassoon by orienting it toward various effects both grotesque and otherwise.

P. I. Tchaikowsky: "Chinese Dance" in the ballet *The Nutcracker*

In his *Concerto in G major for piano and orchestra,* Ravel assigns a melody to the bassoon in its highest register, that, with a jazz accompaniment, acquires a sweet and tender sonority that is a great distance from the ludicrous.

M. Ravel: *Concerto in G major for piano and orchestra*, p. 13, Ed: Durand

At the beginning of *Le Sacre du printemps*, Stravinsky uses the bassoon in its highest register and with the contribution of an uncertain rhythm and of an archaic key signature, he is successful at giving the impression of a new instrument, whose voice seems to resound from the depths of that Russian prehistory.[1]

I. Stravinsky: *Le Sacre du printemps*, "Introduction". Ed: Russe de Musique

P. Dukas: *L'apprenti sorcier*, p. 6. Ed: Durand

In the following example the bassoon functions almost as the first trombone, by playing the first part.

I. Stravinsky: *Chant du rossignol*, p. 66. Ed: S.A. des Grandes Editions

Harmonic and counterpoint evolutions have permitted organizations of new timbral colors. Another example in which two bassoons, playing in parallel fourths and sustained by an intense and lugubrious harmony, reveals an unknown voice, almost celestial, that seems to render one solo instrument.

---

(1) In *I segreti della giara,* p. 162, Casella relates that Saint-Saëns, while hearing the 1913 performance in Paris of *Sacre*, asked him from which family of instruments did that strange voice at the opening come. To which Casella replied that it was a simple bassoon. At that Saint-Saëns became so angry that he exited the theatre, slamming the door. (One should note that in those days the passage was extremely difficult; therefore, the sonority would have resulted in a horrendous sound probably not heard before.)

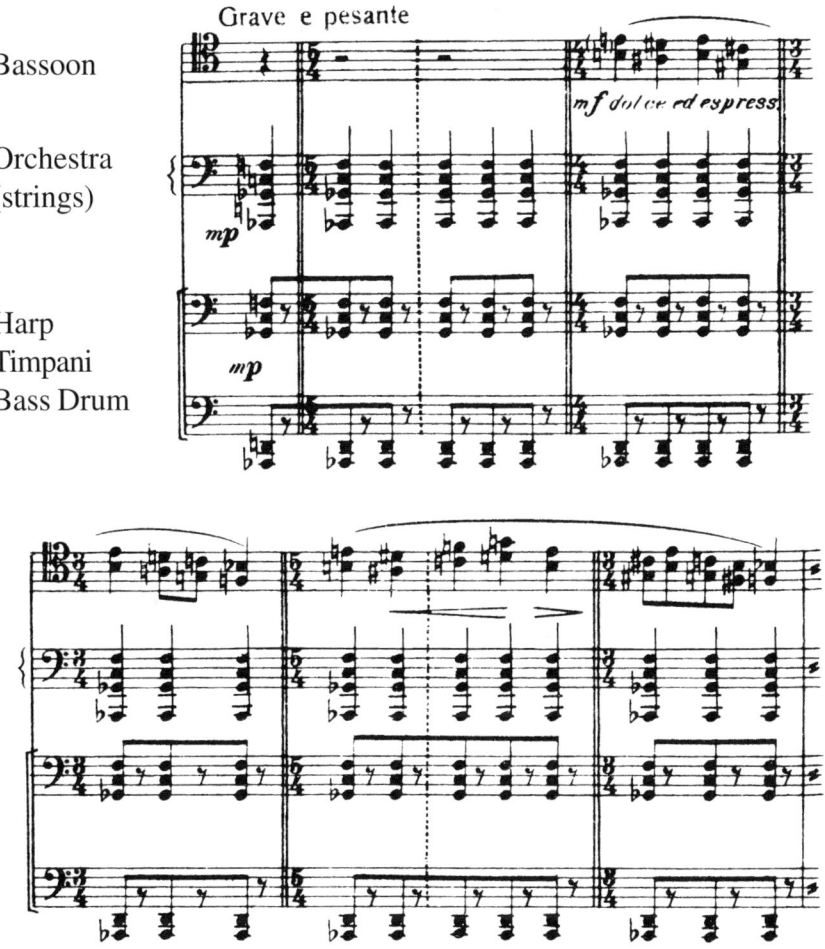

A. Casella: *Elegia eroica*, p. 11. Ed: Universal

The tender sonority of the bassoons in the upper register with bass flutes:

M. Ravel: *Valses nobles et sentimentales*, p. 25. Ed: Durand

In the last ten years the bassoon has made important contributions as a dramatic instrument. Note the rapid and sinister *basso ostinato* under the sound of the other winds.

I. Stravinsky: *Ottetto per fiati*, pp. 22-23. Ed: Russe de Musique

In the *Finale* of the same work, the two bassoons in a counterpoint of great diatonic liberty superimpose a scherzo-like theme over an indifferent and mechanical bass. By doing so Stravinsky acquires a new color.

I. Stravinsky: *Ottetto per fiati*, pp. 40-41. Ed: Russe de Musique

The resources of the bassoon as they appear in these few examples are far from being exhausted, not only for exterior solicitations and circumstances, but also for that wonderful ability of the instrument to adapt to everything. It is, in the orchestra, that which "the horse" is in the game of chess.

CONTRABASSOON

Once the contrabassoon was so defective that the sarrusaphone was often preferred over it. Now, however, the manufacturers have discovered how to correct the many defects, and performers have become most capable at taking the instrument to a notable plane of dignity and precision. Its rounded, full, and warm tone now plays a part in the normal orchestra.

(1) These first two notes are of dubious intonation and are difficult to play.
(2) The notes above this B♭ can be reached easily with an adequate reed, but reeds adapted to the highest tones are often unacceptable to the lowest notes that make the bassoon so endearing.

The best and most useful register is approximately that comprised between the following two notes:  Sounding

Above this register it is best to use the bassoon.

The technique of the contrabassoon is the same of that of the bassoon, but by its best register being lower and its vibrations slower, it is less agile and, therefore, less adapted to acrobatics.

In recent years the old instrument, in the past often condemned to doubling the contrabasses, has been the object of particular attention by composers who have assigned to it important solos. The following is such an example by Ravel:

M. Ravel: *Ma Mère l'Oye* "La belle et la bête", p. 36. Ed: Durand

In *Salome*, Strauss assigns to the instrument a most important part expressing all the furor and the rage of the perverse young woman who meditates her horrible plan.

R. Strauss: *Salome,* final scene 3. Ed: Furstner

SARRUSAPHONE

An instrument of brass with a double reed, it is part of an entire family of instruments. Only the sarrusaphone in C was used as a part of the instrumentation of the orchestra by taking advantage of the lack of the contrabassoon. It was used most often in France where it had a great popularity.

Today, however, this instrument is used only in bands and, if it is indicated in an orchestral score, it is substituted by the contrabassoon. [Translator's note: Now in the 21st century, sarrusaphones are only museum pieces].

THE POSITIONS ON BRASS INSTRUMENTS [1]

The sounds that one can obtain from a column of air excited by the performer's lip with appropriate and different pressures on the mouthpiece are those of the harmonic series. Practically no instrument can produce all of the harmonics in a series. Only the very lowest instruments, e.g., the tuba, can reach the first harmonic (fundamental), but such instruments also do not play above the eighth/tenth harmonic. Generally the harmonic series has a practical beginning at the second harmonic, and only some instruments with a small aperture, e.g., the horn, can reach the highest harmonics (twelfth/fourteenth).

By depressing the valves the length of the instrument is augmented, the sound lowered, and consequently the intonation of the instrument is affected. Therefore, with the valves one can produce the entire harmonic series. Other than their offering the advantage of having the chromatic scale, valves make possible, taking into consideration the rarest exceptions, the obtaining of tones in different series so that a defective harmonic (wind instruments are always subject to inevitable imperfections) in one series, can become a good one obtained in another.

There is the theoretical system of harmonics produced by instruments with four valves; however, the medium and high instruments usually are limited to three valves that are sufficient to obtain the seven positions necessary for every chromatic alteration. (See the following example.) As one will note in the following table the harmonics can be comprised in one series or in a different series, i.e., they can be obtained with one or more positions (valve combinations). For example ♩ can be played with the first, with the fifth, or with the eighth position. The ♩ with the third, sixth, ninth, or eleventh position, etc. The choice of the position, where there is more than one, depends on several factors, but for the most part it is determined by the best sonority obtainable.

The first three positions give the best results and are easier than the others.

---

(1) This treatise contains information on instruments with valves. It does not take into consideration any instruments without valves that were used by composers in previous centuries.

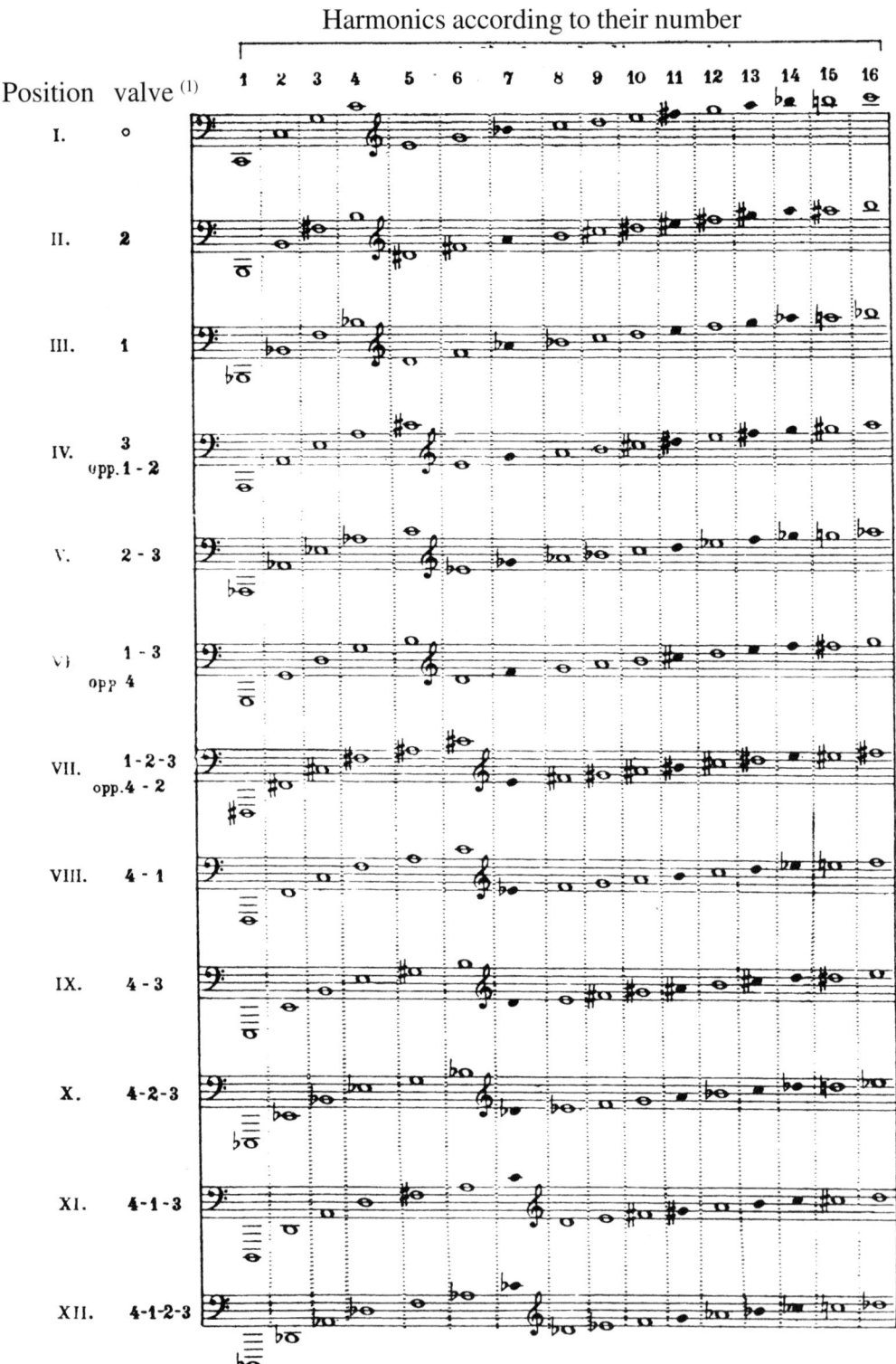

(1) ° = open, without valves; 1 = with the first valve lowered; 2 = with the second valve lowered; 1-3 = with the first and third valves lowered, etc.

The fifth begins to be a little less accurate. In instruments with three valves as they progress toward the seventh position the results are a much less precise intonation. The seventh position, then, is quite bad. In instruments with four valves, the use of the fourth valve helps greatly the sixth and seventh position, but then, as one precedes toward the twelfth position, the sonority becomes again somewhat defective. From the eighth position the intonation is not exact and needs the help of the lip in order to be corrected.

The seventh and fourteenth harmonics are flat. The eleventh and thirteenth are unusable because they are so flat. The greater the number of valves one uses, the worse and more compromised the intonation. In the following table, with the exception of the horn and the trombone for which partial indications are given, one finds listed the different ways of producing each harmonic in the two systems with three and four valves. In the system with three valves the last harmonic is:

Under this note, after a gap of five notes 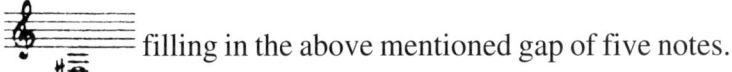, begin the fundamental harmonics, the so called pedal tones 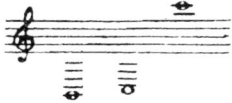. The pedal tones are obtainable only on some low instruments. On the instruments with four valves the use of the fourth valve (as is seen in the table) allows one to play the other positions and, therefore, descend chromatically below the filling in the above mentioned gap of five notes.

The upper range varies according to the number of harmonics that each instrument is capable of producing.

Notation, once equal for all brass instruments even for those on which the sounding note corresponded to tones in other lower or higher octaves – the so called *notazione uniforme*, "uniform notation"– today is generally for the low instruments written as a sounding pitch, i.e., the written note corresponds to the exact sounding note, independent of the size of the instrument or its tuning, [Notes scored in the bass clef regardless of their fundamental pitch, except for contra instruments that sound an octave lower]. This leaves the performer the duty of making the necessary transposition. It is understood, therefore, that for low instruments the notation is necessarily different from that of the "uniform notation" in the table. One must, then, imagine the relative transposition. For example, the range of the tuba in B♭ today is, usually written as follows:

In the "uniform notation" of our table, a notation that is still present in some bands, would be written in this way:

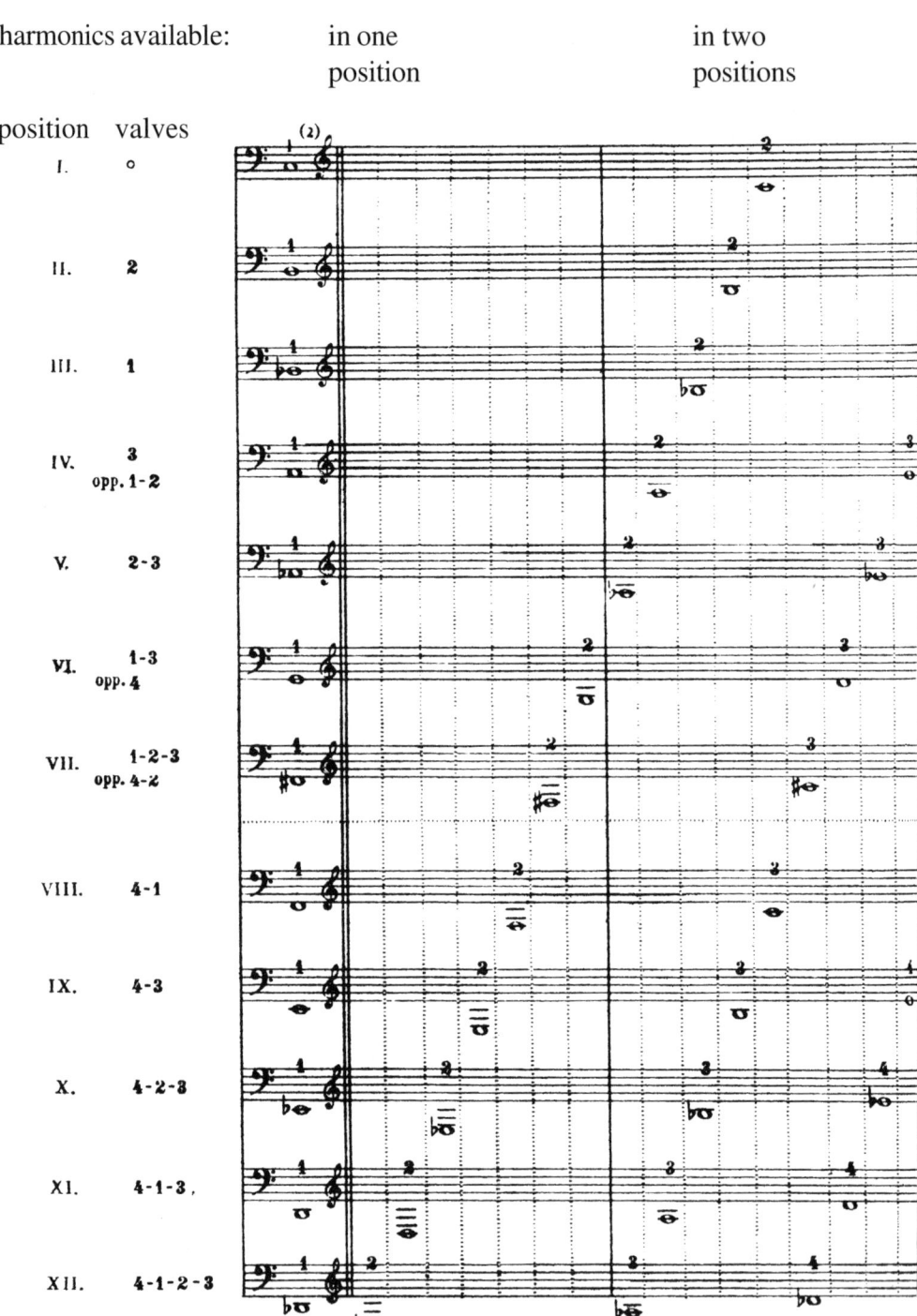

On the instruments with three valves one must consider only the first seven positions. The eleventh and thirteenth are not shown because they are unusable. The seventh and fourteenth are flat.

N. B. - The tables of the positions and of the trills for the trumpet, trombone, flicorno, and the tuba were compiled with the help of the esteemed professor of trombone, tuba, and flicorno at the Conservatory of St. Cecilia in Rome.

in three positions   in four positions   in five positions

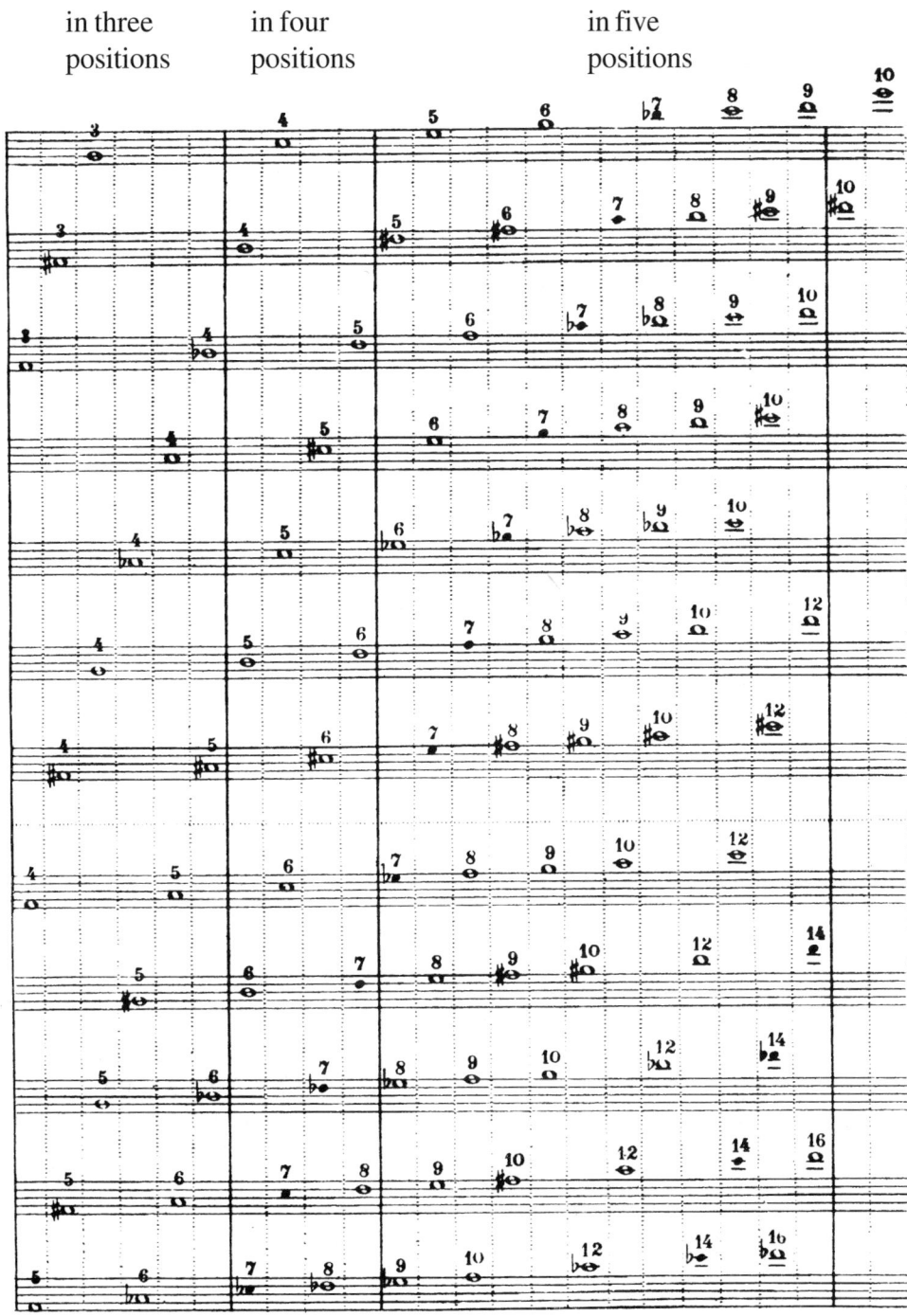

(1) See the note on the positions on the basic overtone series.
(2) The number placed above each note refers to the number of the harmonic in the overtone series.

TRILLS ON THE BRASS INSTRUMENTS
(exclusive of the slide trombone)

The minor trills or those generally that involve only one finger are the easiest, most rapid, and most effective. The third valve, while the only valve that lowers the pitch of the instrument one and one half steps, does not give the same effect as the first or second valves alone. The trills obtained with two or more valves are difficult. If the movement of the two valves is simultaneous, the trill will be poor and will not be as spontaneous as with one valve.

The low trills are generally of mediocre sonority. The tighter the tubing, the more agile and rapid the trills since the tone is more easily produced. Likewise the valves, being shorter and thinner, favor agility.

In the following examples [1] all of the trills on brass instruments are given. At the top of each column the fingering is noted relative to the positions with which one can play the two notes of the trill. For example, the indication

$$
\begin{array}{l}
1 \;\rule{2cm}{0.4pt} \\
\quad\; 2 \\
3 \;\rule{2cm}{0.4pt}
\end{array}
$$

means that the first and third valves must be held down while the second trills.

$$
\begin{array}{l}
\quad\; 1 \\
2 \quad 0 \\
3 \;\rule{2cm}{0.4pt}
\end{array}
$$

indicates that the third valve is held down while the first moves alternating with the second. The 0, placed under the 1 indicates that the second valve must be raised at the moment in which the first is lowered. Trills obtained with alternate movement of two or three valves are difficult and ineffective.

All trills in the same column are played with the indicated position at the top of that column and give, more or less, the same problems. Other fingerings are given that can provide easier trills of better quality.

---

(1) See the note on the previous page.

SUMMARIZED LIST OF BRASS TRILLS

An inclusive list of the trills for double horn in F and B♭. (For the modern transposition, see the section on the horn.)

(x) more or less defective
(xx) not recommended due to difficulty or poor result
(xxx) impossible, or almost, or very poor

For all brass instruments, and above all the horn, trills of a minor second are best. Trills of a whole step must be corrected with the contribution of the movement of the lip: the higher the trill, the more difficult and imprecise, e.g., between numbers 1 and 61. Below the first trill others are possible; however, they should not be considered. With movement of the hand in the bell or of the lip, the performer will almost always know how to correct imperfections. [noted with an x].

An inclusive list of trills for all the trumpets and flicorni (from the very highest flicorno in B♭ to the baritone in B♭).

(x) more or less defective
(xx) not recommended due to difficulty or poor result
(xxx) impossible, or almost, or very poor

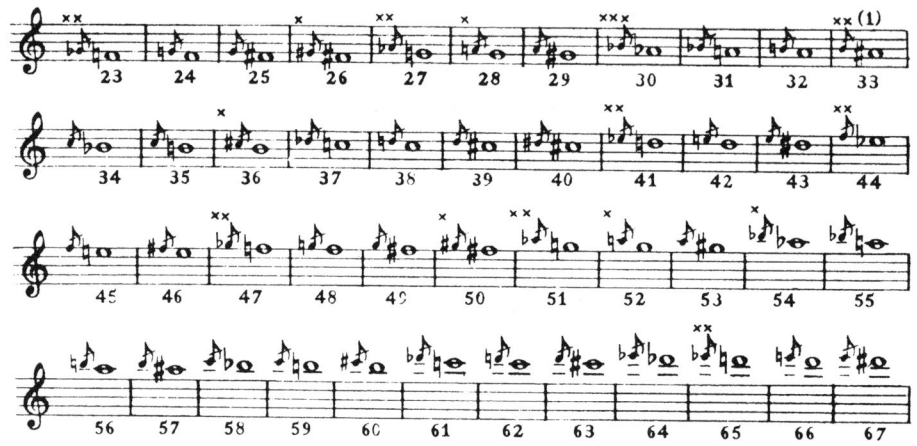

(1) Good on some instruments equipped with the fourth valve.

Register of the trills for instruments referred to in the preceding summary. The numbers indicate the limits of the range. The numbers in parenthesis refer to the exceptional areas that are always more difficult and less spontaneous as one plays higher.

Small trumpet B♭ or in A
and the Small Flicorno in Bb or in A 1-43 (44-49)

High trumpet in F
and Sopranino Flicorno in F 1-49 (50-53)

High trumpet in E♭ or in D and Soprano Flicorno in C or in in B♭ 1-49 (50-55)

Trumpet in A or Soprano Flicorno in A 1-55 (56-59)

Trumpet in F or in in E♭ 4-63 (64-67)

Contralto Flicorno in F 4-55 (56-59)

Contralto Flicorno in E♭ .... 4-59 (no others)

Bass trumpet in C 11-63 (64-67)

Bass trumpet in in B♭ 11-63 (64-67)

Tenor and Baritone Flicorno (Bombardino) in B♭ 5-55 (56-59)

N. B. - The trills under 1-11 are always more difficult

Inclusive list for trills on the Tenor Trombone with valves in B♭ and for all other instruments with four valves in B♭.
(x) more or less defective
(xx) not recommended due to difficulty or poor result
(xxx) impossible, or almost, or very poor

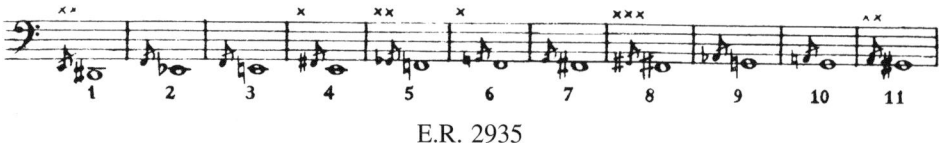

(1) x
(2) xx
(3) xxx in the bass trombone, that has only three valves

Register of the trills for instruments referred to in the preceding summary.

    Tenor tuba or baritone 7-61 (62-69)

    Bass flicorno in B♭ (Euphonium) and Bass tuba in B♭ (Bass-tuba) 3-57 (58-65)

    Contrabass flicorno in B♭ 3-57
    (*Helicon* or *Pellittone*)

    Contrabass tuba in B♭ 7-57 (58-65)

    Tenor trombone in B♭ 12-60 (61-65)

    Contrabass trombone in B♭ 12-60 (61-69)

N. B. -The trills under the lowest limits indicated are most impractical. Under 13 the trills become even more difficult and sluggish and are only usable for effects. For the Flicorno, the tuba, the trombone, and the contrabasses it is necessary to think one octave lower.

Inclusive list for trills on the Tenor Trombone with valves in F and for all other instruments with four valves in F.

    (x) more or less defective
    (xx) not recommended due to difficulty or poor result
    (xxx) impossible, or almost, or very poor

E.R. 2935

(1) x
(2) xx
(3) xxx in the bass trombone, that has only three valves

Register of the trills for instruments referred to in the preceding summary.

    Bass Flicorno in F (Bombardone) 2-57 (58-61)

    Bass Tuba in F 9-61 (62-69)

    Bass Trombone with valves in F 2-64 (66-69)

N. B. – The first trill is considered impractical. Under 13 the trills become increasingly more difficult and usable only for certain effects.

HORN

The horns in use today are those in F and in B♭. The so called double horn that by the use of a special valve can be tuned in either F or B♭, is now in use almost universally. The range of the instrument, therefore, is very large, and through the use of both the F and B♭ overtone series it is possible to correct almost all of the defective notes on one or the other. Since it is in use in almost all orchestras, this instrument will be the only horn discussed.

In the Romantic period the old "*corno da caccia*" enjoyed an immense field of possibilities that were first enunciated by the famous three notes that begin the *Overture to Oberon*: three notes that seemed to have opened a new sound in the world of music.

And, although in the nineteenth century the technical virtuosity of the horn developed rapidly with the invention of valves, its function nevertheless remains substantially that of the amphibious instrument capable of associating itself with either woodwinds or brass, a function that continued through Debussy and that was not even altered with the experimentations of Wagner.

It has been only in the last thirty years that the horn more decisively has become an integral part of the brass: a tendency that is made possible by the extraordinary technical progress of the instrument. Its agility now resembles the trumpet without having had the invigorating jazz influence, like the trumpet. Such new orientation, that with Stravinsky became the property of almost all conductors of the last thirty years, does not exclude however any of the "Romantic" possibilities of the instrument. On the contrary with the always more refined use of the stopped horn and of the mute, the horn competes now in the color areas with its more sensitive colleagues in the modern orchestra.

Range (Sounding)

(1) As one descends from this B♭ toward the lower pitches, the notes speak less easily and require that one leaves ample time for a comfortable attack avoiding any fast moving passages prior to the note. The that at one time was missing on some horns, today can always be obtained. As one ascends above the high F (sounding) the pitches become continuously thinner, less expressive, and of emission so dangerous to discourage the use of them. It is always best that such sounds are reached by adjacent tones.

Almost in order to evoke the black of midnight, Verdi lets the horn descend to the low A (sounding), but had the wisdom to give this note to three horns not only in order to render a bigger sound, but also to guarantee that the note be played. Since the note is perilous, he compensated for it in the event that one of the instruments would remain voiceless, therefore, also giving the players support and reciprocal encouragement freeing them from the panic of the responsibility.

G. Verdi: *Falstaff*, p. 330. Ed: Ricordi

A low A is also found in the works of Mahler.

Mahler: *Sinfonia III*, pp. 4-5. Ed: Universal

(*) On the horn there are cylinders, devices that have the same function as valves.

In the following very well known passage from Strauss, usually, the last two notes are doubled by the second and the fourth horns that are more secure in the lower octaves. Therefore, the accents are assured for those last two notes.

R. Strauss: *Till Eulenspiegel*, p. 3. Ed: Universal

Strauss does not hesitate to send the horn into the very highest range. He does, however, approach these notes stepwise making it easier for the performer.

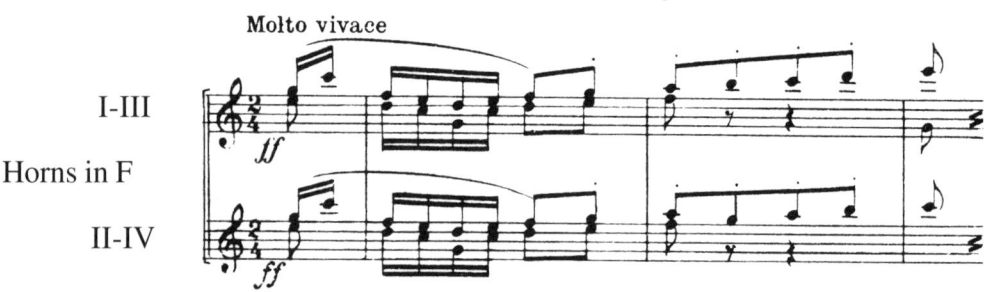

R. Strauss: *Sinfonia domestica*, p. 111. Ed: Universal

Scoring

At one time in all music for horn, as in other brass instruments like the trumpet, accidentals were not put in the part, nor was there a key signature. Each note, therefore, had to be altered when necessary. Today, however, this practice no longer exists nor can it be justified. The key is given as in any other instrument.

Generally the horns are written in pairs. First and Second – Third and Fourth. Since the first and third and the second and fourth are often in unison, it is advised to write horns paired according to their tessitura in order to avoid the useless exhaustive copying of parts, as in this example.

By writing a first/third part and a second/fourth part, one economizes greatly.

The composer, today, always writes as if the horn were in F not worrying about whether the performer is playing on a double horn.

The lowest notes were written in the bass clef and in a manner that today no longer makes sense, for they are written an octave lower than necessary.

Example of the traditional notation:

This habit has now ceased since the modern horn has pushed its tessitura so low that it would be very difficult to read a part with too many additional ledger lines for the lowest notes. To demonstrate this the following example is given:

Fingerings

The mechanism that produces the different overtone series is made up of three cylinders (cylinders that have the same function as normal valves). The modern horn also has a piston (trigger), that, as has been pointed out, transposes instantaneously the instrument from B♭ to F and vice versa. In the following table all the positions (overtone series) are shown for the horn in F and in B♭. The horn is tuned in F when it is used without the piston or trigger. Likewise when the trigger is depressed, the instrument is in B♭. The best partials, generally, are the first ones on the horn in F and the first ones on the B♭. While it is possible to approach the upper most partials, the sound is less pleasing as one ascends. The seventh partial is quite bad. For example, , obtainable with the first, fifth, and sixth partial, is best played with the first valve. The seventh and fourteenth partials are flat. The missing harmonics in the table (11, 13, and 15) are of such defective intonation and uncertain emission that they are not used. Such defective partials were used once on the simple horn that did not have chromatic possibilities and was constricted to the limits of a single series of harmonics.

E.R. 2935

Valve Combinations

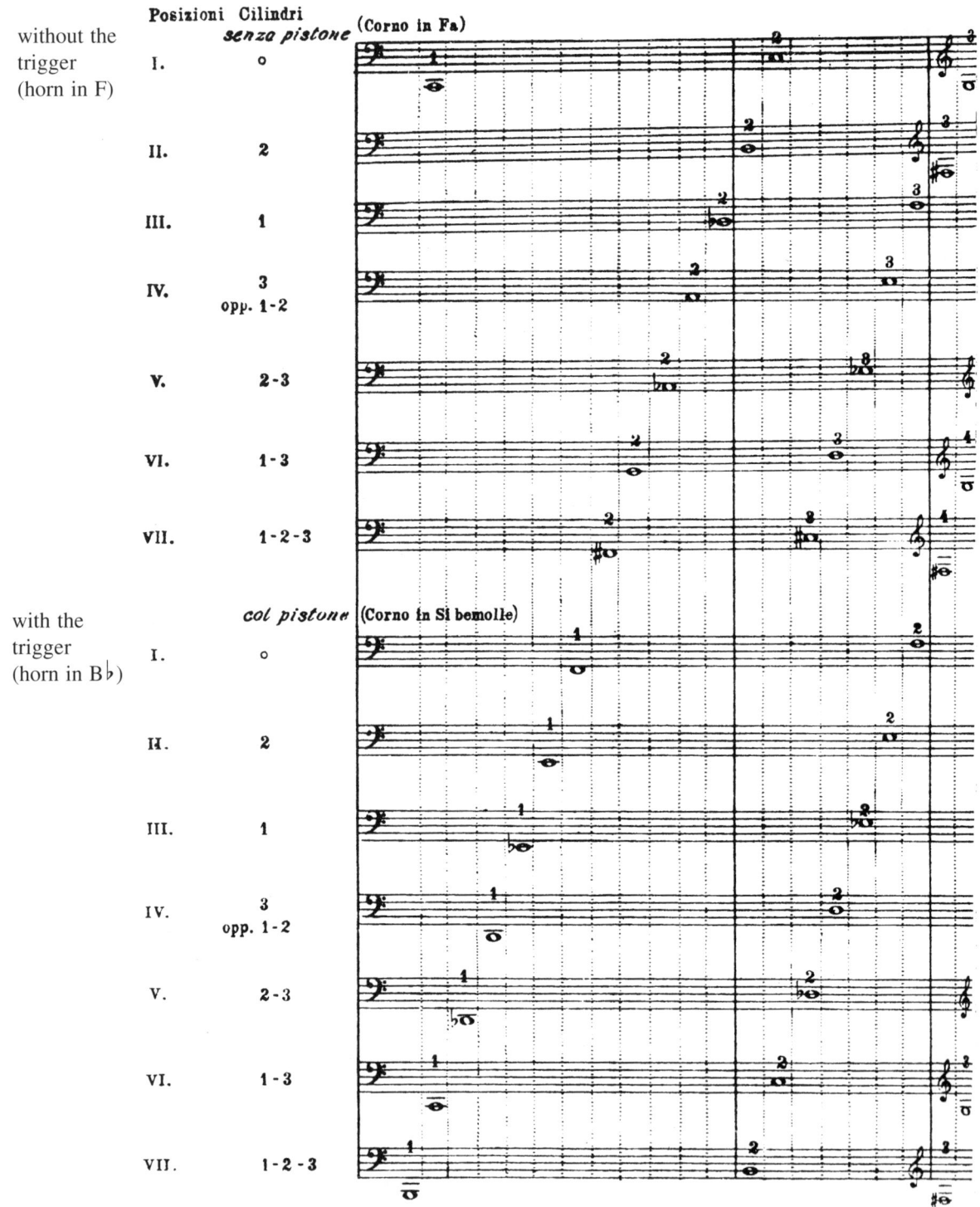

Timbre

The horn in the normal register [♪] has a round and full sonority, of great sweetness with a kind of poetic significance. As from [♪] one descends toward the lower notes, the sonority becomes continuously darker and fuller. The lower notes are, at the *piano*, full of charm, while at *forte*, they remind one of the timbre of the tuba. All the tones on the horn in the normal tessitura indicated above are possible, homogeneous, and in-tune. The small imperfections due to the construction of the instrument must not preoccupy the composer, for it is the task of the performer to correct these by finding the right fingerings for certain problems.

Generally one assigns the highest parts to the first and third horn while the lower ones are given to the second and fourth. It is advised, therefore, that the second and fourth horn do not go above as the highest note , while the first and third do not play in the lower extremes.[1]

Sound production

On the horn one can produce sounds in various ways according to the following varieties:
Open tones or normal sounds.
Stopped tones (*bouchés*), that one obtains by closing the bell with the right hand: their effect is somewhat nasal. The tessitura of the stopped horn is the following:

The *closed sounds* are indicated with a (+). In order to indicate an open sound when it is necessary, one superimposes (o). Such sounds are so sharp that in order to execute them the player must transpose a half step down. And so this effect

(Mussorgski: *A Night on Bald Mountain*) is obtained with the left hand and the lip stopping in the position of the  while the right closes and then opens the bell.

With the indication *Padiglione in alto* (Bell in the air) the player places the instrument so that it offers its most brilliant resources. While placing the bell in the air, one cannot use the hand in the bell.
Metal sounds (*cuivrès*), sforzando sounds of metallic color.
Echo sounds, i.e., sounds not completely stopped. They seem from afar, are most pleasant, and perhaps preserve the purity, softness, and color of the normal horn. Such sounds are so flat that the performer in order to obtain the best intonation must play them a half step higher. They are indicated so: ⊕ ─────

---

(1) Today, however, the four performers are capable of playing the entire range of the instrument.

Flutter tonguing (*Flatterzunge*) is easy and best between the following notes:

As one exceeds these limits the flutter tongue becomes less effective and more difficult, above all in the lower register.

Mute

The use of the mute is normal. However, it tends to suffocate the sound and, though it renders a sweet and dreaming quality, it takes away other possibilities of expression. As pointed out for the correction of defective notes or for a variety of colors, today's performer prefers to exhaust the infinite possibilities of the hand in the bell, a means that conserves the purest of sounds. The mute may be used and taken out while playing.

Slurring

The horn, now, has an agility similar to that of the trumpet and that which applies to slurring on any woodwind would approximately apply to the horn. Slurs ascending and descending of relatively wide leaps are of no difficulty to the performer.

Tonguing

The horn normally is adept at single and double tonguing. Triple tonguing is not usually executed. In the following range one can play 16th notes at a quarter note = 132 single tongued. While with the double tongue one can play 16th notes at 160. Above the as one ascends, the velocity tends to diminish proportionately to the strength of the lip. The speed also tends to diminish as one descends toward the lower register. While diminishing the frequency of the vibrations, the tongue is hindered and the sound becomes sluggish.

Glissandi

It is possible to produce glissandi with each overtone series on the instrument. It is best to begin the glissando on one of the most stable harmonics in the overtone series, i.e., the third, the fifth, or the eighth. Since on the horn the series of harmonics is very extensive, the glissando is quite efficient. It is possible only at forte and must be done rapidly.

86

Maximum range of the glissandi on the double horn in F-B♭.

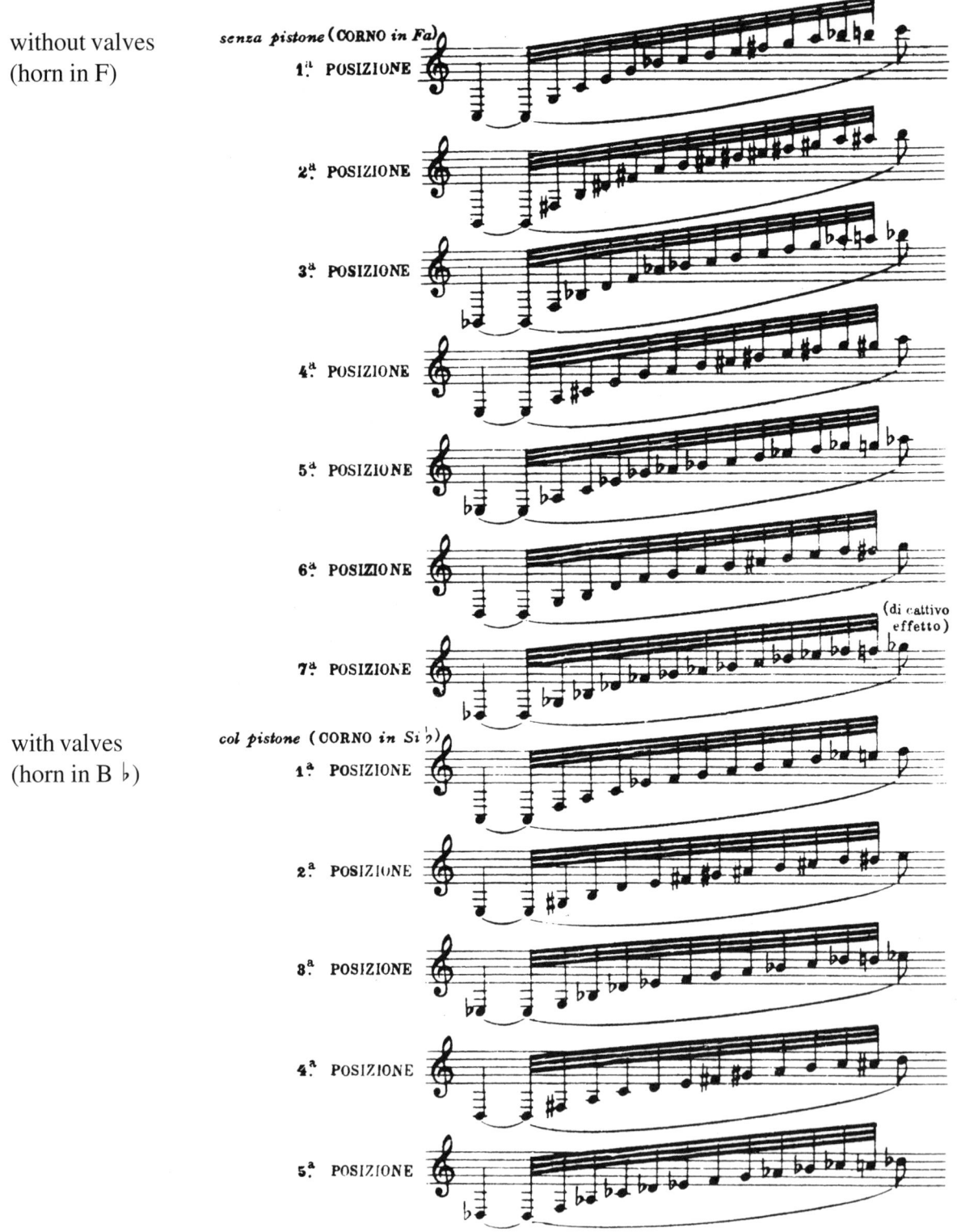

Breathing

The duration of the breath depends on the intensity of the sound and on the quantity of air that is required for the expression of the phrase. The lowest tones require more air than the highest ones. The following are maximum durations for held notes without expression for the average performer in the orchestra:

In the low register ![notation] 10 seconds at *forte*, 20 seconds at *piano*;

In the middle range ![notation] 16 seconds at *forte*, 40 seconds at *piano*.

The maximum times are needed for reference in the orchestra. On the other hand the performer knows how to find the correct moment to take a breath. Breathing in the highest register can be tiring.

Trills

See section on trills for brasses.

Examples of the use of the horn in contemporary scores.

M. Ravel: *Concerto in G major for piano and orchestra*, p. 32. Ed: Durand

Horns in F

A. Casella: *Elegia eroica*, p. 26. Ed: Universal

A. Schönberg: *Fünf Orchesterstücke*, p. 45. Ed: Universal

O. Respighi: *Pini di Roma,* p. 32. Ed: Ricordi

I. Stravinsky: *Symphonie de Psaumes*, pp. 51-52. Ed: Schott

THE TRUMPET

Beethoven, who died without ever having suspected that the trumpet could have performed in such perfect tranquillity with other instruments and could have played a chromatic scale at such rapid tempi, would be quite surprised to know the enormous transformation that has taken place in the character and the technique of an instrument among the oldest in music history. A first and fundamental step had been accomplished in the first ten years of the last century [note: 19th century in this case] with the addition of valves that put at the disposal of the instrument the entire chromatic scale, thus rendering the end to those deplorable gaps against which Beethoven struggled so heroically in his orchestration. But the new invention, by increasing the resources infinitely of the instrument, did not change substantially the trumpet's heroic and warlike character. A true revolution, more in its character than in its technique, was fulfilled in the works of jazz. When black musicians adopted the venerable instrument in the jazz idiom, they gave to the trumpet unexpected possibilities. Its ancient epic and military accents, its heroic masculinity of old were given up to a vast comic, grotesque, gossipy, and exaggerated sentimental prattle. It should be note that it has reached through this medium a very high, fantastic virtuosity that would have appeared unthinkable thirty years ago. It is also necessary to add that a good part of this transformation has been due to the great use, and also abuse, of the mute.

The interesting fact without precedence in the history of instrumental music is that this new technique that one could have supposed should have limited itself to light music, i.e., jazz, has instead rapidly overflown into the field of serious music. This influence has been exercised in two ways: *first*, that of direct assimilation by many European composers (Stravinsky, Ravel, Milhaud, Casella, etc.) by means of special compositions with African-American rhythms like those in Ragtime, the Fox Trot, Blues, etc. *Second* and infinitely more important was the indirect influence produced by jazz technique on symphonic instrumentation. This influence has determined a prodigious virtuosic evolution in the art of the performer that has given to the composer a new symphonic instrument with enormous and unforeseen resources.

The trumpet has affirmed itself, in the last years, as an element not only usable but also precious in the field of chamber music (see *Ottetto* for winds and *L'Histoire du soldat* of Stravinsky, *Serenata for five instruments* of Casella, etc.). This new aspect of the instrument is due to the great virtuosity of the performers who have adapted themselves to the intimacy of chamber music and made themselves part of a group with few instruments without ever overpowering.

The tendency in modern music to push the trumpet toward its highest register has forced manufacturers to make an instrument with a smaller bore in a way to favor the highest tones. Therefore, the trumpet has acquired a more stringent timbre and has lost some of its consistency above all with regard to the trumpet in C, used especially in France. In Italy and Germany one is still quite faithful to the trumpet in B♭ whose sonority in the low register, so important for the music of the past century, is more secure. The trumpet in C is chatty and impish where the trumpet in B♭ conserves the more heroic characteristic of the classic instrument.

Range

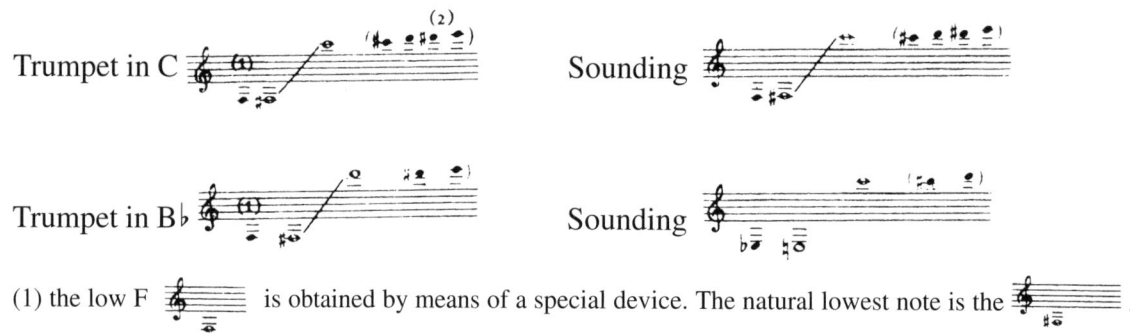

(1) the low F is obtained by means of a special device. The natural lowest note is the .

(2) the highest two notes , on the trumpet in C, are harzardous and of dubious effect. The notes in parenthesis are considered daring on the player's part.

The trumpet in B♭ can be transposed into the trumpet in A by means of a special attachment. The change can be done instantaneously, as on the trombone or the double horn. Such changing is aimed at facilitating certain overtones if the work is in A or in a similar key.

The lowest notes indicated in the standard notation are written in the bass clef with an adjustment to the octave lower, as was pointed out for the horn. The following scoring that is also used for trills is much more logical.

This medium trumpet is quite neglected although it would be very useful in every orchestra for authoritative sonorities and for performing the lower part of the family in a register corresponding to that of the high parts played by the other trumpets. It can be said that it is an analogous requirement to that of the third trombone, even if some indication in the score does not appear. It has a bore with a great diameter and has a large mouthpiece in order to facilitate the playing of the lowest notes.

The trumpet in D, a high trumpet, is generally adapted for the playing of certain types of older music. Its sound is quite small with little expressive quality like that of the *cornetta*. Above the it loses the true timbre of the trumpet. It is, therefore, an instrument that must be treated for its special characteristics without pretending that it can take the place of an ordinary trumpet in C or in B♭.

Timbre

The high register has great strength with the possibility of a ringing, forceful tone that has often attracted the attention of composers. The low register, however, must not be neglected for it is most dignified, rich in charm, and capable of full and solemn sonorities that cannot be duplicated on another instrument. All the notes contained in the following tessitura: [music] are easy and comfortable. As one descends [music] below the tones become more difficult to emit, above all on the trumpet with a small bore, e.g., trumpet in C and in D. Rising above [music] becomes more difficult depending upon the strength of the lip, above all at *piano*. Above this previous G, the sound is more spontaneous if it is launched more at the *forte* and *fortissimo* as one ascends.

This note [music] is quite out of tune. As for the remaining notes that are defective, these are generally those that employ the use of more valves, i.e., the second and third valves in combination. The performer generally corrects these with the appropriate adjustment of the lip. [Note: Casella may or may not have been familiar with the use of the first and the third valve slides. These are quite effective in correcting any of the above problems that relate to notes that are sharp.]

Breathing

For the normal register of the instrument [music] one may think in terms of eight seconds at *forte* and around twenty seconds at *piano* adhering also to the considerations set forth in the opening chapter of the text.

Trills

(See the previous section on trills as they apply to all brass instruments)

Scoring

The trumpet, as the horn, is scored without regard for the key signature.

Slurring

The slur on the trumpet renders an excellent effect. The performer, today, knows how to find opportune devices in order to simulate the slur in cases in which slurring is not possible.

A. Honegger: *Symphonie*, p. 8. Ed: Senart

Trumpet in C

V. Mortari: *Trittico*, p. 2. Ed: Carisch, S.A

I Trumpets II

M. Ravel: *L'enfant et les sortilèges*, p. 131. Ed: Durand

Tonguing

The trumpet is capable of a great agility, by taking advantage of single, double, and triple tonguing. Some approximate metronome markings follow, with consideration to the endurance of the lip.

With reference to the sounds in this tessitura: As one descends below the articulation is more difficult and slower. As one ascends above the articulation becomes more forced and tiring; therefore, the speed tends to diminish.

Single tongue: 16th notes at a quarter = 152
Double tongue: 16th notes at a quarter = 176
Triple tongue: 16th notes at two eighth notes = 104

Flutter tongue

Flutter tonguing is easy and effective. The best register is that between the following notes:

Vibrato

Vibrato is a function of a slight pressure of the lip and/or with the contribution of a light pressure of the finger on the valve. The result is penetrating, sensual, and resembles the human voice. One can use vibrato in the entire range of the instrument; however, it is most effective in the normal tessitura of the instrument.

Glissandi

The effects of portamenti are possible with intervals no greater than a major third. The trumpet, like the horn, can produce glissandi through the overtone series by beginning on the second or the third harmonic and ending on the ninth or vice versa.

Mute

The metal mute can be crackling, metallic, and more harsh as one ascends toward the upper register. Below 𝄞 the tone is not clear, but it does not lose its effect. The mute can also be of fiber or cardboard. The effect is sweeter toward the upper register; however, it renders a better tone in the lower. It is most useful in cantabile sections by giving the effect of a trumpet at the distance.

Another mute is the "wa-wa mute" that originated in America. It has a hole in the front in which one inserts a small funnel. By manipulating the funnel the hand can vary the intensity and color of the sound obtaining mellow, oscillating tones, etc., according to the imagination of the player (this imagination for the jazz virtuoso has no limits). The sound of the wa-wa is sweet and effective over the entire instrument. It seems that the sound comes out of a closed box. The funnel as a mute without manipulation can greatly muffle the sound.

Jazz playing has introduced the so called *sordina muta* or the plunger mute. It is capable of graduating the muffling of the sound increasingly by degrees of the closing of the bell. When the bell is completely closed, the sound becomes opaque and gives only a vague memory of the timbre of the trumpet. It seems as if it is another instrument; soft, sweet, and poetic: an instrument that reminds one somewhat of the saxophone, but more delicate. These special sounds diminish as the bell is opened, giving voice to a richer scale of timbral shadings.

Some uses of the trumpet

Articulations between the trumpet and the strings:

A. Casella: *La giara,* "Finale". Ed: Universal.

An example of very low notes that give very good results even with the mute.

M. Ravel: *Rapsodia spagnuola*, p. 35. Ed: Durand

An agile burlesque where the tuba tries to follow the trumpet.

I. Stravinsky: *Suite per piccola orchestra* (1921), "Galop", p. 26-27. Ed: J. and W. Chester.

The following passage for the Trumpet in F

C. Saint-Saëns: *Sinfonia III*, "Finale", pp. 150-151. Ed: Durand

in France is usually played on the trumpet in C:

(With the trumpet in F the very high D, and all the other D's, would be very difficult to play.)

An example that demonstrates how the mute can be introduced during a played passage

M. Ravel: *Rapsodia spagnuola*, p. 38. Ed: Durand

THE BASS TRUMPET

An instrument of superb timbre, the bass trumpet today deserves a permanent place in the orchestra since the alto trombone is no longer in use. The Italian bass trumpet is usually in B♭, but there are also those in C, in D, and in E♭. (The one in D is now no longer used.)

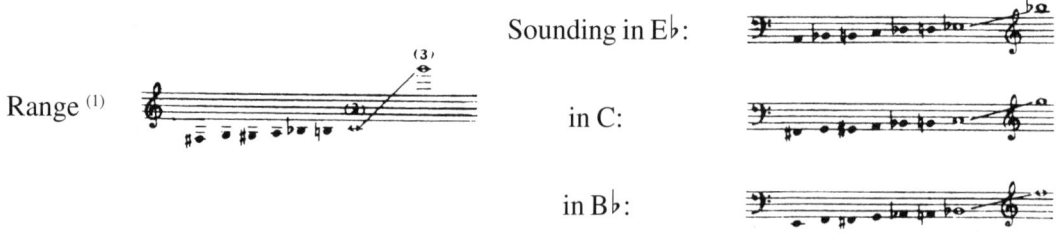

(1) The bass trumpet was also at one time written in the bass clef with a natural transposition an octave higher. It is far more logical to score the instrument as indicated above in the so called "uniform notation."
(2) Above this C the sonority becomes less characteristic and the notes are more difficult to play.
(3) One can play above this G; however, the sonority becomes forced, insecure, and strident. The great pressure on the lip necessary to play these tones is not worth the effort.

Examples of the use of the bass trumpet are plentiful above all at *piano*, for it is in this way the instrument can achieve its special sonority.

I. Stravinsky: *Le Sacre du printemps*, p. 104. Ed: Russe de Musique

(1) This note, below the ordinary range, is obtainable on the bass trumpet in E♭ that has a fourth valve added. In this case the instrument functions as an alto trombone with valves and a smaller bore.

In the above passage for three trumpets, the bass trumpet functions as a trombone; however, the sonority is different.

Trills (See the section on trills for all of the brass instruments)

Everything that applies to the other aspects of performance on the bass trumpet, i.e., tonguing, slurring, articulation, can be assumed from the technique of the ordinary trumpet. One must of course take into consideration that the lower sounds of this instrument are less responsive; therefore, it tends to be less agile.

OTHER TRUMPETS

There are other trumpets pitched higher that are in the keys of E♭ and F.

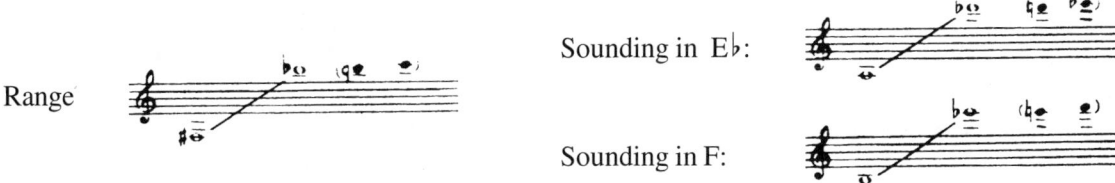

The sounds are smaller, not as expressive, and are quite distant from that of the normal trumpet. The trumpet in F is used often to facilitate the performance of certain very high parts in the music of Bach and Handel.

A very high trumpet in B♭ exists that is a recent invention. It has a very incisive, penetrating, and almost strident timbre, somewhat similar to that of the *clarinetto* in its high register. It is reminiscent of the sound of the highest trumpets that were called *clarini*.

It is unclear whether these trumpets were indicated in scores or whether their use was left to the performer. The modern trumpet is not adapted to perform such parts.

A very high trumpet in A also was built and could be most useful for music in that key.

Trills (See the section on trills for all of the brass instruments)

CORNET

The cornet is a most agile instrument and was an enormous resource in the bands of the 19th century. Until mid-century (20th century) the cornet was unique; however, today the modern trumpet has the same possibilities of lightness and mobility. The bore of the cornet is conical and it has a special mouthpiece. Its timbre is rounder and more subtle (veiled) and quite spread. There are cornets in C, in B♭, and in A that is the least used. The ranges are those of the corresponding trumpets and those aspects of tonguing, vibrato, muting, etc., also apply. Despite its spontaneous agility, for the most part, the modern trumpet has taken its place and it has almost disappeared from the modern orchestra.

The term "*Cornetta a pistoni*" no longer applies, for now no brass instrument lacks a chromatic mechanism except the military trumpets and some antique instruments.

I. Stravinsky: *Petrouchka,* III scene, p. 2. Ed: Russe de Musique

Cornet in B♭

I. Stravinsky: "Marcia reale" in *L'Histoire du Soldat*, Ed: Universal

Cornet in B♭

A. Casella: "Polka" in *Pupazzetti*, Ed: J. and W. Chester

THE TROMBONE

The tenor trombone in B♭ is generally no longer used. Likewise the use of the bass trombone has fallen into decline, supplanted by the tenor/bass trombone. The alto trombone, so valuable to many 19th century composers, has also now almost disappeared from the orchestra. In some venues, however, in order to be faithful to the spirit of the original works, the alto is still used. It should be said that the tenor is a poor substitute for the alto trombone, for an alto part played on the tenor will result in a sound that is forced and unnatural simply due to the difference in the tessituras of the two instruments. The tenor lacks the facility and spontaneity of the alto in its high range, and the timbre is certainly different.

The old trombone with valves, known for its agility, has been substituted in almost all orchestras by the "slide" trombone (*trombone a tiro*) (*à coulisse*). The slide trombone has become the instrument of preference simply due to its homogeneity of sound.

The valve trombone has the same range and the same timbral characteristics as the slide trombone. Its technique is similar to that of other instruments that have valves and similar proportions. The slide trombone has all of the same technical possibilities and prerogatives as the valve trombone; however, it provides a technique unattainable by the other instrument through the addition of the valve or trigger attached to it near the bell. This attachment allows one to transform the instrument from an instrument in B♭ to one in F so that notes unattainable on the B♭ may be played on the F. Today the following notes, missing on the normal slide trombone and the valved trombone, are possible.

The following notes, are obtainable only in the seventh position on the trombone in B♭. One should note that the seventh position is the most uncomfortable due to having to use the maximum length of the slide. These notes then are quite delicate and efficient with the use of the special key or trigger that places the instrument in the key of F. The trombone in B♭-F that is referred to as the trombone tenor-bass does not produce a gap. With the use of the trigger it enjoys a purity of sound, accurate intonation, and agility simply by avoiding both the difficult and uncomfortable sixth and seventh positions. One note only is played in the seventh position, the

. It is quite sharp and must be corrected carefully by the player with the lip. Although all trombones today are not equipped with the trigger, there is no doubt that this system will soon be universal.

In order to write for a simple trombone in B♭, the following limitations of the instrument must be considered.

Range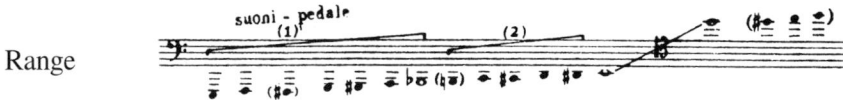

(1) The F♯ should not be used, but the preceding E♭ and F are usable.
(2) As has been pointed out, these notes exist only on the trombone tenor-bass. For the low B see above.

The lowest notes, the pedal tones, must be used with caution and reached by step-wise motion. Rapid movement must be excluded and all passages must have a tempo slow enough for comfortable execution. It is also recommended that notes in this area be given length. These two notes [notation] are quite difficult, and it is better that they are given to other instruments more secure in the bass region of the orchestra.

The highest notes above the [notation] are difficult and forced. Moreover, when one plays a part written for the alto trombone on the B♭ instrument, at least to [notation], the performer is faced with a certain difficulty.

One writes for the instrument in the bass clef and the higher notes are written in the tenor clef. The use of the slide (the sliding double tube that the arm manipulates making the column of air longer or shorter and therefore producing the seven series of harmonics that constitute the seven positions) gives to the player the responsibility of intonation as much as the fingerboard of a string instrument. The performers, then, cannot attribute out of tune notes solely to a defect in the instrument as was said of the low B [notation].

Positions

The positions on the trombone are seven, but on the tenor-bass trombone there are fourteen (14) positions: seven on the trombone in B♭ and seven on the F. The positions used are only twelve, for one does not use the sixth and seventh on the B♭ instrument simply because these positions give two series of harmonics that are much more easily obtained on the trombone in F. (See the following pages for positions on both instruments.)

Timbre

In the middle and high ranges at *forte*, the trombone has a brilliant and heroic timbre. In the low region it can be quite dark, fat, and menacing. At *piano* the sonority is full, mysterious, and always somewhat heavy. The pedal tones have a lacerating timbre, all with a particular and recognizable quality.

Once an instrument of grand, majestic, solemn, dramatic, violent, and even ferocious timbre, the trombone had to come under the influence of the African Americans who not having known the noble instrument of Mozart or of the *Ring Cycle* of Wagner took charge of this noble sound in the jazz idiom. They set into motion a virtuosity of unthinkable technique and joy of which they would have never dreamed. The strict performers of an earlier time never dared to suppose such. Everyone remembers the extraordinary virtuosity of the trombone that was the center of the famous film, *Il re del Jazz* (The King of Jazz). By comparing that frenetic, pyrotechnic, and acrobatic technique to that of massive Wagnerian gravity, one may have a clear idea of the prodigious movement, that in few short years, has created modern trombone technique, let alone the timbral and expressive functions of the instrument.

Flutter tonguing

Flutter tonguing is easy and secure on the instrument. The best range for the technique is as follows: [notation]

Vibrato

(Not to be confused with the tremolos that are great resources of the soloist in the band)

Vibrato is a function of the lip and, at times, a very slight use of the slide. The sound resembles the same as vibrato in the human voice. One can produce vibrato on the entire instrument; however, on low notes it is less effective.

Glissandi

The glissando is a characteristic effect of the trombone. It may be produced either ascending or descending. Provided that its limits do not exceed the interval of a diminished fifth, the effect is obtainable with the play of the slide between the first and the seventh positions.

Contemporary music is rich with examples of the procedure. It produces comic, grotesque, and characteristic effects along with sentimental and insinuating accents of jazz.

J. Ibert: *Suite symphonique*, p. 39. Ed: Peters

M. Ravel: *La Valse*, p. 127. Ed: Durand

M. Ravel: *L'heure espagnole*, p. 15. Ed: Durand

The trombone, like the horn, can produce the harmonic series with glissandi that are quite curious. These harmonic series glissandi are not as wide as those on the horn since they must begin on the second, better the third, harmonic and can not go farther than the tenth harmonic. With the use of the slide one can change positions during a glissando and therefore, produce different keys from the key from which the effect began. This type of glissando is possible only at *forte* and must be rapid.

102

The positions on all of the trombones written at the sounding pitch

without the F attachment
(Trombone in B♭)

with the F attachment
or trigger
(Trombone in F)

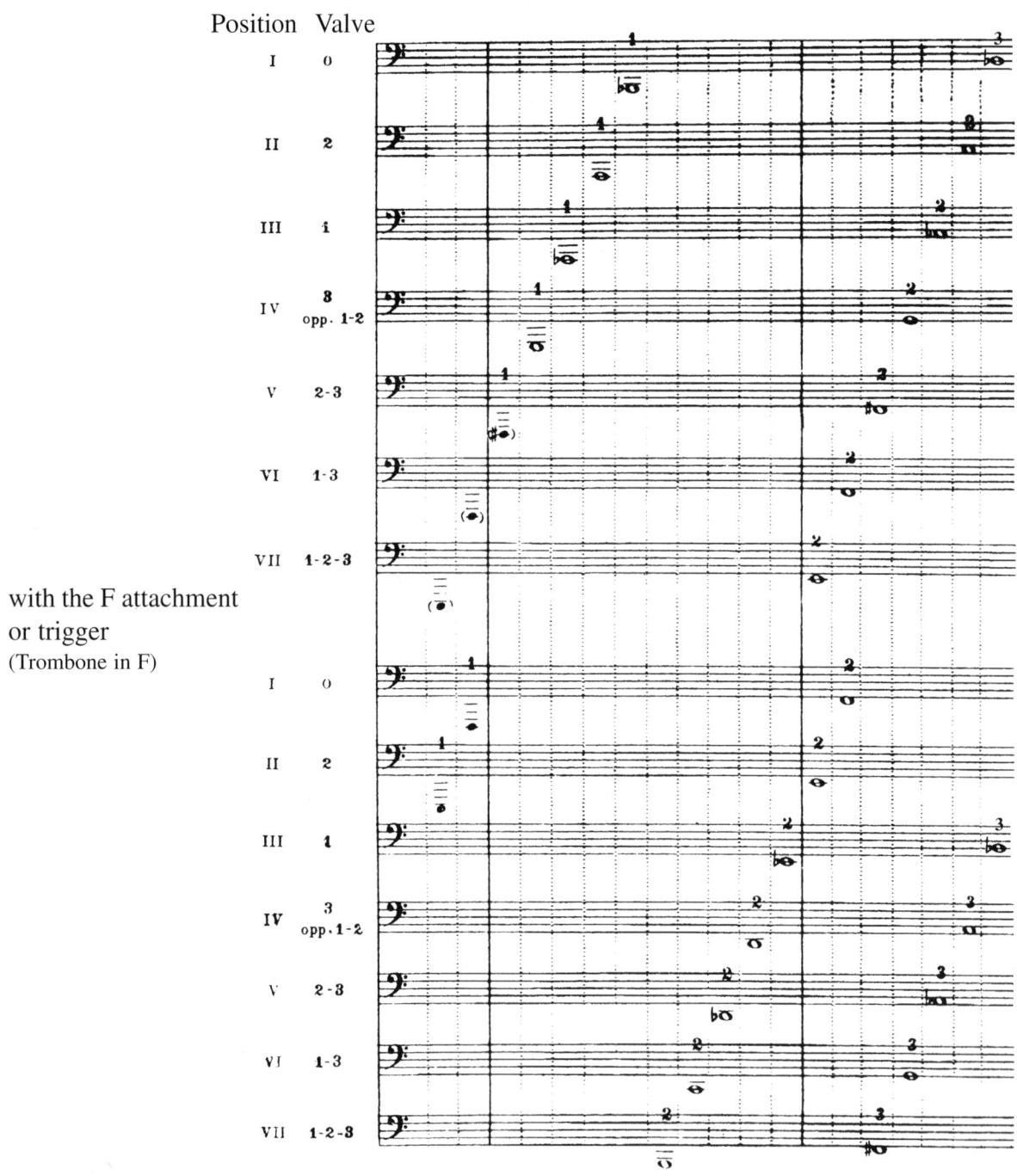

N. B. - The seventh partial is flat and generally not used, since the same tone can be produced much better in other positions. [Note: It should be realized, however, that there are seventh partials that must be played on the instrument to achieve adequate technique.]

E.R. 2935

Mute

Muting is well known on the trombone either with the metal or cardboard types. A mute renders dark sounds on the lower notes and quite harsh and "thorny" qualities in the highest areas of the instrument. Jazz has introduced other types of mutes among which the *wa-wa* and the plunger mute have been described in the chapter on the trumpet. The *wa-wa* mute produces a timbre that is somewhat nasal often suggesting grotesque or possibly even pastoral effects.

Slurring

It has always been said that the nature of the trombone does not favor the slur. In truth, sometimes the slur is quite impossible without their being a portamento or a slight glissando between the notes. The performer, however, knows how to use clever manipulations of the lip that can overcome the impossible nature of some slurs. One must not think that the slur is impossible, for notes in the same harmonic series (same position) are very easy to slur.

One can slur wide intervals either ascending or descending provided that the sounds from slurring are not of equal number in the order of the harmonics.

(1) G, the fourth harmonic, slurs well with E♭, the third harmonic.
(2) E, the third harmonic, slurs well with B♭, the fourth harmonic.
(3) G, the fourth harmonic, cannot slur with F♯, the fourth harmonic.
N. B. – It is easier to slur an ascending interval than it is a descending one.

Here is a beautiful example that demonstrates the excellent singing ability of the trombone.

W. A. Mozart: *Requiem*, "Tuba mirum"

Tonguing

The performer may use single and double tonguing in the following tessitura.

With the single tongue one can reach an approximate tempo of 16th notes at a quarter note = 120: with the double, one may reach a tempo of 16th notes at a quarter note = 144.

While one may tongue faster than the limits provided above, the effectiveness of the tongue is reduced at the lowest and highest pitches. It is recommended that one write agile passages with some brevity due to the tiring of the lip and the necessity for air. If the passage does not exceed more than one or two markings than that above, the tempo will be comfortable for the performer.

Since the agility of the lip is superior to that of the slide, one should write passages that permit a certain ease in the changing of the positions.

G. Petrassi: *Concerto per orchestra*, p. 58. Ed: Ricordi

(1) Rapid articulation in the low register in this case is not averted since the double tonguing at the octave above absorbs the attention of the listener.

Breathing

The trombone demands a lot of air. At *forte* the performer must breath very often, at almost every beat and sometimes every note. At *piano* instead it can reach a longer duration. One should be aware that for the length of a sound, besides the needed air, the resistance of the lip is also a factor for the lowest and highest registers above all.

In the following tessitura one may write ♪ around six seconds at *forte*, around sixteen seconds at *piano*, keeping in mind the considerations set forth previously. On the lowest notes the duration is less because the largest quantity of air is needed. On the highest notes, also, the duration is less depending on the least resistance of the lip necessary to produce the notes.

Trills

Trills are possible with a manipulation of the lip between two notes in the same position [same overtone series] or they may be achieved with rapid movement of the trigger. The following is a list of trills.

(x) defective
(xx) not recommended

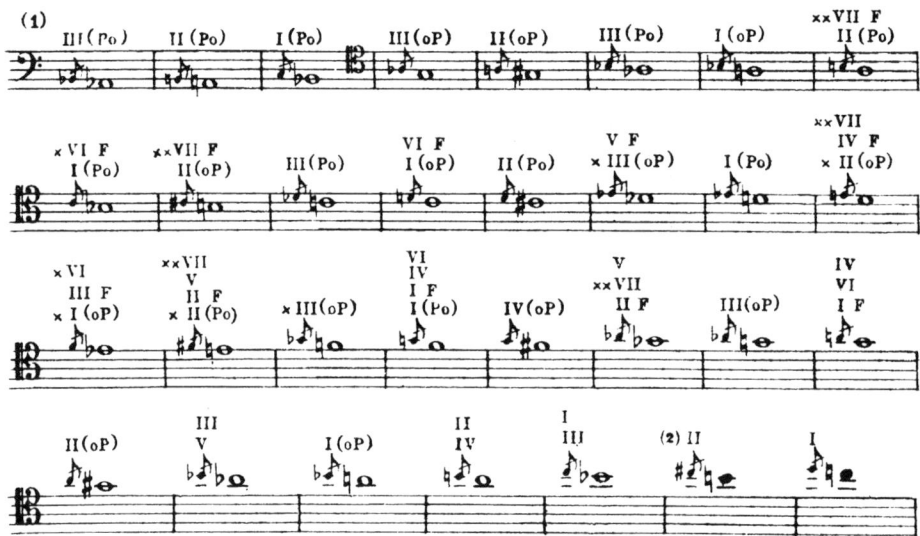

(1) The indications superimposed above the notes refer to ways in order to perform the trill. P° or °P indicates the alternated play of the piston (P = piston lowered; ° = piston raised). The roman numeral indicates the position with which the trill is executed. A number followed by an F refers to the instrument in F, i.e., with the piston lowered.
(2) The two last trills are difficult since the strength of the lip in the high register is an obstacle.

A half-step trill may be played with the movement of the slide. On such a trill, however, one must not expect precise tone quality or intonation. Due to this uncertain oscillation between two tones, the duration must not exceed approximately that of a double or triple mordent. The range is as follows:

(1) Difficult and bad
(2) Impossible

E.R. 2935

Grace notes

Grace notes are easily performed if they require only a minor movement from the slide (adjacent positions). That which was said for the trill applies to the grace note.

Position:
Number of the harmonic:

These are not as easy, but possible with the movement of two positions. With more movement the difficulty is augmented.

This passage could be written:

Analogous to the trumpet, the trombone in recent years has taken its place in chamber music that represents another and very important enlargement of the possibilities of the instrument. This new employment is found in the *Ottetto per fiati* of Stravinsky, where two trombones (and two trumpets) place themselves opposite a flute, clarinet, and two bassoons without ever overpowering. Another magnificent example of this kind is the *Concerto* of Hindemith for piano, brass, and harp. Neither must one forget the amusing *Sonata* of Poulenc for horn, trumpet, and trombone in which three instruments conserve a delicate language among themselves without "hardness."

In summarizing, one can affirm that the trombone, like the trumpet, is among the instruments that in the last forty years has demonstrated major evolutionary strides and its transformation, like that of the trumpet, has enriched the possibilities of the orchestra greatly. One might also say that this evolution is due to the potent influence of jazz.

A typical solo in somewhat a jazz style:

M. Ravel: *Bolero*, pp. 28-29. Ed: Durand

A passage of agility:

R. Strauss: *Der Rosenkavalier*, p. 240. Ed: Fürstner

108

A. Casella: *Scarlattiana*, p. 65. Ed: Universal

A solo of paradoxical character in the style of a "circus."

I. Stravinsky: "Marcia reale", in *L'Histoire du soldat*. Ed: Universal

A. Schönberg: *Fünf Orchesterstücke*, p. 57. Ed: Universal

Below are pedal tones that form a "fat" and welcoming pillow.

Albéniz-Casella: *Rapsodia spagnola per pianoforte ed orchestra*, unedited

OTHER TROMBONES

Other types of trombones exist that now are more or less in disuse. The Alto Trombone and its substitution in the orchestra for the tenor-bass trombone with less than good results has been discussed. It may be though that one day it will return to standard use. The instrument is tuned in E♭ and has the following range (the trombones, like the tubas, are written in sounding pitch).

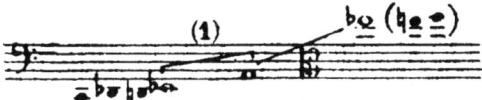

(1) The five tones between these two notes cannot be played.

The bass trombone also, as has been pointed out, has almost disappeared from the orchestra with the substitution of the tenor-bass trombone. This instrument has taken the role of the third trombone, i.e., with a larger bore and a larger mouthpiece, so that it can descend comfortably in the lowest notes demanded by composers. The true bass trombone is in F and has the following range:

(1) The five tones between these two notes cannot be played.

Finally, there exists a contrabass trombone. It is in B♭ bass, i.e., an octave below the tenor trombone, and has four pistons or triggers.

Wagner used it in the *Ring*. The instrument serves to give body and security to the lowest sounds and to maintain with the lowest notes of the harmony the same timbre of the trombone family. Its pedal tones are unusable. Today the function of the contrabass is generally given to the tuba.

FLICORNI AND TUBAS

The Flicorno (also called the Saxhorn) is an instrument with a notably developed conical bore that flows into a voluminous bell. The largeness of the bore gives an advantage naturally to the lower notes; however, it impedes the development of the upper register. A number of the instruments exist in the family especially enriching the lower unit, that of the tubas. The tuba, however, has a less conical bore than the flicorno. The mouthpiece of the tuba is smaller than that of the flicorno and has its own characteristics that consequently influence the timbre. One might say that the tuba mouthpiece falls somewhere between that of the horn and that of the trombone. The sound comes easily to the tuba and with the help of valves it can perform technical passages much easier than the slide trombone. Likewise, the less conical bore allows for an easier performance of the upper notes.

Instruments with three valves

Range

Smallest Flicorno in B♭ or in A *(sopracuto)*

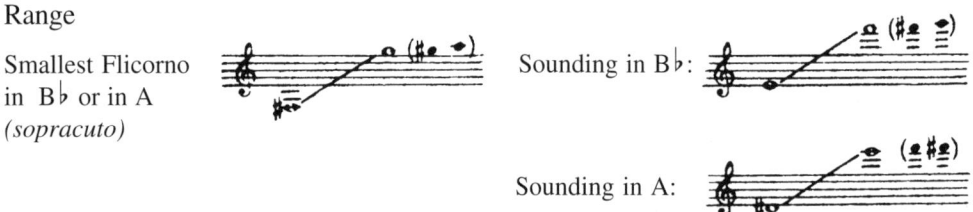

This instrument is most useful in B♭, but the one in A can be helpful for certain keys in order to reduce the number of accidentals.

Sopranino Flicorno

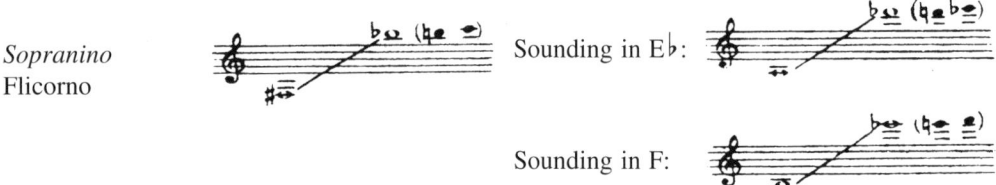

The *sopranino* in E♭ is at times used as a substitute for the trumpet in C or the small trumpet in D. Its smaller and less shrill tone and great facility, especially at *piano,* makes it particularly adaptable for singing lines. The following is an example:

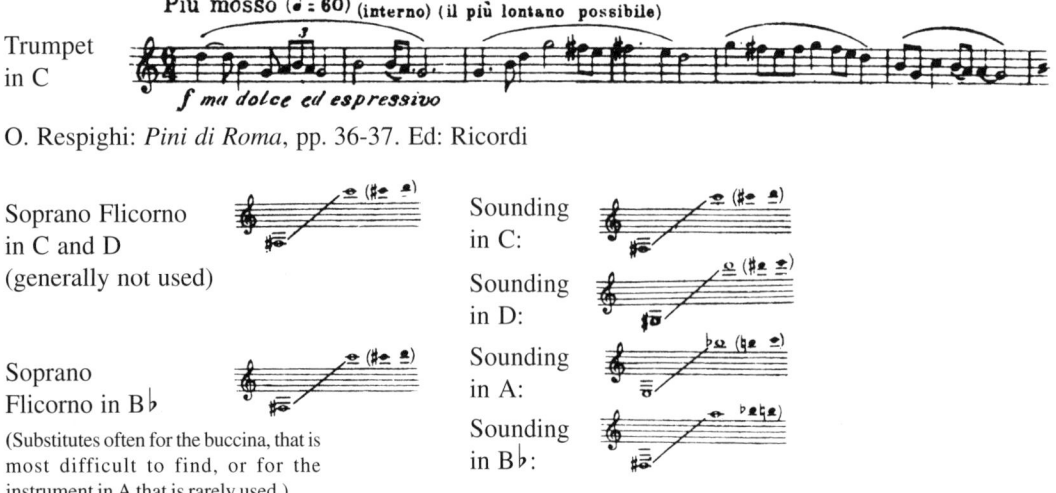

O. Respighi: *Pini di Roma*, pp. 36-37. Ed: Ricordi

Soprano Flicorno in C and D (generally not used)

Soprano Flicorno in B♭

(Substitutes often for the buccina, that is most difficult to find, or for the instrument in A that is rarely used.)

Alto Flicorno in E♭ and F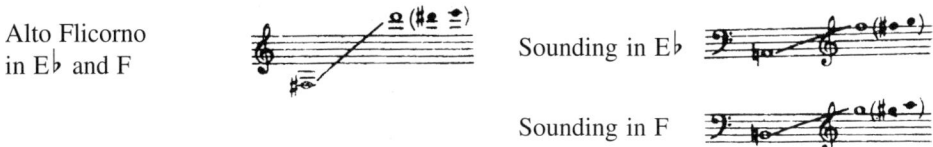

Limited generally to use in the band, these instruments can also give very good results in the orchestra. In fact parts have been found in some scores for an instrument called the *Tuba contralta in mi bemolle*, Alto Tuba in E♭. Since a certain confusion exists between the words flicorno and tuba, not to mention the terms used in other countries, e.g., saxhorn, bugle, one should not be amazed that some call the tuba a flicorno and vice versa.

Tenor or Baritone Flicorno in B♭ (also called *Bombardino*)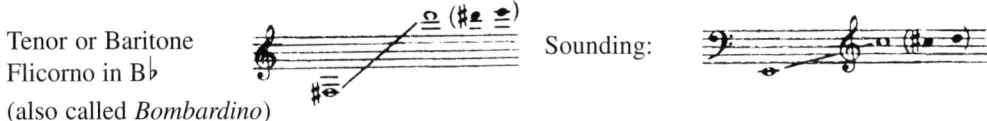

The baritone flicorno has great facility in the lower register, while in the upper it is better that one does not write above the ♪.

Instruments with four valves

To this category belong the tubas that are indicated here along with the flicorni due to their close relationship to the bass flicorno. The theoretical range is the same, but the tuba, with its smaller bore has greater possibilities especially in the upper register.

Bass Flicorno in B♭ (also called *Euphonium*) and the Bass Tuba in B♭ (in Germany called *Bass-tuba*)

(For this instrument one still writes the same notations of the flicorni above, i.e., uniform notation.)

(1) These two pedal tones ♪ are quite good.

(2) These five notes are possible, as pointed out previously, with the use of the 4th valve. The B ♪, by not being able to be executed in the 7th position, results in poor intonation and is ineffective.

(3) These two last notes are forced and very difficult.

N. B. - It was the first instrument to substitute in the orchestra for the *Oficleide*, now in disuse.

The difference in the construction between the bass flicorno in B♭ (Euphonium) and the bass tuba in B♭ is so small that the two instruments can not be given separate identities.

Flicorno basso-grave in E♭ and F
(also called *Bombardone*)

and Tuba basso-grave in E♭ and F

(1) The pedal tones are excellent and sonorous, but not easy to play.
(2) This note is defective for the same reason given in note 2 for the bass tuba in Bb.
(3) Tones not advised.

This instrument has now disappeared from the orchestra, especially the one in E♭. Its place has been taken by the contrabass tuba in B♭, and in some countries, also by the contrabass tuba in C. The contrabass tuba serves as the second instrument to have replaced the *Oficleide* after the *Euphonium* in order to serve as a bass for the trombones.

Contrabass Flicorno in C and B♭   in C
(also referred to as the *Helicon* due
to its elliptical shape, or *Pelittone*
from the name of its inventor, Pelitti)
and the Contrabass Tuba in C and in B♭   in B♭

(1) The fundamental is very difficult to produce.
(2) Very sharp.
The final low notes are difficult and require a notable effort of the embouchure.

The contrabass tuba is the normal instrument used in orchestra and now is a part of the low brass section with the trombones in substitution for the bombardone.

Double contrabass tuba in F-B♭.
(A flicorno of this type is nonexistent.)

The instrument is capable of immediately transposing to the key of B♭ with a simple added key. The mechanism is not unlike that of the trombone with a trigger that affords the instrument the possibility of finding the note with the best intonation and tone quality.

The mechanics involved are those of four rotating valves [rotary valves] which are more easily manipulated than piston valves on an instrument of this size. The intonation on the instrument is quite satisfactory in all ranges rendering an enormous service in the extremes of the orchestra. Although its use is still expanding, it does not exist in all orchestras. [Note: Certainly during the time of publication the instrument may not have been universal.]

Timbre

The timbre of the flicorno is not as incisive as that of the trumpet or the trombone, for it is much darker, almost resembling the horn in its lower regions. The tuba, however, although not losing the characteristics of the flicorno, has a color much nearer to that of the trombone.

Wagner for the *Ring* had two flicorni constructed and used two tenor tubas in B♭ with four pistons to accompany two bass tubas in F, also with four valves. These Wagnerian tubas have some special characteristics due, above all, to their using the same mouthpiece as the horn giving them a similar timbre to that of the horn. Wagner places these instruments in an alternating group with the horns. Playing the instrument is easier than playing the horn. This coupling of the tubas with the horns created, at least in Italy, tubas that were called *corno-tube*.

The range of the Wagnerian tuba in F is as follows:

The range of the tenor tuba in B♭ is as follows:

(1) With the use of the 4th valve one the lowest notes may be played, however with difficulty.

Besides the Wagnerian tubas, two other like instruments are in use: the *tenor tuba in B♭* and the *bass tuba in F*, both with four valves. Both have the same range and differ only slightly from the Wagnerian tubas, e.g., the Wagnerian tubas use a mouthpiece like that of the horn. For these tubas, like the others, it is recommended that one use the same notation, i.e., sounding pitch. Such notation unifies the notation of all tubas without having to make a change for the tenor tuba in B♭ and the tuba in F whose parts are regularly performed by the trombone with valves that plays at the sounding pitch.

All that was discussed in the chapters on trumpet and trombone concerning flutter tonguing, vibrato, muting, slurring, tonguing, etc., applies to the flicorni and the tubas taking into consideration that the lower one plays the less easy and spontaneous the technique. Likewise the lower the instrument, the longer the pistons must be and, therefore, the more time required to press them down. The same requirements for breathing set forth earlier for the other brass instruments (horn, trumpet, trombone) apply for the flicorni and tubas.

At times composers use only the generic term *tuba* without specifying the type. Strauss in *Don Chisciotte* asks for a *tenor-bass tuba in B♭* for the comic representation of Sancio Pancia. In reality the instrument used is an ordinary tenor tuba in B♭ with four valves (the fourth valve, as one knows, permits extending the lower tessitura). Today the term, tenor/ bass tuba, is generalized. In Mussorgski's *Pictures at an Exhibition*, Ravel wrote for a *tuba* without an indication of the type instrumentation to be used. Through an examination of the score one finds that the best instrument to be used is the tenor / bass tuba (i.e., the tenor tuba with four valves) or, better, the *bass tuba in B♭* (*Euphonium*). It is strongly advised that the composer, however, indicate the type tuba to be used.

Here is an example of lip agility that cannot be entrusted to the trombone.

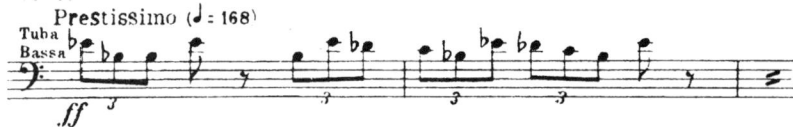

I. Stravinsky: *Le Sacre du printemps*, p. 71. Ed: Russe de Musique

The following is another magical color, almost sulky, that only the tubas, semi-brilliant, but a little opaque are able to render, a special color that is unforgettable.

I. Stravinsky: *Le Sacre du printemps*, pp. 56-57. Ed: Russe de Musique

The following shows the famous example of the tuba in *Don Chisciotte*. The character is evident: the instrument is "fat," a little "cafone" [Note: *cafone* is a word in the Italian language that in Casella's time would have referred to a person somewhat culturally deprived.] The impression is one of a person who wants to be gallant, invoking most efficiently the rough personality of Sancio. The doubling in the bass clarinet has a prudent reason.

R. Strauss: *Don Chisciotte*, pp. 86-87. Ed: Peters

A. Casella: *Sinfonia op. 63*, mvt. II, Ed: Universal

G. Gershwin: *An American in Paris*, pp. 82-83. Ed: New World Music - New York

This instrument [1] – that seemed until yesterday to be the "Cinderella" of the brass group has inspired the fantasy of composers in most recent times. Its low, round, rather pachyderm-like voice, was used in its singing character for the first time by Mahler in the third movement of his *First Symphony*. Another genial use is that of Stravinsky in the fourth scene of *Petrouchka* at the entrance of the bear tamer with his animals who seems to find his natural voice through the melodic element of the bass tuba.

(1) The simple indication, tuba, in modern scores refers generally to the contrabass tuba in B♭.

I. Stravinsky: *Petrouchka*, fourth scene. Ed: Russe de Musique

One anticipates even more surprises from the latent possibilities of this instrument whose construction continues to be perfected.

[Translator's note: Certainly since the time of Casella, we have seen untold uses for the tuba in bands, orchestras, and solo literature. The instrument is considered today a melodic instrument as are any of the other instruments of the orchestra. Its facility can be compared to any brass instrument with valves or cylinders.]

SAXOPHONE

The saxophone is a metal instrument with a conical bore with a mouthpiece not unlike that of the clarinet. An entire family exists with each instrument distinguishing itself according to its tuning.

Range

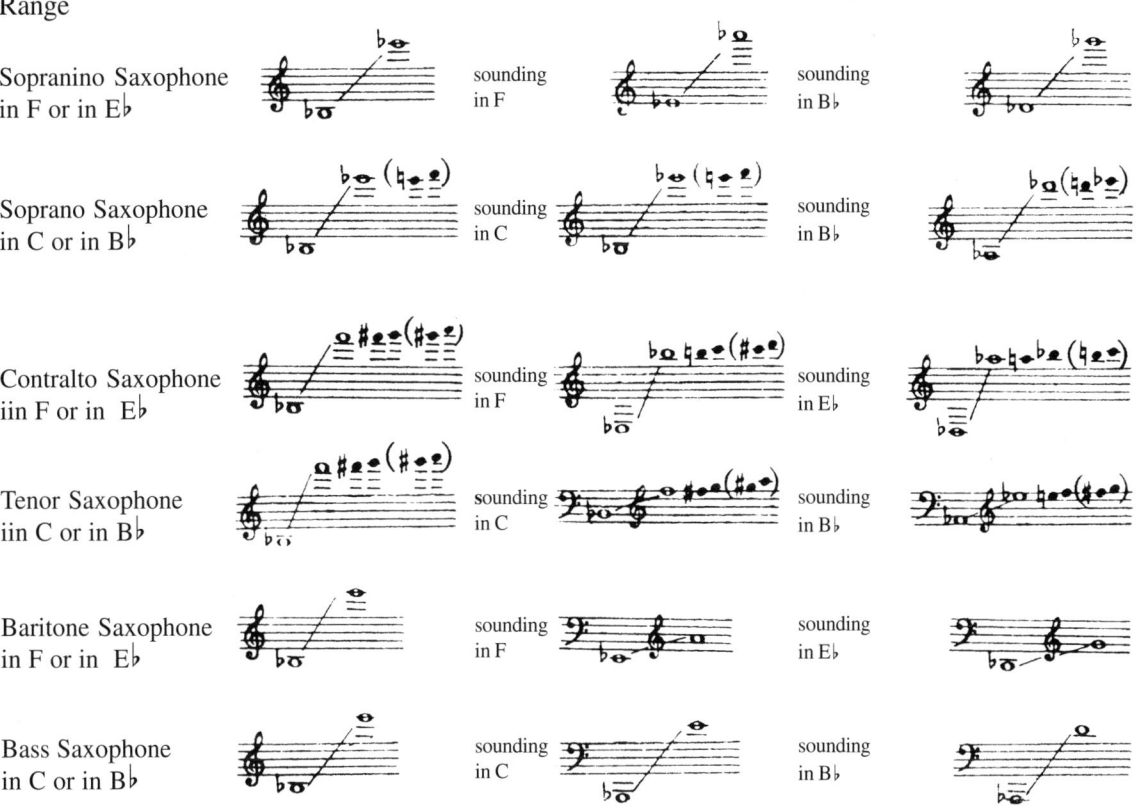

The most used of the above are those in in E♭ and B♭. The lowest notes are a modern edition for the range began with the . Moreover, American manufacturers have added these other tones to the low register. Below the , however, the sonority tends to become more harsh and difficult to play, and playing below the is almost impossible at *piano*. One is discouraged from using this B♭ just as one should not use the corresponding note on the oboe. The highest tones above become more forced as one ascends. Those above are reserved for the virtuoso and generally for virtuosic effects.

Timbre

The saxophone's sound is penetrating, somewhat veiled with a certain sensuality that allies it with the ingratiating timbre of the first string of the violoncello. Its sonority is very intense at *forte* which can be compared to the intensity of the horn at *forte*. At *piano,* morbid, weak effects are possible. Three registers are evident on the instrument.

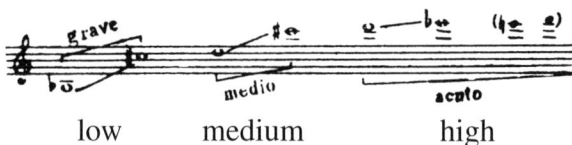

low   medium   high

The lowest register comprises all of the fundamental harmonics as in the corresponding chalumeau register of the clarinet. The middle register is produced from the first harmonic and reached by the use of a special key called the octave key. The highest sounds are reached with various harmonics. The lowest is the most sonorous. It is intense, open, rich, and has a natural sound, i.e., it is not achieved through any artificial means. The ♩ is somewhat voiceless.

From ♩ (1) the sound becomes more velvety, quiet, and almost closed. As one ascends in the highest register the sound becomes smaller, loses body, and transforms its timbre. Moreover, with recent mechanical improvements done by the French manufacturer, Henri Selmer, the high register has developed a sound much more sympathetic with the rest of the instrument. The saxophone in general tends toward harshness with a metallic and nasal sound. Likewise its intonation deficiencies must be treated delicately. Therefore, not withstanding a certain ease in producing a sound, one must take special care to produce a quality timbre.

In the orchestra the soprano, alto, and tenor are generally used; however, Ravel used the sopranino in *Bolero*.

Trills

In the following range, all of the major and minor trills are available to the performer.

Three are impossible:

(1) This trill can be played on the Selmer saxophone

---

(1) The modern devices added to the instrument have made this D much more homogeneous with the instruments timbre.

Tremolos

(x) defective
(xx) difficult and of poor quality
(xxx) almost impossible and very heavy
(1) good on the Selmer saxophone

Note: The tremolos below the letter A are not rapid and difficult to execute. The tremolos between A and B are better and more rapid. After B they are rapid and spontaneous. Between C and D, E and F, and from G above they are again less rapid and spontaneous. In general one should remember that the tremolo becomes less rapid and less spontaneous as the interval becomes larger.

Slurring

The saxophone as a melodic instrument lends itself particularly well to the slur. Slurring is easy even at the octave; however, after a leap of an octave, it becomes more difficult. As with all of the wind instruments, it is easier to slur up than it is to slur down.

Tonguing

Only single tonguing is available to the performer. The instrument is less facile than the clarinet, e.g., the clarinet in the low register becomes continuously more "lazy" and on the lowest notes only passages with moderate speed are possible. It is best not to write single tonguing faster than 16ths at a quarter note = 112 in the medium register. As for the rest of the instrument, the tongue is less rapid.

Flutter tonguing

The flutter tongue is not a spontaneous technique on the instrument as it is not on the rest of the instruments that employ a mouthpiece that goes into the mouth. It is possible, however, and can be done effectively.

Mutes

Mutes can be use on the saxophone and are generally employed in the low register. As one ascends to the medium and high registers the mute loses its effect. With such devices as mutes, it acquires a more muffled tone, and the intonation tends to sharp.

Portamenti

The portamento is accomplished with the lip and is quite possible within the range of an octave. In passages that require portamento between registers [Note: more than an octave in the same register] the portamento can become interrupted with a fracture in the sound that is difficult to overcome. In the jazz style they are of the utmost importance and play a tremendous part in the jazz timbre.

Breathing

The saxophone requires much air especially in the lower register.

The enhanced construction of the saxophone in the last thirty years has brought about notable improvements to the instrument. The thousands of personal demands of the jazz improvisers have excited the imagination of the manufacturers to offer untold mechanical resources. A type of race based on personal initiatives, secrets of certain odd and eccentric effects by performers, and on a total assent of method has taken place. These elements, including performers and manufacturers, have created good and bad advancements often without worry for the purity and beauty of the sound.

For approximately a century, since the saxophone was created by the ingenious imagination of Adolph Sax, much has been said and much has been done in favor of this instrument beginning with Berlioz. But its ordinary use with only some exceptions has not exceeded the limits of the band. Were it not for the deliberate diabolical spirit of jazz, the saxophone could have been given serious consideration. From jazz, then, it has passed to the orchestra with timid apparitions, dragged for the most part by the influence that the spirit of jazz has exercised on so-called learned art. Its adaptation in the instrumentation of the orchestra is not yet apparent, not withstanding the isolated use by Strauss in the *Sinfonia domestica* where the saxophones only are used as doubling instruments and are given the indication *ad libitum*.

As an absolute function of necessity the saxophone plays a part in the Gershwin orchestra, as a direct derivation from jazz. Note the beautiful use of saxophones with the trumpet in the following example:

G. Gershwin: *An American in Paris*, p. 51. Ed: New World Music - New York

As an isolated instrument in the orchestra the saxophone appears in *L'Arlesienne* of Bizet.

Here is another beautiful modern example:

G. Petrassi: *Partita*, p. 13. Ed: Ricordi

In the following famous work of Ravel the sopranino saxophone, after the singing opening of the melody, descends into its lower register and acquires a color that seems almost in miniature, somewhat of a caricature of the chest voice of a dramatic soprano. Then, the sound of the soprano saxophone is so pure that it takes the melody of the sopranino from its extreme lowest limit and continues it to the conclusion.

M. Ravel: *Bolero*, p. 16 and following. Ed: Durand

Most distant from any influence of jazz appears this example of the use of the saxophone in the orchestration of Ravel in the *Pictures at an Exhibition* of Mussorgsky. No timbre could have been more adapted for the sad atmosphere and, at the same time, demonstrate the fantastic and fairy-like air of the melody.

Contralto Saxophone in E♭ (Alto)

Mussorgsky-Ravel: *Pictures at an Exhibition*, p. 24. Ed: Boosey and Hawkes

PERCUSSION

a) INSTRUMENTS OF DETERMINED PITCH (timpani and keyboard instruments in current use)

Timpani

It is said that without a good timpanist, a good orchestra cannot exist.

The timpani are constructed of a metal bowl to which a membrane made of skin is attached at the top. The membrane is struck with mallets of various qualities (hardness, softness). The timpani that are used today in Italy and that have taken the place of the older models with a different system of tuning are the turning timpani on which one adjusts the intonation by means of rotating the metallic bowl. These timpani allow for rapid tuning and are considered superior by most performers. For some time, however, a model that is tuned by means of a pedal has been in general use. This permits the use of the glissando.

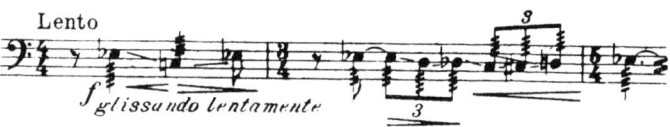

A. Casella: *Elegia eroica*, p. 13. Ed: Universal

or passages such as this:

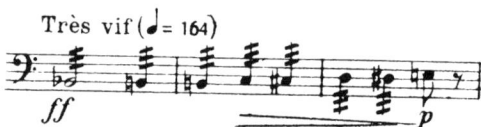

V. D'Indy: *2nd Symphony*, p. 111. Ed: Durand

The timpanist uses today normally three instruments that have the following ranges.

The black notes above on each timpani are perfectly usable when needed. For example, the low E on the first instrument is good at *mezzo piano*, and at *piano* one can also use the low E♭. The high notes in parentheses have a dry, muffled, and taut sonority.

Besides these three normal instruments, models exist of small timpani that can, depending upon their dimensions, reach unusual heights as in this example.

M. Ravel: *L'Enfant et les sortilèges*, p. 67. Ed: Durand

Some timpani are made that can descend to the C below the E♭ indicated; therefore, it is difficult to state an exact tessitura for timpani in that the range depends entirely on the size of the instrument.

The mallets in current use in the great orchestras of today are normally made of hard or soft felt or of wood. It is advised that one not use sticks made of sponge since they are hard and deliver an ugly sound. The indication *bacchetta di spugna* [sponge stick] refers generally to the softness and not to the true material from which the head of the mallet is made. It would be better simply to indicate "soft mallet" or "hard mallet," for the good timpanist would know that which to use.

Xylophone

The xylophone is an instrument of Asian origins formed by a chromatic series of bars of wood of various thickness placed on two long wooden narrow planks and suspended above the planks by string or other material so that they resonate.

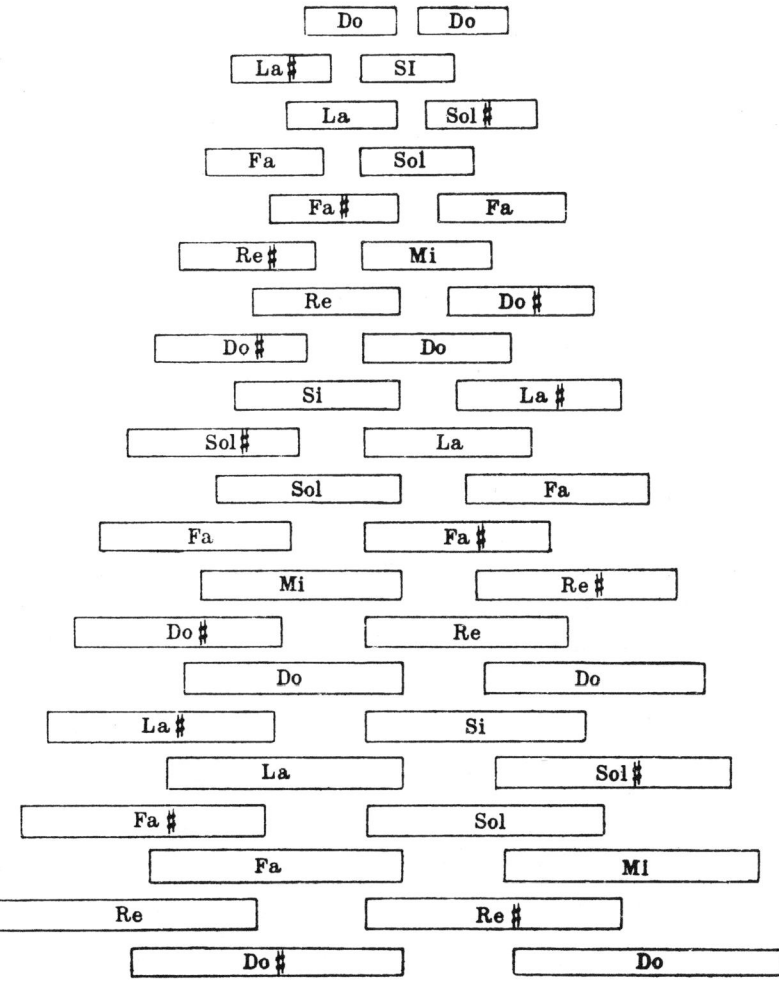

(Trapezoidal placement of the Xylophone)

E.R. 2935

Until the end of the last century it seemed that the instrument would be destined, above all, as in the celebrated example in Saint-Saëns' *Danse macabre*, to evoke the funereal creaking of bones. In any case it seemed to have been relegated to lugubrious and sinister situations. Impressionism, however, enlarged greatly the performance sphere of the instrument, an enlargement that fortunately contributed to improvements in the instrument's construction. Its voice has therefore become one of sweet refinement as in the wonderful example in the opening of Debussy's *Les parfums de la nuit* from *Iberia*.

A trapezoidal model exists as shown in the previous example; however, the model that is now universally used is that which places the bars of wood like the keyboard of the piano making possible the use of the glissando in C major. The glissando is accomplished by sliding the mallet up or down the keyboard, and it is found in numerous contemporary works.

In the last twenty years a model has been developed in the United States that places thick bars of wood above resonating metal tubes of appropriate length for the note. Hence a larger sound and new singing capabilities were created. The model, *"Deagan"*, has a range of four octaves: and is that which Puccini used in *Turandot* calling it the bass xylophone. Not often having the opportunity to find such an instrument in Europe, it is advised, then, to use the instrument with the normal range:

It is necessary to take into consideration also that the written note sounds an octave higher.

It is important to note also that a xylophone exists that is called the *silofono a tastiera*, keyboard xylophone, that uses a mechanical system commanded by a keyboard like the piano instead of mallets. Its aim is to facilitate the use of the xylophone and offer particular possibilities, e.g., producing chords of three or more notes. The sound is less pleasing than that of the normal instrument, the possibilities of color are limited, and it does not lend itself well to the tremolo. [Note: As in all discussions of instruments in this text, one must take into consideration the publication date. At present percussion instruments are completely similar worldwide and the performers employ a variety of techniques associated with them.]

Celeste

This noted instrument is constructed of a series of metal tuning forks, called *coristi* (diapason), that have pure sounds without harmonics played by means of an ordinary keyboard. The instrument resembles a small piano (model Mustel).

The normal range is: 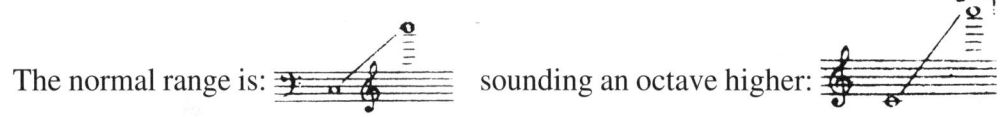 sounding an octave higher:

The instrument may be played by two performers (four hands) as one encounters in the fourth scene of *Petrouchka* or in the *Danza delle vecchie dame* from *Convento veneziano* of Casella.

The sudden use of the piano scored as an orchestral instrument has corresponded to the diminished use of the celeste and the harp, instruments that reached their maximum favor in the lyric impressionistic period from approximately 1895-1914. It is possible also that for a continued period of time that this will continue. No one can hypothesize the use of these instruments, and it is possible that in the near future that the celeste and the harp will retake an important function in the orchestra, even if this appears to be quite improbable.

b) INSTRUMENTS OF INDETERMINATE PITCH

This category of instruments made its entrance in the orchestra in the *Sinfonia militare* of Haydn and in the *Ninth Symphony* of Beethoven. But it was above all the Russian school, defined as orientalist, who conferred upon these instruments their autonomy. The symphonic poem, *Tamar*, of Mili Balakiref (1884) contained six parts for percussion other than the timpani, and five (always with timpani) were used in Rimsky-Korsakov's *Sheherazade*. In the new century, the use of percussion (of indeterminate pitch) has enlarged even more until reaching its highest level in the work of the American, Edgar Varèse, in his *Ionisation* (1931) for piano and 42 percussion instruments. One might also say that jazz with its use of the drum set could have influenced serious music in this use of percussion. But instead the historical examples stand to prove that the development of percussion was prior to and independent of jazz. One has only to remember the *Rapsodia spagnola* of Ravel written in 1907. On the other hand the evolution of percussion is characterized by a constant qualitatively refined research that is not, nor cannot be, confirmed in the much more primitive jazz technique. In fact, although the sounds of these instruments remain always indeterminate (percussion always lives in the margins of music as a type of spice, e.g., paprika), nevertheless, a tendency is evident in many works of the last 25 years to create new and unceasing contrasts among these instruments, as for example, the simultaneous use of various tuned tambourines of different diameters (see *L'Histoire du soldat* and *Les Noces* of Stravinsky), the use of large and small tam tam, the use of bass drums of various sizes, etc. Finally these instruments have created a vast group of contrasting timbres in that sector of the orchestra that finally has built a particular conversational sound with its own timbral mixings.

The list of the instruments of percussion with indeterminate sounds could today extend to infinity, since in the last 25 years it has been made up of elements heretofore never thought of, e.g., the whistle, the siren, the cheese grater, and even the typewriter! But, looking past the above attempts, in most cases, one can adhere to the following list that corresponds to the instruments used by serious composers:

Bass drum, cymbals, crotali, military drum, snare drum, tambourine, Tam tam, triangle, castanets, sleigh bells, ratchet, whip, temple block, wood block, wind machine, guiro, cow bells, anvil

Bass drum

The instrument is so well understood that it is not necessary to explain its construction and its various aspects. It is superfluous to remember as well the past use of the bass drum and cymbals played simultaneously by the same musician (right hand with the mallet for the bass drum and left hand with the cymbal to strike that cymbal that was attached to the bass drum). Such ignoble use is today extremely limited, and if one finds its use today, one can determine that the composer made knowledgeable and almost malicious use of the combination. (See *"Polka"* in *Pupazzetti* of Casella.)

The instrument offers limited resources. Among those that one can consider important are the imitation of the sound of thunder and that of the canon (this last can be found in *La Damnation de Faust* of Berlioz). Good opportunities for development still exist, e.g., the substitution for the timpani when they are not present, and above all, when they are used in isolated places, best at *piano*, fused with other percussion colors. One plays the instrument either with one simple mallet, with two, or with a mallet with a double head for rolls. [Note: Today the double mallet is rarely used and is for the most part inefficient for the subtleties demanded by contemporary composers.]

Cymbals

The classic use of the pair was to make noise (*far baccano*). This practice has now almost fallen into disuse. These effects were used, however, in the works of Berlioz, *Symphonie fantastique,* and Wagner in the third act of *Lohengrin*. The suspended cymbal remains in great favor. It is set into vibration by means of the following: a timpani mallet, a mallet used for the bass drum, a triangle beater, a piece of iron (*Turandot*), or simply with the hand (*Tanzsuite* of Bartók). The tremolo *ff* obtained with two cymbals by means of rotating the two as in the celebrated example from Wagner's *"Ouverture"* to *Tannhäuser* has been abandoned due largely to its crudeness.

It is always necessary to indicate the exact value of the duration of the sound or in other cases to write, l. v., *lasciare vibrare* [let vibrate].

Crotali (antique cymbals)

The *Prélude à l'après-midi d'un faune* of Debussy and *Les Noces* of Stravinsky offer two excellent examples of the use of these cymbals. Other scorings, just as interesting, can be found in the works of Berlioz, Gounod, Saint-Saëns, etc. They are small discs of variable diameter from 15 to 20 cm. and of one thickness greater than that of two ordinary cymbals. Their small size limits their use in that they must be touched very lightly, excluding the employment of a mallet or larger stick. One may also use the metal rod used for the triangle. They are tuned and are constructed with varying intonation within the following proximity:

Military drum and snare drum

This instrument is constructed of two sheepskins [heads] mounted on two sides of a small circular metal casing and tightened generally with small keys [lugs] opposite each other on the casing. [Note: Today many synthetic materials are used for the construction of the heads.] On one of the sides are stretched cords of metal or gut. The instrument is played with two wooden sticks and is capable of rendering great rhythmic precision that has made it the inseparable companion to marches and music with a martial character. In recent years, however, the snare drum has enjoyed a great increase in the possibilities for its use in the sense of color, e.g., the use of a cloth to cover the instrument rendering a fantastic and lugubrious sonority.

The so called *caisse claire, cassa chiara* is a variety of the military drum with somewhat the same dimensions; however, its skins [heads] are stretched much tighter producing a higher sound than that of the military drum. The instrument does not have snares, and therefore, its timbre is different from that of the military drum. Stravinsky made great use of it. (See *L'Histoire du Soldat*, in which he uses two *caisses claires* with timbre, tuned as one would like, however with different pitches).

Cassa rullante (also refers to an old type of military drum)

The *Cassa rullante* has an oblong form with a wooden shell and uses two skins (heads) on either end as the above. The skins are often stretched by means of a cord with a V shape on the sides of the drum. Among the best examples is that from the *"Battle"* in *Heldenleben* (*A Hero's life*) of Richard Strauss.

Tam-tam

If the instrument were not destined to be associated with lugubrious and catastrophic situations in orchestras, it would have already had a place in the world as that which announces the hour of meals with its ringing on transatlantic ships and in large hotels. (This humorous observation probably would have made some musicians into travelers.) Today the instrument does not necessarily function solely for dramatic situations, but often reinforces moments of great power. As shown in Varèse's *Ionisation*, other types have begun to be introduced: large, medium, and small. (See *Ionisation* of Varèse and the *Preghiera di Maria Stuarda* of L. Dallapiccola in the orchestral examples section of the text.) The true danger in the use of the tam-tam is that rarely does it sound a note of indeterminate pitch. Composers generally do not take this into consideration, for they explore its use simply for its beautiful deep sound. The instrument is normally struck with a large mallet, like that of the bass drum with strips of cloth. There are numerous examples, however, of the use of a felt mallet (*Elektra* of Strauss), with a triangle beater, with a drum stick (*Petrouchka* di Stravinsky), or, yet scraping the circumference of it with the triangle beater (*Le Sacre du printemps* of Stravinsky). One must always write the duration of the sound either with l. v. (*let vibrate*) or with an exact notation as with the cymbal.

Tambourine

The classic tambourine is very well known to everyone; therefore, it is not necessary to describe a sound that everyone knows. The true *tamburo basco* does not have the small discs that rattle. In order to avoid confusing it with the known type it is better to indicate the type instrument that one wants, e.g., *tamburo basco senza sonagli* (tambourine without rattles) or *tamburo basco con sonagli* (tambourine with rattles). The instrument is played in several ways:

a) striking the skin with the bottom of the hand

b) shaking it rhythmically

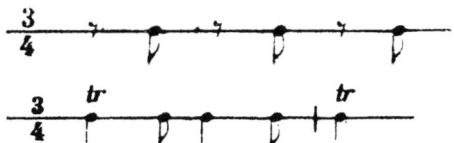

c) rubbing the skin with the thumb (notation as seen in the preceding example, but specifying "with the thumb"

d) with the knee (*Le chant du Rossignol* of Stravinsky)

e) with a drum stick by having the tambourine placed on the top of the snare drum

For a special effect, Stravinsky at the end of *Petrouchka* asks that the tambourine be dropped from "not too high to the floor."

Triangle

Different from the tam-tam, the triangle seems uniquely to be reserved for sounds that are luminous, festive, and joyous. Everything that is drammatic or sorrowful is foreign to its use, unless as often happens in contemporary music, it is used in a paradoxical sense. Then it may assume any kind of lugubrious or perhaps macabre significance. One characteristic of the instrument is that it may be heard above the orchestra playing at *fortissimo*. For this reason one should score it with caution. It should also be noted that effective use of the tremolo or roll may be made.

Castanets

These have been associated forever with the rhythmic traditions of Spanish music: *fandango, bolero*, etc. But, as for almost all of the percussion instruments in modern times, composers have pushed the instrument to new horizons. Once reserved for joyous expressions, now they are also found in use in dark and sinister situations.

Sleigh Bells

Sleigh bells are constructed of a series of small bells attached to a leather strap and shaken with the hand. [Note: Of course today they are attached also to a wooden shaft with a handle. These are much easier to control and are used far more often today than those described by Casella.] Examples are: The "delicious" [Casella] use on the first beat of the *Fourth Symphony* of Mahler and the interesting case in the ballet of Casella, *La Giara*, where they accompany each entrance of the old character, Zi' Dima, associating in this way his miserable, grotesque figure with that of a beast of burden.

Ratchet

The instrument is constructed of a wheel of wood with teeth-like appendages that when turned scrape against a fixed piece of wood. A beautiful example (maybe the first to-date) is found in Strauss' *Till Eulenspiegel* when the hero appears suddenly in the middle of the market. Among its few other uses are the beginning of *Pini di Roma (Pines of Rome)* of Respighi where the instrument is justified by the infantile climate and the noisy sounds in the music. [Translator's note: Casella refers to the children's songs in the opening of the *Pines of Rome*.]

Whip

The final movement of the *Concerto in G major for piano and orchestra* of Ravel is among the few extant examples of its use. Needless to say one never uses a true whip, but two blades or strips of wood approximately 35 cm. each fixed together by a hinge. When struck together they produce a dry noise or slap that simulates the crack of a whip.

Temple block

The temple block is normally made of a small coconut hollowed out in which a small crack has been made on the top half. One strikes it with an ordinary stick (or a small mallet) producing a dry somewhat nasal sound which is above all used in the jazz orchestra. [Translator's note: It goes without saying that today's temple block (s) are far superior to the one (s) described by Casella, for there are extremely advanced models of tuned temple blocks made of both natural and synthetic materials.]

Wood block

There are two types: that referred to as the Chinese made of an oblong hollow block of wood in which a narrow opening in the wood has been taken out according to the length of the instrument.

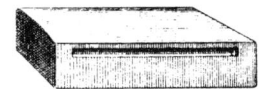 

Wood block, Chinese model   Wood block, American model

The other model, referred to as the American model, is constructed of two cylinders of hollow wood with an opening on either side according to the length of the instrument.

One or the other model is played with a stick or mallet and produces a sound which is near to that of the croaking of a frog. [Translator's note: As with the whip, there are enormous numbers of these instruments made today of every conceivable type of material and rendering every possible sound.]

Guiro (adopted by Stravinsky in *Le Sacre du printemps* and by Varèse in *Ionisation*.)

Constructed of a dried squash with lines in relief along the side, it is played with either a wooden or metal stick. Its origins are North American Indian.

Wind Machine *(Eolifono)*

This is an old machine used in theaters to produce the sound of wind. It was used most effectively by Strauss in his *Alpensymphonie* and by Ravel in *Daphnis et Chloé*.

Cow bells *(Campane da gregge)*

One encounters an example that is extremely characteristic in the *Fourth Symphony* of Mahler where this fluctuating and indefinite sound contributes powerfully to the creation of an atmosphere of the very high mountains.

Anvil *(Incudine)*

A true anvil with a hammer constructed in various pitches can be found in the *Sixth Symphony* of Mahler.

Summary of the Percussion Instruments

Although previously discussed, it is important again to note the addition of an extremely large number of instruments to the orchestra in the last 25 years. In the creation of these new instruments we have seen develop many expressive possibilities. It is impossible to predict the advancements of the future in the orchestra of these instruments when one takes into consideration their expressive, evocative, and often psychological values. They have become one of the first levels of consideration in the art of orchestration. It is, therefore, perfectly logical to visualize new rich and exotic timbres in the future. This vast evolution seems to have directed today's European thought toward an art where the timbre little by little becomes, as in the ancient art of the Chinese, the predominant factor in music.

The most important and definitive example of a percussion group is found in Stravinsky's *L'Histoire du soldat* (1918) which uses:

a) two snare drums without snares of different sizes;
b) a military drum without snares;
c) snare drum with snares;
d) cymbals;
e) a bass drum;
f) a tambourine;
g) a triangle

The part is written for one performer. [Note: It is this important contribution of Stravinsky that has spurred the enormous development of the multi percussion solo.] One other important Stravinsky work with six percussionists is *Les Noces* and its instrumentation is as follows:

Timpani	Xylophone
Tambourine	Triangle
Snare drum without snares	Cymbals
Military drum without snares	Bass drum
Snare drum with snares	Crotali
Military drum with snares	One chime 

Other more recent and important examples regarding the use of color can be found in the dramatic madrigals, *Coro di morti* (1940-41) for men's chorus, brass, three pianos, and percussion of Petrassi, and the three *Canti di prigionia* (1938-41) for voice and small orchestra of Luigi Dallapiccola.

* * *

It is superfluous to say that all considerations for writing for percussion instruments of indeterminate pitch can be understood as one. It is never advisable to use any percussion instrument without in-depth knowledge of all of its aspects as to timbre.

Various Instruments More or Less in Normal Use in the Orchestra

Orchestra bells (*Glockenspiel* or *Jeu de timbres*)

This instrument was once diversely referred to simply often due to its construction. Today, however, all are unified in what is called the orchestra bells. Found in every orchestra, the bells are arranged chromatically resembling the keyboard of the piano. They are sometimes struck with the mallet of hard wood. [Note: Of course today we find many models of orchestra bells that are struck with many types of mallets that create many types of sounds. The available sounds are truly limitless.] The timbre of the instrument is quite scintillating, and the use of it limited, except in rare exceptions, due to this luminous and brilliant sonority.

The normal range:

When writing for the orchestra bells, the written note sounds two octaves higher. The instrument is not sensitive to touch and therefore it is often played at *forte*. [Note: This on the modern instrument is not a true statement, for percussionists are capable of creating great subtlety with the bells.]

One other variety of this instrument is the so called *sistro*, bell lyre, the keyboard of which is made of bars of steel.

Chimes

The chimes have been continuously used for their religious connotations. One noted example is that festive sound evoked by Stravinsky in the *finale* of *Les Noces*. Given the enormous weight of the true chime(s), the use currently of the tubular type made of steel strung on a bar is universal. The sound is the same and the range is as follows:

Normally, the effect wanted is the octave higher than that written; however, today one tends to write at the sounding note. There are also smaller and larger models of the instrument (see the low chimes in Puccini's *Tosca*); however, they are of dimensions difficult to maneuver.

Mandolin

After the celebrated use of the mandolin in Mozart's *Don Giovanni* (preceded by others like Vivaldi who wrote a concerto for two mandolins), this most precious instrument to the Neapolitans has been abandoned in the orchestra for more than a century. It can be found today in the works of Mahler, in a particular way in the third *Nachtmusic* of the *Seventh Symphony* and in the *finale* of *Das Lied von der Erde*. As in the percussion instruments it is possible to see a constant evolution in the employment of the mandolin for color prevalent in impressionist works. In the case of the two works of Mahler the color reaches a sweet and unreal poetry. In the *Danza delle vecchie dame* in the *Convento veneziano* of Casella, one finds the mandolin used for its humoristic character.

The range of the instrument is:  It is useless to say that the instrument is played with a pick.

Guitar

The Guitar has had little use in the orchestra. One is found next to the mandolin in the same works of Mahler (cited above) in which the instrument was used solely in an impressionistic sense. One other very interesting example is found in the *Serenata* (*da camera*), op. 24 of Arnold Schönberg for clarinet, bass clarinet, mandolin, guitar, violin, viola, violoncello, and bass voice. Nevertheless, the great resources of the guitar, so superior to those of the mandolin, allow one to surmise that in the future it will find occasion to be a part of the orchestra, particularly in a chamber group. [It is difficult not to recall the great prodigy, Andrès Segovia who performs often the *Chaconne* (for violin) of Bach!! on the guitar.]

The instrument is tuned as follows with a notation to the octave above. One should note that its technique, however, is quite complex and requires considerable study.

Saw

This instrument that emerged approximately 20 years ago in the so called light orchestras and in use still in jazz, consists of a blade saw of flexible steel that one plays with the bow of a contrabass on the opposite edge to the teeth. It may also be struck with a felt stick. The pitch depends on the curvature of the blade. When it is played with a bow, it emits a sound that is in constant glissando or portamento. The sound could be compared to that of a flute, possibly the string instruments, or the human voice. This type of sound is that which is recognized in jazz through the saxophone and the banjo. Even if the saw has remained limited in the jazz idiom, nothing impedes the thought that one day it might be used in the symphonic orchestra that is enriched each day with exotic and bizarre voices.

The range of the instrument is approximately two octaves.

Flexaton

This instrument, used by Schönberg in his *Variazioni per orchestra*, is a variety of the saw. The instrument was before used exclusively in jazz except for the example cited above of Schönberg. One other should also be noted: Krenek's *Johnny spielt auf*. Schönberg's use of it in a very serious work is enough to authorize future exploration of the flexaton in the orchestra. The range is much greater than that of the saw and depends on the dimensions of the instrument. It can reach the extreme high regions of the orchestral tessitura as seen in the *Variazioni* of Schönberg.

Vibraphone

The vibraphone is an instrument that resembles the American xylophone with a series of chromatic bars of steel that are struck with two mallets. Under each bar is found a metal tube or resonator. Attached to the resonators is a small electric motor that is used to vibrate the sound by means of small cylinders below each bar and above the resonator for the bar. One can use the instrument without vibrato and in that case its sound resembles the bell lyre. When the vibrating mechanism is used, the instrument acquires a poetic beauty that cannot be compared to any other instrument in the orchestra. The range is:

Notable examples are found in the *Canti di prigionia* by Luigi Dallapiccola, in the *Sinfonia sacra* of Antonio Veretti and in the *Missa solemnis pro pace*, *Crucifixus e Agnus Dei* of Casella. One can hold two or more mallets with each hand thereby permitting the use of chords.

Accordion

The only significant use known in orchestral literature of the accordion is in Alban Berg's *Wozzeck* and involves a group of musicians on stage playing in a small special orchestra. The particular nature of the instrument seems to preclude any use of it in the orchestra. However, one cannot affirm with absolute certainty that in the future some composers will not have the need to turn to the accordion for timbral needs. Today the principal obstacle that impedes its use in the orchestra is without doubt the ugliness of its sound that does not blend with any other instrument or group of instruments in the orchestra.

Ondes martenot [1]

This instrument probably is the most conspicuous orchestral enrichment of the last 25 years. Even if it has up until now found little application, it offers such enormous possibilities. It is obvious that composers will find means to use this supernatural and fantastic voice for unforeseen drammatic and expressive possibilities.

It is constructed of a radio/electric device formed by: a) a lamp with an oscillating circuit (a type of silent reed); b) a group of electric batteries to furnish the energy necessary for the vibration that substitutes for the breath; c) the timbral variations reach and are intercepted by circuits that absorb in a variable way the harmonics of the fundamental sound.

The range at present of the instrument is enormous:

The low octave is very light and (*calante*) flat. The highest octave does not work well at *fortissimo*. Otherwise the instrument in all of the remaining areas of its range can perform well at an imperceptible *piano* and at the most heavy *fortissimo*.

---

(1) So called by its inventors, the Martenot brothers

It possess a great variety of timbres: that of the horns or of the brasses; that of the small instruments; that of the saxophone; and finally it imitates the flute. These are, however, limited to its keyboard. These rich timbres, added to the capacity to put forward the most tenuous *pianissimo* and a *fortissimo* with limitless power, make the Ondes Martenot a new orchestral element of infinite possibilities. One very good example of its use is found in Honegger's *Jeanne d'Arc au bûcher*.

It is advisable, however, not to use this powerful means, this unreal, superhuman voice, without having studied closely the instrument and its singular characteristics.

JAZZ

Although the division between "learned" music and so called "light" music still exists, it is not possible in a treatise on contemporary instrumentation not to speak, although briefly, of the musical phenomenon of jazz. As we have seen in previous chapters, jazz has exercised a decisive influence on the technique of almost all of the instruments.

* * *

Jazz of the United States, the only art form truly unique to North-America, developed from African-American and European materials. The rhythms, first among them African syncopation, the polyphony, and the instrumental technique are respectively African-American and American, while the harmony is without a doubt the only element that is truly European. It is necessary to add that the commercialization of jazz has been the exclusive work of "white" America, especially in New York. [Note: This was certainly true in Casella's time.]

The art of jazz rests essentially on two characteristic elements: African-American syncopated rhythms and instrumental technique. The syncopated rhythm was introduced in North America by African-Americans and Mexicans, and one can surmise that these were present even before the American civil war of the last century. When speaking of contemporary jazz, it is necessary to establish a borderline between the rhythms of "rag-time" that was popular until approximately 1926, and that of the "fox-trot" that is the true typical rhythm of jazz. In "rag-time" the syncopation has a very limited function. While instead, modern jazz has introduced in its polyphony an entire kaleidoscope of rhythms that weave themselves in the general rhythmic division of a work. They live in every part of the life of a piece, unfolding melodies in complete rhythmic contrast to the piece's fundamental rhythm.

	Melody (eighths)	123 123 12	etc.
	Accompaniment (quarters)	1 2 3 4	etc.
or:			
	Melody (eighths)	123 12 123	etc.
	Accompaniment	1 2 3 4	etc.
or:			
	Melody (eighths)	123 123 12 3 123	etc.
	Accompaniment (quarters)	1 2 3 4 1 2	etc.

Therefore, a true polyrhythm exists, or better, a rhythmic counterpoint as never dared before in music. It is interesting to compare this rhythmic technique with that of Stravinsky. In the music of the Russian composer the struggle against the metronomic monotony of the old symmetrical rhythmic system takes place in a constant feverish movement of the line of rhythmic division by altering beats constantly, always conserving the value of the eighth and quarter notes for the entire piece.

In jazz the liberation from the arithmetical demands takes place by means of violent shiftings of rhythmic accents that recreate in the traditional meters of **4/4**, **2/2**, or even **3/4** a world of contradictions and rhythmic conflicts, the efficacy of which is not inferior to that of our western composers. The difference, above all, lies in the success that jazz has in canceling the romantic *cantabile* with modern rhythmic mechanics. One can see in fact superimposed in the same work a sweet, tender, and passionate melody of the purest rubato over an impassable, rigid bass.

* * *

That which is of most interest for this treatise is the instrumentation of jazz. Above all the makeup of the instrumentation that has been standard almost since its beginnings.

2 trumpets in B♭
1 tenor trombone
2 alto saxophones in E♭ (the first is often asked to perform clarinet in B♭ parts as a soloist).
1 tenor saxophone in B♭ (sometimes employed with the second contralto saxophone on a B♭ clarinet part so that the three saxophones may be substituted with three clarinets).
1 piano
1 contrabass (*a pizzico* - slap)
1 guitar or banjo
1 drum set

Around 1939 this instrumentation became enlarged and reached the following size that was that of the orchestra of Glen Miller:

4 trumpets
3 trombones
2 alto saxophones in E♭
2 tenor saxophones in B♭
1 baritone saxophone
1 piano
1 electric guitar (with a microphone attached to the inside and connected to a speaker so that it could be used as an audible soloist)
1 contrabass, played arco
1 drum set
And eventually a section of strings (violins and violincelli)

Except for the use of special instruments, e.g., the vibraphone, the electric violin (amplified with a microphone as the guitar), and the celeste, all of the major orchestras adhere to this model. It is important to observe that in general the violins and the violoncelli are used only in the "white" orchestras (the "black" orchestras adhere to the preference of using a group entirely made up of winds.) The greatest and most celebrated orchestras are those made up of the above instrumentation. Among these are those of Duke Ellington (with electric violin), Harry James, Tommy Dorsey, Charlie Spivack, and that of Lionel Hampton (Hampton's of course always having the addition of the vibraphone).

It is necessary immediately to say that the secret of the success of this instrumentation lies in the use of the saxophone. The instrument had to wait seventy years in order to find its proper place as a member of the jazz orchestra. In this new family of instruments the saxophone represents with its large and ample sound the human voice. This quality allows it to blend with all of the instruments in the ensemble: strings, brass, piano, and drum set. It is to jazz that the saxophone owes its typical soft sound serving as a large oriental rug. This sonority, however, does not exclude its ability to be extremely forceful and even brutal at times. Another secret of the jazz sonority is found in the fact that the brasses play almost always with a mute. This muting permits an intimate and delicate mixing with the rest of the instrumentation and in a special way with the saxophones. One can in short consider that this grouping of instruments is something completely new in the history of music a union that offers enormous coloristic, rhythmic, and expressive possibilities.

But this instrumentation would not be enough to constitute the art of jazz if the instruments were not played according to new and special techniques that are a product of the African-American influence. The jazz technique with its perpetually unstable sounds represents a typical manifestation of the African-American spirit, a spirit that does not know the past and that can therefore exempt itself from European prejudices by discovering, or better, daring to do certain things that would have been totally foreign to the European tradition. Thus it has occurred precisely in the field of jazz, for in jazz, the African-American genius discovered how to reveal a new world of possibilities by exploiting certain instruments that were known to Europeans for centuries but were never used outside of traditional boundaries. In Europe the traditional understandings of instruments were born, e.g., the solemn and majestic trombone, the heroic trumpet, the pastoral oboe, the soldierly snare drum, the lyric violin, and the romantic piano. No European would have ever thought of creating an agile trombone that was capable of continuous glissandi that sings as a violin or that comes back like an athlete. Nor would anyone have thought to create a neurotic and hysterical trumpet or to make of the piano an instrument, formerly lyrical, now a percussion instrument. These ideas could not have risen in the minds of *enfants terribles*; however, they were exactly the creations by the makers of jazz.

The remaining instruments have been discussed in other chapters (clarinet, trumpet, trombone, percussion, etc.) in light of the influence of jazz technique on serious European music of the last twenty five years and further on how much one can still expect from an instrumental revolution that is just at its beginnings.

The large use of variation in jazz performance, inherent in the extreme virtuosity of the musicians, has taken two avenues: 1) Straight jazz that requires the music be played as written, without allowing any modifications, and 2) hot jazz, performances of which are based on the spontaneous transformation and improvisation of the vital elements of the composition. It is a style that resembles greatly the *commedia dell'arte* in which the actors improvise the action and the words above a canvas of the author. The African American has achieved in the second of these types an improbable bravura by being successful at improvising a polyphony in which each instrumentalist develops his part according to a perfect independence and autonomy, realizing never-the-less a totally perfect togetherness in an often crazy and frenzied performance.

In recent times, however, "hot jazz" has diminished in daily practice and the great improvisatory groups are seen less. The parts are written for the entire group and the improvisatory sections are left to the soloists. This implies a certain regrouping on the old ideas of the "straight" form, a renunciation of the convulsions and the frenzy of the "hot." It is necessary to recognize that this renders a less original performance in the sense that it tends toward an ordinary style of playing that accommodates more or less the entire orchestra. The characteristics that differentiate among the various orchestras are few. Only the Duke Ellington orchestra stands out among the others due to its harmonic and timbral individuality.

In substance, jazz at present is not different from that of ten or fifteen years ago if one excludes the rhythmic variants brought about by the *Boogie woogie* that came into vogue around 1937-38. The *Boogie woogie* substitutes the old bass with quarter notes, found in the fox trot or blues, with one of eighths. Therefore, instead of four quarters to the measure, we now have eight eighths. This is not a great innovation nor is it so audacious. Nevertheless it has influenced in certain cases the melody that must necessarily assume rhythms that concur with those below.

One often dares to say that jazz is only an instrumental technique lacking any spiritual content. This affirmation is absurd since no art can be without spirit. Instead each technique is made up of an organic aspect coming from a single artistic thought. Jazz is infinitely more profound than some would like to think. It is an integral part of the spirit of a new country, of a new civilization. Under that apparent optimism, American life hides vast nostalgic feelings, great aspirations toward the infinite, all well defined by Paul Whiteman in *Sad Gayety*. These emotions find their lyricism in the over excitement and dynamic of jazz. This strange music is a pure emanation of the American soil and the American soul. Of the rest, jazz is not, above all, a black creation, i.e., of a more nostalgic and melancholy race. (One must remember the admirable spirituals of these people.) This art was not developed and brought to perfection by one or another race but by parameters without country or exile.

This lengthy discussion about jazz is short when one considers the enormous importance that it has had on universal musical life. But it was necessary in a treaty on instrumentation above all to indicate not only the existence of the art, but to underline the profound technical importance that it has given to modern European orchestration. Nothing can be said today for certain regarding the future reserved to this art. For some it seems next to extinction for lack of renewing elements. For others instead it contains a future world. Therefore, it is infinitely probable that jazz, since Europe seems today to be heading toward its decline as a revolutionary force on instrumentation, can still contain many fertile seeds for the future foundation of a symphonic American school.[1]

---

(1) Most of the information in this chapter was given through the courtesy of my colleague, Luigi Colacicchi.

HARP

The enormous development reached by the harp in the golden impressionistic period often assumed aspects of playing that were more near abuse. (One is reminded of the miles of glissandi associated with the celeste and the xylophone during the French/Russian epoch.)

Therefore, anti-impressionistic composers in many cases prefer the metallic and powerful sonority of the piano to that of the outdated harp. This dissatisfaction is of little significance, for in the near future the harp will not have to once again find its lost favor. Numerous are the "virgin" resources of the instrument, and no one can foresee what the future will bring.

The so called chromatic harp, that had a period of favor in France at the beginning of this century (20th), is now no longer in use. The diatonic harp, however, has prevailed and is used worldwide with the Erard system of double movement. It is a harp tuned in C♭. The normal position, therefore, aligns the strings according to the order of the scale in C♭ major. By means of the pedals the pitch of the strings can be raised by a half or a whole step. There are seven pedals corresponding to the seven notes of the diatonic scale. The pedal can be in normal position, or lowered in part where it can be inserted into a notch with the result of raising a note by a half step or a corresponding note on the entire range of the instrument. Likewise the pedal can be lowered completely by inserting it into a second notch in order to raise the string another half step (or whole step from the original). One neither indicates sharps or flats for the harp. The F double sharp, for example, would have to be written G.

The pedals; three at the left for B, C, and D and four at the right for the E, F, G, and A, are used by the left and right feet respectively, and their manipulation cannot be done by a crossover of the feet. The playing of the pedals can reach great technical levels. The harp remains an instrument exquisitely diatonic; therefore, one needs to be prudent with chromatiscm and poly-modality. An excessive use of gymnastics by the feet is contrary to the nature of the harp and can be quite noisy due to the mechanics of the pedals.

The exceptional harpist can manipulate more than one pedal at once; however, this technique is not advised for use in normal playing in the orchestra.

Range

The two lowest notes are excluded from the pedal mechanism. They are, therefore, two isolated notes of fixed pitch by the performer before beginning a work. This intonation can vary, normally, within the limits of a tone, without being modified with the use of the pedals. These two notes are so distant from the overtone series that they have little resonance, especially the lowest. The best register is that between:

Ascending in the high register, the sonority becomes little by little less full, less harmonious, and the highest octave is weak with few singing possibilities. It can be adapted to light and decorative passages. At *forte* it is dry and harsh. While descending in the low register the sonority becomes muddled and is not adapted to rapid passages, above all to scales or to a succession of notes in small intervals.

When one writes chords, it is preferable to leave a certain amount of space between the notes especially in the low register. Moreover one must note that the maximum stretch between two fingers may be produced between the thumb and the index finger. The natural position of the hand, therefore, is favorable to the large intervals that can be played just with two fingers, i.e., those intervals written at the top of the chord.

If the chord comprise notes below the first line G in the bass clef, it is best that the two lowest parts be written in an interval of a certain width, preferably an octave. The alternating of the hands permits arpeggiated chords of notable range.

V. Mortari: *Studi galanti*, p. 2. Ed: Forlivesi

When rapid successions of chords, either arpeggiated or not, are written, it would be better to employ simple groupings of three notes in each hand, allowing the keeping of the hands in close proximity.

A. Casella: *Sonata per arpa*. Ed: Suvini-Zerboni

If there are no indications, chords are rapidly arpeggiated. If one wants the arpeggio to be more subtle, the sign in the preceding exercise by Mortari must be used. If instead one wants a contemporary execution of the notes, one must write either *non arpeggiato* or *secco*.

The enharmonic interpretation of sounds presents rich combinations of simultaneous sounds or rapid arpeggios; however, it is necessary to be prudent in order not to write unplayable combinations.

(1) This chord is impossible since there is no way to produce simultaneously G♯, G natural, and A. One could consider the G♯ as A♭ and then lower the pedal in order to play the last upper note of the rapid arpeggio; however, then the effect of the G♯ would disappear by the raising of it by a semitone with the movement of the pedal.

Arpeggios

The arpeggio is the specialty of the instrument and is usable in any form, above all if divided between the hands. It is preferable to write only four notes in each hand. It should be noted that the harp unlike the piano is played with only four fingers, i.e., without the little finger.

Tremolos

Tremolos are produced by alternately plucking two strings with two fingers. They can be quiet rapid, but they become more rapid if they are executed on two strings conveniently tuned.

Naturally tremolos are possible between two notes of different pitches, but it is best if the interval between them is quite small.

Trills

The best range for trills is as follows:

(2) Below this E, the trill is muddled.

Trills are preferably alternated between the two hands:  however, one can also play them with the right hand.

Production of the sound

The sound of the harp can be produced in various ways other than plucking the strings in the ordinary manner.

Sulla tavola – The strings are plucked near the sounding board resulting in a clear sonority much like that of a guitar.

Étouffés – Is a very characteristic effect on the harp achieved by plucking the strings with the thumb and then muffling them immediately after with the palm of the hand. While only the left hand is used, the entire range of the instrument is possible.

The following example demonstrates an approximate maximum tempo.

The right hand, due to its position on the instrument, has limited possibilities for this technique. In order to muffle the sound, one can use the same finger that plucked the string. This technique of muffling, adapted naturally for the left hand, limits the tempo and is used mostly in order to play chords *étouffés*. If these chords are four notes, they must be in the closed position.

If instead the chords are of two or three notes, the position can be open.

If the succession of chords requires a noticeable movement of the hands, the tempo must definitely be limited.

The *étouffés* technique is indicated with the word or with the sign ⊕.

For a passage of length using *étouffés* one should follow the indication with a series of dots, or the sign ⊕ followed by a line indicating the duration of the passage.

étouffés. . . . . ⊕ ─────

Glissando

The glissando is a much used and abused characteristic effect on the harp. It can be ascending or descending, and each hand can perform it in single, double, or triple notes provided the stretch of the hand does not supersede the interval of a sixth. (The double glissando in octaves can be performed exceptionally well.)

The tuning of the harp for the glissando is predisposed according to the harmonic needs of the work. The overworking of homophonic sounds produces the immediate repetition of some sounds. The effect can be produced more efficiently by the simple scale *glissate* in which such repetition of sound does not occur.

The movement of the pedals permits numerous combinations.

The *glissando* can be played also with the fingernails with an almost crackling effect. It is more evident and efficient at *piano* and when played slowly. The glissando *sulla tavola* is also a curious effect and is more characteristic if it is made with the fingernails.

Harmonics are obtained by plucking with the thumb while the palm of the hand touches the string in the middle. They are very subtle and almost transparent. Their range is as follows:

for the right hand: Sounding an octave higher.

for the left hand: Sounding an octave higher.

The right hand, hindered by the instrument itself, can not play a single harmonic, while the left can produce two, three, and even four of them at the same time. The technique is natural provided that the harmonics require that the hand be in a closed position. Harmonics are indicated by placing a small "o" on the note. The harmonic produced on the harp is the second overtone. Others exist, but are not used. The third overtone, moreover, can also be achieved with quality. It is produced utilizing a third of the length of the string and one should indicate it as follows:

(The ordinary sign for indicating the string used is the small squared note indicating an harmonic effect.)

Mute

The mute is made of a tight strip of paper that is placed between the strings in the highest area. The timbre that it produces is one of a brief sound that resembles the harpsichord.

Portamento

It is possible to produce a portamento with the movement of the pedal while a string is in vibration. This must necessarily be limited to the interval of a half step or to one tone comprising of the movement of one pedal. The changing of pitch is accompanied by a very small non-annoying metallic noise that gives large relief to the note reached by the portamento. This process can be very effective in rapid chromatic passages.

A)

G. L. Tocchi: *Canzone, notturno e ballo* for harp, flute and viola, p. 20. Ed: De Santis, Roma

B)

Tocchi, p. 23.

Among the many brilliant inventions of Carlos Salzedo the following are illustrated.

Aeolian tremolo – One scrapes the hand rapidly forward and backward on the strings within the desired limits and with the desired tuning.

(The tuning of the harp is indicated by the small notes in parenthesis.)

Aeolian ascending chords – One obtains these by rapidly scraping the fingers of the hand, one after the other, with the exclusion of the thumb on a group of notes limited to appropriately tuned strings. One indicates the technique with the sign, 〖, shown in the example below followed by a line for the entire duration of the passage.

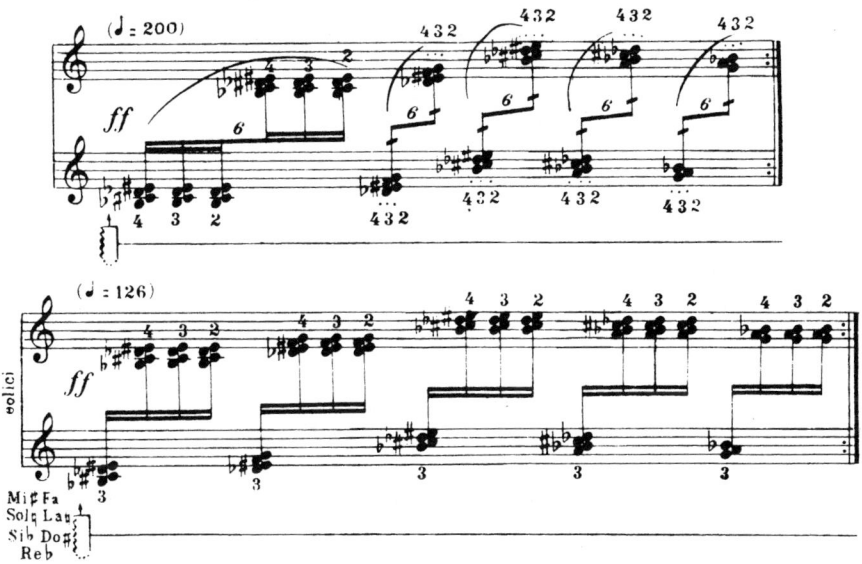

C. Salzedo: *Modern Study of the Harp*, p. 14. Ed: G. Schirmer, New York

Aeolian descending chords – They are like the preceding example except that the glissando is descending and is played with the thumbs of both hands alternating. One indicates the technique with the sign, 〗, followed by a line for the entire duration of the passage.

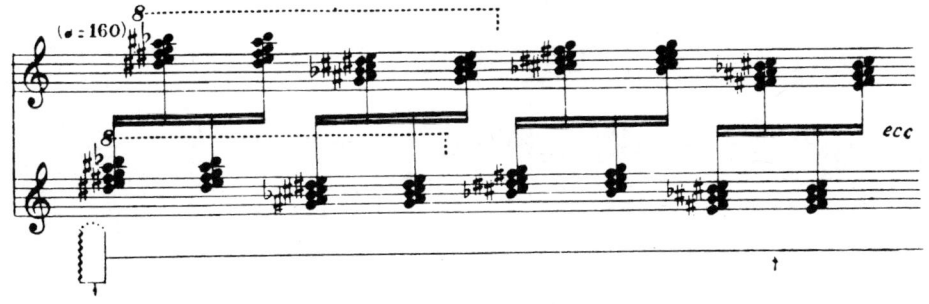

C. Salzedo: *Modern Study of the Harp*, p. 14. Ed: G. Schirmer, New York

Suoni fluidi – The left hand hooks the string in its highest extremities with the steel of the tuning key and while the right hand more or less rapidly plucks at the extreme lower portion of the string, the key is allowed to descend on the string with little interruptions (stoppings) at each half step. One can obtain a chromatic scale, if needed, rapidly, in a range approximately two octaves by going from the note that stays at least a perfect fourth above the note of the string used. The best result of this effect is obtained with the strings in the following tessitura:

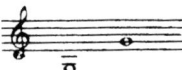

In scoring, the small squared note indicates the string used and plucked by the left hand, the normal note is that really produced according to the position of the key excited by the right hand. For the best clarity it is advised to write the indication: *suoni fluidi* (fluid sounds).

The *suoni fluidi* are particularly effective for the glissando on the same string by letting the key slide uniformly, i.e., without stop, while the left hand plays a rapid tremolo at the extreme lowest point of the string. An enharmonic scale results.

The following is an excellent example of a combination of glissando and harmonics.

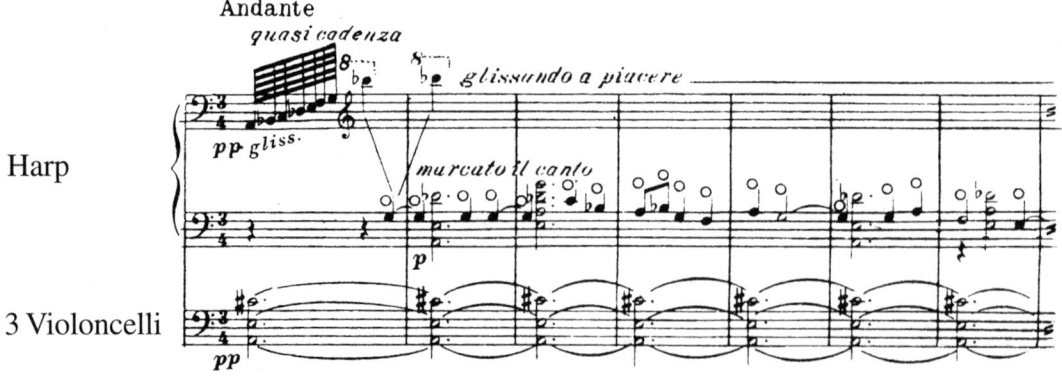

M. Ravel: *Concerto in G major for piano and orchestra*, p. 29. Ed: Durand

A very beautiful sonority is obtained by playing in unison both harmonics and ordinary tones.

V. Mortari: *Sonatina prodigio*, p. 2. Ed: Carisch

Banjo effect:

G. L. Tocchi: *Canzone, notturno e ballo* for harp, flute and viola, Ed: De Santis, Rome

Many passages in double notes render a wonderful effect as follows:

P. Hindemith: *Sonata per arpa*, Ed: Schott's Söhne

L. Perrachio: *Sonata popolaresca per arpa*, p. 12. Ed: Carisch

PIANO

For many years the rapport between the piano and the orchestra has been that of an instrument for soloists. The rapport, therefore, has always rendered the concept of a certain hierarchical status, i.e., in front of the orchestra. This status of course excluded any possibility of its being used in the midst of the other instruments as part of the orchestra. Nevertheless, it is not impossible to find in the *Concerti* of Mozart and Beethoven passages that are in some ways prophetic in which the piano assumes the function of an orchestral instrument, e.g., the end of the *Adagio* of the Beethoven *Concerto No. 5* in which the piano seems to have been thought of as a type of celeste. Other than these isolated examples, however, one must realize that the piano as an integral part of the orchestra is essentially a modern concept. Among the very few examples that one can cite in all of the 19th century exists in the very curious use of two pianos in the *Fantasia sulla Tempesta di Shakespeare*, the sixth part of the monologue *Lelio ou le retour à la vie* by Berlioz in 1833. A second and extremely beautiful example is found in the *Third Symphony* of Saint-Saëns (1886) in which the piano, two and four hands, was used. A third case occurs in the symphonic suite, *Printemps* (1887), of Claude Debussy in which the piano is only treated as four hands. Along with these few isolated examples one must remember the curious case of the *Petite Messe solennelle* of Gioacchino Rossini (1863) in which two pianos modestly cooperate or coexist to sustain the chorus for the entire duration of the work. The use merits noting not only for it singularity but also because Rossini's *Messa* anticipates the Stravinsky of *Les Noces* (1924), a work in which four pianos along with powerful percussion support all of the weight of the vocal polyphony.

Entering into the twentieth century, one finds the piano in the orchestra of the poem *Jour d'étè à la montagne* (1905) of Vincent d'Indy and in the *Eighth symphony* of Mahler (1910). After these sporadic attempts, one reaches finally 1911, the year of *Petrouchka* and Stravinsky's celebrated burlesque scene in which the piano was used as an obligato instrument of the orchestra. The bravura character is derived probably from the fact that the author conceptualized from the beginning the *Danse russe* and the second scene, *The room of Petrouchka*, as a concerto for piano and orchestra. *Petrouchka* is today recognized for the genial association of the piano with a dazzling and virtuosic orchestration; an orchestration in which the sonority of the piano assumes its own intense psychological expressivity. André Schaeffner is quoted as saying, "for the first time music finds in the dryness of the sound a plastic material; in the mechanism an expression of humanity."

* * *

With *Petrouchka* one begins the musical epoch that will be called anti-impressionistic, and that corresponds to a great diffusion in the use of the piano as an orchestral instrument. Here one must hesitate a moment in order to see the reasons that this instrument, until now held at such a distance from the orchestra by the majority of composers, has suddenly encountered such favor. It must be said, however, that the piano is not the first instrument that has had to await its own epoch or the discovery of its resources. One can cite the example of the saxophone that although invented 1840, found a sudden and immense circulation only by means of the jazz idiom seventy years later. Without returning to the prevalently lyric character of the romantic orchestra, the sonorities of the piano would not have found a place. Likewise in impressionistic orchestration it would have supplied in the middle of that diffuseness a contribution of precise and coherent sound. The instrument, therefore, would have been totally out of place. Composers instead found important the use of the lunar colors of the celeste and the playful sounds of the harp. Instead the piano found a full utilization of its characteristics in the music after the first world war and in a particular way in music that greatly reacted to romanticism. By contrast to those lyrical outbursts, to those coloristic atmospheres made of harmonic vagueness, this music established a most vigorous art, more steadily constructed without interference of painting or of literature. It is necessary also to say that the addition of the piano to the orchestra profoundly modified the equilibrium of the ensemble especially in the extremes. The basses were enormously enhanced by its dark and metallic sonority and the high sounds of the small instruments were greatly reinforced by its shrill and scintillating timbre.

* * *

In summarizing, the piano seems today to assume in the orchestra a primarily timbral, rhythmic, and percussive function. While this is true it can be expressive and lyrical. A beautiful exception is found in *Petrouchka* in this moving moment.

I. Stravinsky: *Petrouchka,* III scene, Ed: Russe de Musique

I. Stravinsky: *Symphonie de Psaumes*, p. 57. Ed: Russe de Musique

152

Employment of the dark and metallic bass:

Chorus
Orchestra

Piano
with Vc.
and Cb.
pizz.

A. Casella: *Missa solemnis pro pace*, from the "Agnus dei". Ed: Universal

Note: Parts of this chapter are taken from Casella's *Il Pianoforte*, Pbl: Tumminelli, 1937, Roma-Milano; now Ricordi.

HARPSICHORD

The harpsichord that flourished under the fingers of Frescobaldi, J. S. Bach, and Domenico Scarlatti has risen again to new life in the last forty years principally due to the great virtuosity of Wanda Landowska, Ralph Kirkpatrick, Alice Ehlers, Eta Harich-Schneider, and our Ruggero Gerlin and Ferruccio Vignanelli. The reason is probably due to the new and previously unthought-of uses for the instrument in chamber music. It is necessary then to give a technical illustration since this instrument is not at all simple and since it is so very different from the piano (The piano's ancestry is not from the harpsichord, as commonly believed, but from the clavichord.)

Range

The harpsichord consists of two keyboards each with a range of five octaves.

N. B. - Some old harpsichords had keyboards of various ranges, e.g.:

Pedals

The harpsichord has pedals that have registral functions, i.e., they serve to determine the quality of sound that one wants to obtain. The pedals number from five to eight according to the model of the instrument. The most current instruments have six pedals. In fact all of the harpsichords in use today (1946) have six pedals with the exception of the Pleyel grand model that has seven. The Erard and the Mendler-Schramm small models have five.

In some models, e.g., in the Pleyel, Mendler-Schramm, Steingräber, and Neupert, the pedal activates when it is raised. In others, e.g., Gaveau, Assmann, and some others, the pedal activates when it is lowered. However, the coupling pedal activates always when it is lowered, regardless of the model. This pedal functions only on the lower keyboard: coupling, i.e., is obtained only by playing on the lower keyboard after having lowered the relative pedal.

The pedals number from left to right. Their effect is as follows:

1. Register of 8 feet, written: (8'). Renders the note with normal pitch.
2. Register of 4 feet, (4'). Renders the note one octave higher.
3. Register of 16 feet, (16'). Renders the note at the octave lower.
4. Coupling. Unites the two keyboards.
5. Mute. A device of strips of cloth that impedes the vibration of the string is pushed against the string when the pedal is used. The sound becomes muted, like a light pizzicato in the strings of the orchestra. The register of the mute effects only the upper keyboard with the exception of the instrument made by Mendler-Schramm that has the mute also at the 16' or lower keyboard.
6. Register of 8 feet reinforced. This is always an 8' register; however, the string is plucked two times simultaneously in two different points.
7. Pedal of 8' muffled. The pedal places in action an order of small pulses that pluck the string at its extremity obtaining a sound of great sweetness. This register exists only on the Pleyel (large or small models), the Mendler-Schramm (large model), and the Assmann.

The pedals are placed in different ways according to the harpsichord.

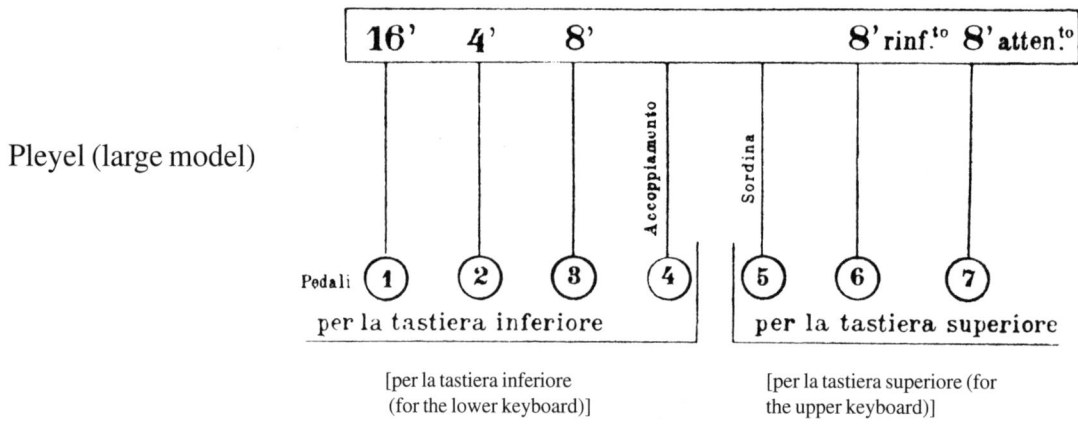

Pleyel (small model)

Erard (the only model)

Assmann (As the large Pleyel)

Gaveau (the only model)

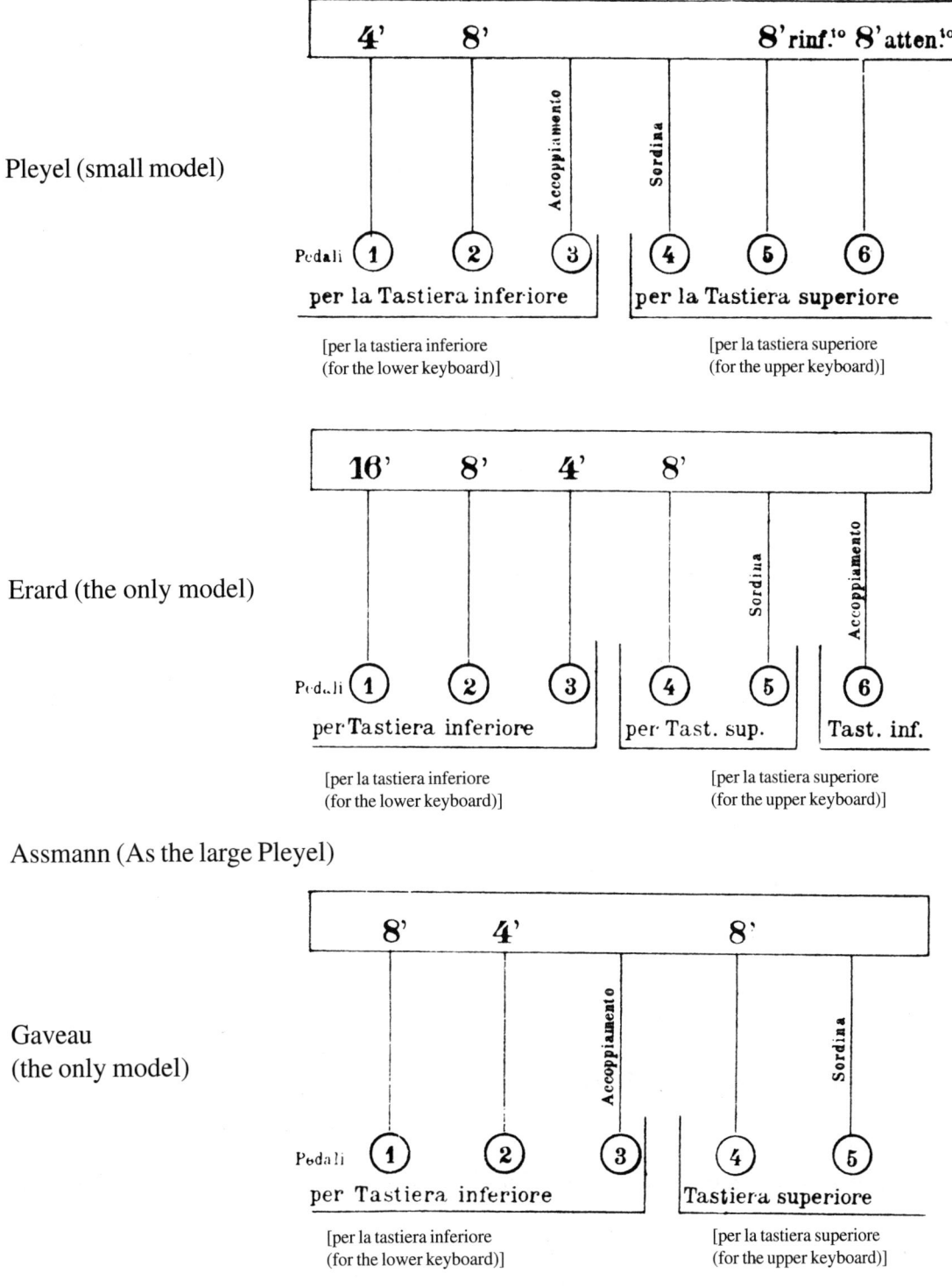

Mendler (Schramm-Mendler)
(large model)

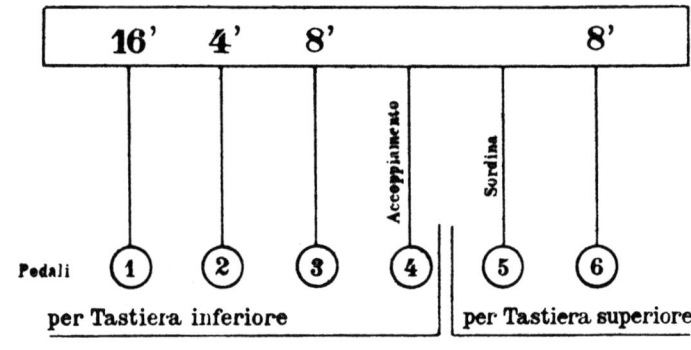

Mendler (small model)

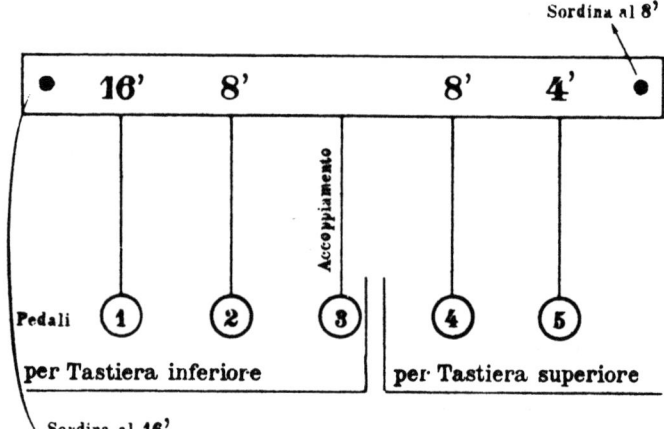

Steingräber (as the lar
Neupert (as the Gaveau)

Use of the pedals and different combinations

I – On the Pleyel (large model)
Key to terms: Tastiere = Keyboard; Infer. = lower; Super. = upper; rinf. = reinforced [1]; combinazioni = combinations

Tastiere

Infer.	Super.	Infer.	Super.
8' . . . . e . . . . 8'		16' . . . e . . . . 8'	
8' . . . . » . . . . 8' rinf. ([1])		16' . . . » . . . . 8' rinf.	

---

(1) This pedal acts for lowering.

Infer.	Super.	Infer.	Super.
8'	e . . . 8 atten.(¹)	16'	e . . . 8' atten.
8' Acc.	» . . . 8'	16'	» . . . Sordina
8' Acc.	» . . . 8' rinf.	16' Acc.	» . . . 8'
8' Acc.	» . . . 8' atten.	16'	» . . . 8' rinf.
8'	» . . . Sord. (²)	16'	» . . . 8' atten.
4'	» . . . 8'	16' 8'	» . . . 8'
4'	» . . . 8' rinf.	16' 8'	» . . . 8' rinf.
4'	» . . . 8' atten.	16' 8'	» . . . 8' atten.
4'	» . . . Sordina	16' 4'	» . . . 8'
4' Acc.	» . . . 8'	16' 4'	» . . . 8' rinf.
4' Acc.	» . . . 8' rinf.	16' 4'	» . . . 8' atten.
4' Acc.	» . . . 8' atten.	16' 4'	» . . . Sordina
8' 4'	» . . . 8'	16' 8' 4'	» . . . 8'
8' 4'	» . . . 8' rinf.	16' 8' 4'	» . . . 8' rinf.
8' 4'	» . . . 8' atten.	16' 8' 4' Acc.	» . . . 8' rinf.
8' 4'	» . . . Sordina	(Gran giuoco. *Plein-jeu*)	
8' 4' Acc.	» . . . 8' rinf		

Totale: n° 36 combinazioni

II – On the Pleyel (small model)

Tastiere

Infer.	Super.	Infer.	Super.
8'	e . . . 8'	4'	e . . . Sordina
8'	» . . . 8' rinf. (³)	4' Acc.	» . . . 8'
8'	» . . . 8' att. (²)	4' Acc.	» . . . 8' rinf.
8'	» . . . Sordina	4' Acc.	» . . . 8' atten.
8' Acc.	» . . . 8'	8' 4'	» . . . 8'
8' Acc.	» . . . 8' rinf.	8' 4'	» . . . 8' rinf.
8' Acc.	» . . . 8' atten.	8' 4'	» . . . 8' atten.
4'	» . . . 8'	8' 4' Acc.	» . . . 8'
4'	» . . . 8' rinf.	8' 4' Acc.	» . . . 8' rinf.
4'	» . . . 8' atten.	(Gran giuoco. *Plein-jeu*)	

Totale: n° 19 combinazioni

---

(1) This pedal functions for lowering.
(2) In order to obtain this color it is absolutely necessary first to lower the corresponding pedal, i.e., the 7th, putting in motion the 6th pedal (8' rinf.). If this 6th pedal is not lowered, the muted keyboard will result.
(3) The mute can be of three gradations: used with 1'8' normal, 1'8' rinf., or 1'8'soften.
(4) See first note.

III – on the Gaveau (only model)

Tastiere

Infer.	Super.	Infer.	Super.
8' . . . . e . . . . . . 8'		16' . . . . e . . . . . . Sordina	
8' . . . . » . . . . . . Sordina		16' Acc. . . . . . » . . . . . . 8'	
8' Acc. . . . . . » . . . . . . 8'		16' Acc. . . . . . » . . . . . . Sordina	
4' . . . . » . . . . . . 8'		16' 8' . . . . . . » . . . . . . 8'	
4' . . . . » . . . . . . Sordina		16' 8' . . . . . . » . . . . . . Sordina	
4' Acc. . . . . . » . . . . . . 8'		16' 8' Acc. . . . » . . . . . . 8'	
4' Acc. . . . . . » . . . . . . Sordina		16' 4' . . . . . . » . . . . . . 8'	
8' 4' . . . . . . » . . . . . . 8'		16' 4' . . . . . . » . . . . . . Sordina	
8' 4' . . . . . . » . . . . . . Sordina		16' 8' 4' . . . . » . . . . . . 8'	
8' 4' Acc. . . . » . . . . . . 8'		16' 8' 4' Acc. . . » . . . . . . 8' Gran	
16' . . . . » . . . . . . 8'		giuoco. *Plein-jeu*)	

Totale: n° 21 combinazioni

IV – On the Mendler-Schramm (large model) as the Pleyel (large model)
V – On the Mendler-Schramm (small model)

Tastiere

Infer.	Super.	Infer.	Super.
8' . . . . e . . . . . . 8'		16' . . . . e . . . . . . 8' 4'	
8' . . . . » . . . . . . Sordina		16' Sordina . . . » . . . . . . 8'	
8' . . . . » . . . . . . 4'		16' » . . » . . . . . . 4'	
8' . . . . » . . . . . . 8' 4'		16' Acc. . . . . . » . . . . . . 8'	
8' Acc. . . . . . » . . . . . . 8'		16' Acc . . . . . » . . . . . . 4'	
8' Acc. . . . . . » . . . . . . Sordina		16' Acc. Sordina » . . . . . . Sordina	
8' Acc. . . . . . » . . . . . . 4'		16' 8' . . . . . . » . . . . . . 8'	
8' Acc. . . . . . » . . . . . . 8' 4'		16' 8' . . . . . . » . . . . . . 4'	
16' . . . . » . . . . . . 8'		16' 8' . . . . . . » . . . . . . 8' 4'	
16' . . . . » . . . . . . Sordina		16' 8' Acc. . . . » . . . . . . 8'	
16' . . . . » . . . . . . 4'		16' 8' Acc. . . . » . . . . . . 8' 4'	
		(Gran giuoco. *Plein-jeu*)	

Totale: n° 22 combinazioni

VI – On the Assmann [as on the Pleyel (large model)]
VII – On the Steingräber [as on the Mendler (small model)]
VIII – On the Newpert (as on the Gaveau) IX – On the Erard

VI - Nel clavicembalo Assmann: come il Pleyel (grande mod.)
VII -   »   Steingräber: come il Mendler (piccolo mod.).
VIII -   »   Neupert: come il Gaveau.
IX -   »   Erard:

Tastiere

Infer.	Super.	Infer.	Super.
8' . . . . e . . . . . . 8'		4' . . . . » . . . . . . Sordina	
8' . . . . » . . . . . . Sordina		4' Acc. . . . . . » . . . . . . 8'	
8' Acc. . . . . . » . . . . . . 8'		8' 4' . . . . . . » . . . . . . 8'	
8' Acc. . . . . . » . . . . . . Sordina		8' 4' . . . . . . » . . . . . . Sordina	
4' . . . . » . . . . . . 8'		8' 4' Acc. . . . » . . . . . . 8' (Gran	
		giuoco. *Plein-jeu*)	

Totale: n. 10 combinazioni

Manufacturers

The principal manufacturers are the following:

In France:
    Pleyel
    Gaveau
    Assmann

In Germany:
    Erard
    Mendler-Schramm
    Neupert
    Steingräber

In Great Britain:
    Dolmetsch

In the United States:
    Chickering

A typical modern example of harpsichord writing that is quite sonorous.

Manuel de Falla: *Concert for Harpsichord and 5 Instruments*, pp. 22-23. Ed: Chester

THE STRING INSTRUMENTS

This group of instruments, besides having been the foundation on which the modern orchestra was based, have enjoyed a privileged place in the hierarchy of instruments for a very long time. This privilege comes, above all, from the violin's being referred to by many as "the king of instruments", a deserved appellative stemming from the great instrument makers and performers of the past. Today the situation is somewhat changed. The wind instruments, and even the percussion, have made such progress in a century that they have threatened seriously the ancient supremacy of the strings. The other instruments have thus compelled the strings to an equality that no one would have dreamed of in the past. Stravinsky wrote concerning the prelude of *Le Sacre du printemps* in which the strings are almost excluded: "*J'ai mis au premier plan les bois, plus secs, plus nets, moins riches d'expression facile, et par cela même plus emouvants à mon grè*". (I placed in the first scoring the winds...rich in expression and more moving). In the words, "ease of expression therefore more moving", resides the entire aspect of music today. The abandonment of the old romantic lyricism that became through its last decadence, "easy". The music of today finds a new emotion by means of instruments less exploited.

In the orchestra, the mass of the strings appears today to us as a perfect instrumentation in itself. This appears so either because the construction of the single instruments has reached a defined end (nor does it seem that the construction will change) or because the technique of the performers is based on a tradition of great consistency. What matters above all for the violins (and the viola, the violoncello, and contrabass) is that they have recently entered in an evolutionary phase that has already enormously renewed their possibilities. We can, however, maintain that the strings, even after losing some of their absolute supremacy, remain the basic element in the normal orchestra representing an unsubstitutable technical and expressive resource. The future may hold, however, that one could also do without the quartet as in the *Symphonie de Psaumes* of Stravinsky, in which the strings are reduced to the violins and the contrabasses while the mass of the winds is reinforced. No matter how much the recommendation of Widor [1] appears to be so removed, "*quand le quatuor sonne bien, tout va bien!*" [when the quartet is capable, everything goes well], every orchestrator knows that it is not enough to know how to write well for the strings. He must also be aware that is also indispensable to demonstrate the same expertise in the treatment of woodwinds, brasses, and percussion.

---

(1) Ch. M. Widor: *Technique de l'orchestre moderne*. H. Lemoine & C. Ed., Paris.

THE VIOLIN

Of the instruments that make up the string quartet, the violin was the first to reach a point of structural perfection: perfection in the construction by such great builders as Gaspare da Salò and Antonio Stradivari, and perfection in the virtuosity of the great performers such as Nicolò Paganini. Most recently the violin has reached a certain perfection due to the expressive necessity demanded by modern composers who have employed new sonorities, new positions, new ways of using the bow, new means, in short, of improving the technique of performers due to their emerging musical demands. Today the parts for the bravura soloists are filtering little by little into the parts for all performers. The following are examples of the technique of the *Capricci* of Paganini transported to normal orchestral technique.

A. Casella: *Paganiniana*, pp. 45-49. Ed: Universal

A. Casella: *Paganiniana*, pp. 54-56. Ed: Universal

The violin is tune to a perfect fifth but in some rare cases composers have imposed special tunings. Mahler, for example, raised all of the strings by one step to obtain from the violin a color more taut and brilliant.

In these cases when the tuning is altered the written notes do not correspond to the sounding notes.

In the cited example of Mahler all of the violin parts are written a step under the sound wanted since the instrument is tuned in D.

G. Mahler: *Fourth Symphony*, II movement, p. 73. Ed: Universal
*As a "violinaccio" (bad violin)

The first violinist, then, has two instruments of which one is tuned a note higher than the other. Every violinist is aware of the many times Paganini modified the tuning of the violin. In those days the pitch, most probably, was lower than it is today, and for taut and brilliant sonorities Paganini had need evidently of a higher tuning. Sometimes the tuning of a single string was altered.

Range

The boldness of Richard Strauss forced the addition of notes to the highest range of the violin. Note the following example:

R. Strauss: *Tod und Verklärung*, pp. 103-104. Ed: Peters

The limits of the violin in the orchestra, however, are normally as follows:

The virtuoso can achieve notes higher than above; however, they are and should be approached with exceptional respect. The highest note achievable on the instrument is:

It is advisable that the highest notes be written so that they can be reached stepwise or with small intervals, for the left hand must have a way to find its place with ease among the very tight positions of the keyboard in that extremity. Modern technique tends to go beyond these prudent suggestions, and it is not rare that the violinist finds that he must perform in the extremes using larger intervals than those indicated above. The result can cause a preoccupation to the performer that betrays musical expression as well as rendering poor intonation.

For the highest limit on the instrument the following is indicated:

This note is often played as a harmonic (see the paragraph on harmonics) with ease and a sonorous result.

Timbre

The violin, and in general all of the string instruments, excluding the contrabass, has an essentially lyrical nature. The violin has a great variety of color, and each of the four strings has its own particular timbre. The first string, called also *cantino*, is brilliant, open, and incisive. The second is persuasive and gentle. The third delivers a great sweetness capable of noble, poetic effects. And finally the fourth has almost a contralto timbre and with certain kinds of bowings, it can render a hard and coarse sound.

As one ascends above [♪] the sound becomes smaller and is often subject to greater preoccupation on the part of the performer. This preoccupation stems simply from the violinist's trying to maintain the beauty and expressiveness of the sound as he ascends.

In the last thirty years the soloistic and orchestral technique of the instrument has been noticeably enriched, e.g., the development of the use of harmonics. The instrument, therefore, has adapted itself to a more rigid and inexpressive style imposed upon it by the necessities of the evolution of the music. Continuing on this path, one has only to note the three *Mythes* of Karol Szimanowsky. This work which is now limited to the virtuoso soloist will no doubt in time be extended to the full section of the strings. The instrument, therefore, is without question destined for new expressive timbral changes.

Production of the sound

The sound of the violin has different aspects according to how and where the string is set in vibration. Notable also in addition to the above is that the sound is influenced by the position of the left hand on the keyboard. When the left hand is near the center of the string, third and fourth position (see the paragraph on the positions), the color is soft and persuasive and the most characteristic that can be obtained on the instrument. As the left hand moves toward the bridge, the vibrating part of the string becomes shorter and the sonority becomes more strident and taut. If instead one moves toward the *capotasto*, i.e., the point on the handle of the instrument where the strings rest against the wood, the vibrating part of the string becomes longer and the sound acquires a clearer and more open timbre. The best ranges for each of the strings follows:

I. String II. String III. String IV. String

If the composer wants a beautiful sonority from the third and fourth positions, he must indicate the string on which he wishes that the passage be executed. Otherwise, the performer can play in the position most easy and comfortable on the highest string. This example demonstrates that without the indication, II (second string), this passage could be played on the first string with a different result.

II. String

The ordinary means for placing the string in vibration is the bow. All of the notes under a slur must be played with the same movement of the bow. The bow moves down (⊓) or up (⋁). The importance of a good placement of the bow is fundamental, for the use of the bow influences above all the ability to play expressively. This example from Beethoven demonstrates.

The meaning of the phrase would change greatly if the bowing were modified as follows:

The down bow has an intensity of attack and therefore the violinist tends to use the down bow in strong sections of music and for expressive accents. Chords are also usually played with a down bow. Immediately after the attack, however, the sound tends to diminish with the down bow while the up bow that emits a weaker attack tends to sustain or reinforce the sound. It should not be said, however, that all *forte* attacks and accents should be played with the down bow nor should one assume that one cannot play softer attacks and crescendi with only the up bow. Both up and down bows can be made to do similar expressive gestures.

The violinist follows the so called spontaneous tendencies of the bow. Above all the player must put the bow in the service of musical expression. One must not avoid the traditional habitual rules for bowing, but one must also keep in mind that the bow should follow the expressive accents more than the rhythmic accents.

1. The down bowings are on each strong point, as the norm would advise, but the expressive accent falls on the E♭ . The sonority then diminishes immediately. Therefore, this E♭ must be played down.

2. The diminuendo is followed by the down bow to the third measure; therefore, the attack on the up bow of the last note can be played with great and spontaneous sweetness.

The following example demonstrates a two-note grouping, the second note of which is short and played usually with the same bow.

L. V. Beethoven: *Ninth Symphony,* First movement.

Another way of writing the same bowing:

Observe the following example:

V. Mortari: *Concerto per quartetto e orchestra.* p. 2. Ed: Carisch

In part the imbalance of the bow in the first two measures (the first and the third bowing have a length disproportionate to the second and the fourth) is evident in the banality of the movement of the bow in the third measure. Below, instead, demonstrates how one can balance the bow and give to it the possibility of a fullness of development and excellent expressive accentuation.

The indication, *alla punta*, or the point of the bow produces a subtle and sweet sound, for the point of the bow has little weight and must be made to exert more energy for a louder sound. The bow *al tallone*, at the heel of the bow, instead is needed for energetic and rough sounds.

The bowing *sul ponticello*, on the bridge, renders a metallic sound, somewhat harsh at *forte*, silvery at *piano*. Sustaining the sound on the bridge is almost impossible, but a melody in notes that are not long and one that does not require a certain effect can be very effective *sul ponticello*.

H. Wieniawski: *Le carnaval russe,* 7th variazione. Ed: Eschig

The sounds indicated by *sulla tastiera*, on the fingerboard, are sweet and veiled. It should be noted that the position of the string where the vibration has its maximum fullness is the most favorable for the purest production of the sound. Therefore, as the bow moves toward the fingerboard it moves closer to the loop of the vibration, if not the axis of the wave itself; hence, the sound acquires probably its most beautiful quality.

The marking *col legno* produces a crackling, dry sound of little fullness. When the mass of the strings employ the technique, the result can be most curious.

The tremolo that was used for the first time by Claudio Monteverdi has lost favor in the last half of the century (20th century) due to its abuse as a melodramatic device. It did, however, gain favor among the impressionist composers who found new and noble effects for its use. This is the tremolo that one obtains by moving the bow rapidly up and back . Another type of tremolo is that achieved by two notes on the same string that are rapidly alternated with one bowing.  The most comfortable stretch of the left hand for this type of tremolo is that in the limits of a minor third. As the stretch becomes larger (the maximum achievable easily is that of a diminished fifth), the result is a higher string from the fingerboard; therefore, one must exert a greater and more uncomfortable force on the string for the rapidness of the tremolo. The string, then, by being higher, produces higher movements that disturb the regular movement of the bow endangering the resulting sonority. The more one ascends toward the highest positions, the more the stretch of the left hand must be augmented; therefore, again the greater the height of the string is from the keyboard, the greater the disturbance of the bow. One should avoid, then, in writing for orchestra tremolos with greater stretches than those indicated. If the tremolo is not rapid, and it is measured, it can be played on two strings making the bow rock back and forth alternately from one to the other string. In this case the maximum stretch is stabilized by the possible use of the two strings. The following example demonstrates:

on only one string   on two strings

Grand détaché

This effect is one of great and imposing sonority. One uses it at *forte* in passages of notes that are non legato, of equal value, and generally at a moderate tempo. One obtains the effect by letting the bow flow rapidly at its full length with adequate pressure. The technique is somewhat difficult, for by letting the bow rapidly bound forward, it can displace itself on the string easily producing serious sonorous defects, e.g., whistles, false harmonics.

Successive down bows

If one wants a harsh and violent effect, one can attack all of the notes with the down bow with the result being an intense accent on each stroke. A short pause then is required prior to the next down bow. It is a bowing that, more than the preceding, requires a moderate tempo.

G. Pugnani-Kreisler: *Preludio e allegro*. Ed: Schott

N. Rimsky-Korsakov: *Sheherazade*, p. 93. Ed: Belajeff

Martellato

The martellato gives a dry and cutting effect. One uses it at *forte* for the most part with notes of equal value at a tempo that is moderate. A variety of this bowing is that which is termed *martellato alla punta* (martellato at the point of the bow) that is generally used at *piano* with a very small part of the bow for notes that are very short. This bowing is analogous with martellato only for the incisiveness of the bow on the string. Its musical expressiveness is totally different. For the *détaché* and martellato the tempo should be limited to 16th notes at a quarter = 100.

Staccato

The ordinary staccato is performed according to the tempo and intensity required with more or less bow and with a maximum of three quarters of the bow. It is neat, precise, and easy to execute.

W. A. Mozart: *Le nozze di Figaro*. Final scene

Liscio (simple bowing)

Each time that the bow moves either up or down it produces an articulation. With simple bowing the violinist works in a way that the articulation is almost not heard.

Alla corda (on the string)

One plays *alla corda* (on the string) by articulating with precision each note but without the rigidity with *souplesse*. The sound must be sustained for the duration of its value. In place of the indication alla corda, one can place dashes above each note.

Legato

Today in good orchestras one knows how to use the bowings that generally respond to the expressive needs of the music. Moreover, it is always advisable that the composer, perhaps with the help of a performer, indicates all of the bowings in a way as precise as possible so that they are easily played by the performers and avoid useless waste of time in the rehearsals.

Separato (separated – linked bowing)

The articulation of some sustained sounds are played with the same bow but not legato. The procedure is most elegant and renders a beautiful effect. Often it is opportune to employ an equal distribution of the bow.

M. Castelnuovo-Tedesco: *Ouverture per il "Mercante di Venezia"*, p. 40. Ed: Ricordi

Picchettato (staccato volante or flying staccato)

This bowing is executed by playing a group of rapid and staccato notes under the same bow. Usually the technique is done with the up bow, but it can be also played down bow. Not all violinist are capable of executing this technique just as not all percussionist are capable of the finger roll on the tambourine.

Balzato (saltellato or saltarello)

The *saltarello* is generally executed in the center of the bow with a very light rebound. It is quite efficient in rapid and light passages as follows.

L. v. Beethoven: *Seventh Symphony*. "Allegretto"

Two or more notes can be taken under the same bow as follows. In an arpeggiated passage as many as four notes may be played under the same bow.

Gettato (Jeté)

This bowing requires that the upper part of the bow be allowed to rebound on the string two, three, or more times. The technique is indicated by a staccato marking with a slur as follows.

Suoni flautati (Flageolets)

(Translator's note: *Flageolett* is a general term for harmonics on the violin)

The technique is one that emits soft, veiled, and very sweet (*dolce*) sounds. The bow is used with the very maximum lightness of pressure with the fastest stroke that can be done without sacrificing the tone. If equilibrium is missing between the velocity of the bow and the pressure, the sound will be vague and impure with a kind of halo that is more or less distant. The effect is undetermined but can be useful in the effort to find new timbres.

(Not to be confused with harmonics, in Italy inappropriately called *flautati*).

Pizzicato

Pizzicato is a very noticeable effect on the violin that is usually executed with the right hand but may also be played with the left. In the first case one places the indication, pizz. In the second one writes a small cross above or below the note.

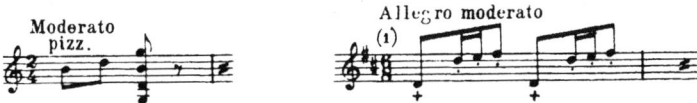

(1) The notes marked by a cross are played with the left hand; the others, not having any indication should be played with the bow.

The pizzicato should not be written at a fast tempo, above all if the passage is long, simply due to the endurance of the hand. It is advised to maintain a tempo of not more than 16th notes at a quarter = 92. One can execute pizzicato more rapidly, however, if the hand has time to rest.

As one ascends to ![notation], the pizzicato becomes less sonorous and dryer. There are few examples of the technique in this range. One may also play arpeggiated passages pizzicato if they are not rapid. The example below demonstrates an ascending arpeggiated group of notes that are played with the same finger.

(In this case the notes are tied.)

One can play the violin as if it were a guitar. In this way one can also use the thumb and obtain new speeds and effects by moving the hand without rigidity as if one were playing the guitar. This procedure that has been for the most part used for picturesque effects is naturally more comfortable when the violin is placed on the knees or is held under the arm. It is also possible to execute the technique in the normal position.

(like a guitar the violin under the arm)

Cl. Debussy: *Iberia*, p. 102. Ed: Durand

B. Bartók: *Fourth Quartett*, p. 41. Ed: Universal

(1) This indication means that the hand must be moved up and down alternately on the string.

For chords formed by the superimposition of perfect fifths one can overcome the performance difficulty with the violin played under the arm or on the knees, because, in this case, the finger of the left hand can be extended flat across the string as if it were a moveable *capotasto*, or the point of the fingerboard where it meets the strings.

The pizzicato has a soft vibration and is a sweet sonority if it is played on the fingerboard. As one descends toward the bridge the technique becomes more marked and dry. Very close to the bridge it is quite harsh. (See the Bartók example above)

Natural harmonics

Harmonics are produced by touching very lightly or by brushing over the strings at a determined point so that one obtains the 2nd, 3rd, 4th, 5th, and 6th harmonic. (Remembering that the 1st is the fundamental and all above are the harmonics). One should not venture beyond the 6th harmonic and even including the 6th, for the 6th is most insecure, weak, and inefficient.

Artificial harmonics

The harmonic is produced with the index finger pressing on the string making the *capotasto* moveable while another finger brushes against the string producing another note. The result, then, is a harmonic above that note pressed by the index finger. This harmonic, however, can be somewhat uncomfortable because it requires an extension of the left hand. Below are the indications for artificial harmonics: the perfect 5th which produces a 12th; the perfect 4th which produces a 15th; the major 3rd or the 6th which produces a 17th, and the minor 3rd which produces a 19th. Of all these artificial harmonics the best, the easiest, and almost the only one used in orchestra is that which one creates with the 4th of the primary note. (#4)

Very often the harmonic is indicated with a small note, but this is not obligatory. Some composers write only the effect leaving the selection of the way to produce the harmonic to the player. The highest limit for the production of artificial harmonics is the following.

Glissando

The glissando or small portamento is often used in contemporary music and is of little difficulty to the player.

E.R. 2935

M. Ravel: *L'heure espagnole*, p. 191. Ed: Durand

One can perform double chord glissandi and also pizzicato glissandi. The pizzicato glissando is achieved by scraping the finger after having plucked the string in exploitation of the vibrations of the pizzicato. This effect, more easily achieved on the more sonorous violoncello, is not very effective on the violin especially on the fourth string. It has been used rarely, generally only ascending. Descending should be always avoided.

In modern scores one finds harmonic glissandi that produce most effective and mysterious passages.

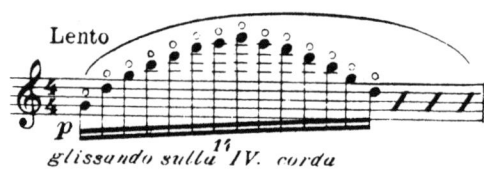

The complete series of all the harmonics that are obtainable with the gliding of the finger pushing against the string are below: (Avoid fast tempos in the use of the very high harmonics due to their uncertainty and unpredictable intonation.)

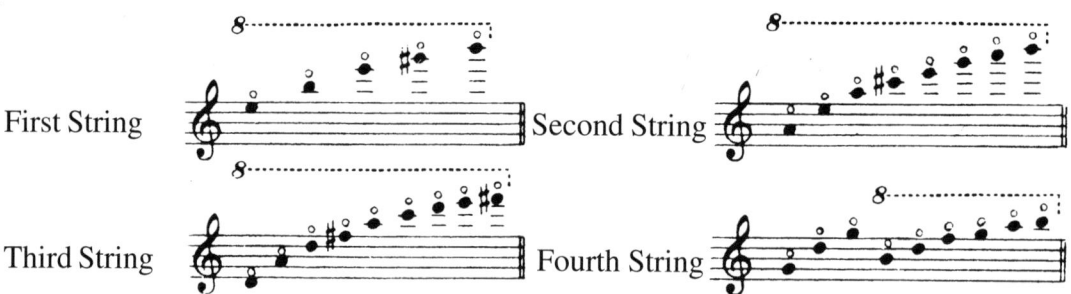

Fingerings and positions

Since the thumb is not used, the index finger is considered the first finger; the middle, the second; the ring finger, the third; and the little finger, the fourth. The open string is indicated with an "o".

The first position of the left hand on the fingerboard is that which stays immediately above the open string in the order of the diatonic scale. By moving the hand up the fingerboard the other positions are available.

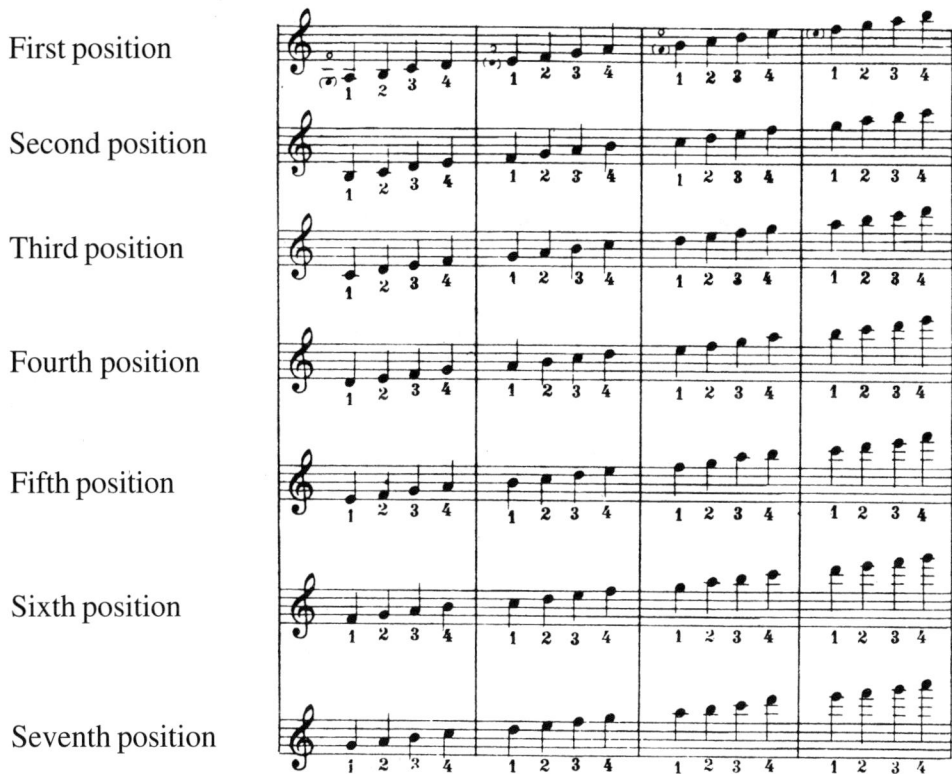

There is also the so-called half position, i.e., a half step above the first position.

Modern technique on the instrument has brought other criteria that have enriched its virtuosic possibilities. These criteria render certain passages more comfortable and expressive above all in the chromaticism of contemporary music. They have also led to the avoidance of an inexpressive open string or an inopportune changing of a string that of course would give way to any disadvantage to musical expression. The research into the perfections of the positions is still in progress, and one does not know where it will eventually arrive. For example, the chromatic scale was once played with the following fingering. (The half step was played with the same finger.)

It is easy to understand that the performance of this scale could not have been more than approximate regarding clarity and intonation. Today the same scale would be played as follows. This fingering permits good articulation and intonation.

There was a time that one did not go beyond the first string. Today, however, in avoiding the so called *smanicamento* (*démanché*) (movement of the left hand to distant positions) some fast and high passages are played by using that which the French call the *restez*, i.e., remaining in the same high position passing from string to string. This passage, for example, once would have been played with a movement of positions easily controllable in the previous table of positions.

Today's modern technique prescribes this alternate that permits the *restez* in fourth position in the left hand.

Double, triple, quadruple strings

For the study of double, triple, and quadruple strings the following chromatic table is proposed that conserves the relationship of the perfect fifth among the four strings.

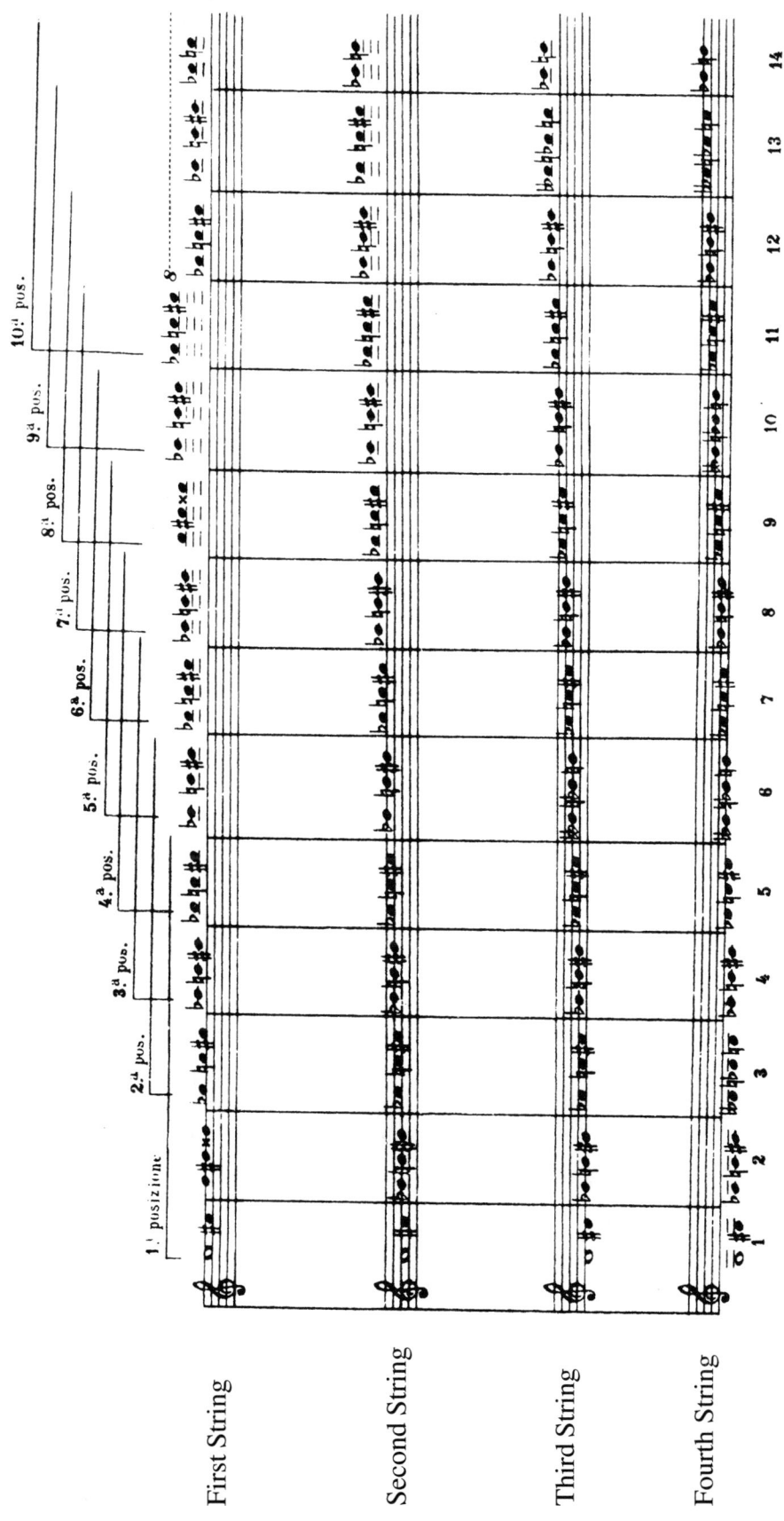

The normal placement of the left hand on the fingerboard corresponds in the table to a group that embraces four boxes. In the limit of this four box group the composer may select notes that are desired for combinations of two, three, or four tones distributed on two or three consecutive strings or on all of the four strings. By acknowledging any group, e.g., that which from box 4 moves to box 7 (inclusive), the following examples are given of two, three, and four combinations.

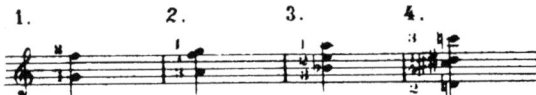

The note that one finds in the first box at the left of the group must be played, as a rule, with the first finger. The notes that stay in the successive boxes must be played with the second, third, and fourth finger. The second combination, for example, is formed by the G of the first string (placed in the first box of the group is played with the first finger) from the A of the third string (played with the third finger because it stays in the third box of the group) and from the F of the second string (that touches the fourth finger because it stays in the fourth box).

The notes included in the same box should be played with the same finger. In practice, this takes place only with the notes of two consecutive strings that stay in rigorous vertical alignment with the intervals, i.e., of the perfect fifth.[1] Since the same finger cannot be used at the maximum for two immediately successive strings, it is evident that two superimposed fifths are quite uncomfortable simply because one of the fifths must be pressed with one finger while a second finger must try to find a place near to the first in an identical position. Three superimposed fifths, then, are quite unperformable. If notes in the middle box are not in the order of superimposed perfect fifths, the player will provide, with an enharmonic interpretation, a possible fingering.

In the third example the three notes are placed in the same box and therefore must be played with the same finger that, as has been noted, is impossible. But the perfect fifth (G♭-D♭) interpreted enharmonically (F♯-C♯) can be given to the finger of the preceding box, rendering possible the performance of this chord. Therefore, in order to perform the fourth chord, one will have to interpret the D♯ as E♭.

To these expedient devices the composer can take into account that the modern performer will adapt rapidly to the most comfortable and playable positions.

---

(1) The perfect fifth is easier in the 1st and 2nd positions, better if it can be played with the 1st or 2nd finger. In the positions above the 2nd, the fifth with the 3rd finger is quite uncomfortable, with the 4th it is much ill advised, above all in orchestral playing since the distance between the strings becomes greater as one approaches the bridge and the little finger cannot easily embrace two strings that are not in close proximity.

The following examples by also using the open strings give an idea of the infinite combinations available to the composer.

N. B. The Roman numeral indicates the string. This indication is important at times when or because a string will not sound above the successive strings; or for purposes of explanation, the fingering might not be clear.

Through extension of the fingers of the left hand, a combination is possible of more sounds other than the limits of the same group, but it is opportune that this crossing (at least in orchestral playing) does not fit in an entire box in the system of the box in this text.

As one proceeds toward the highest notes, the extension can become greater, but it is advised not to extend pass an entire box.

At the beginning of the third act of *Aida*, Verdi gives to the first violins a most challenging passage in regard to the extension of the left hand, i.e., a group of seven boxes in the system of boxes. The execution is possible, however, since after the left hand is placed, no finger must move during the entire lengthy passage.

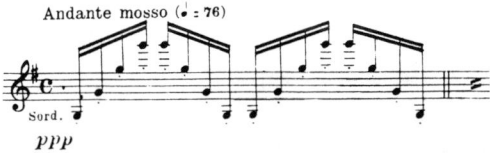

G. Verdi: *Aida,* Preludio atto III. Ed: Ricordi

Double, triple, and quadruple strings are played by beginning from the lowest note; however, for special effects, one can also play by beginning from the highest note. In this second case one puts an arrow in the wanted direction as noted in the following example.

B. Bartók: *Fourth Quartett*, p. 62. Ed: Universal

It is also possible to play double harmonics; however, when doing so it is better that at least one of these is a natural harmonic or that the harmonic(s) are not employed by only one finger, i.e., they are in relationship to the perfect fifth.

Karol Szymanowsky: *La fontaine d'Aréthuse,* from *Mythes*. Ed: Universal

In Paganini one finds most complex and difficult combinations. Naturally these are for the virtuoso performer and would be useless when used in orchestral writing.

Mute

The mute stops in part the vibration of the body of the instrument with the result of altering the timbre. In short it deadens the sonority of the instrument. The very sweet and mysterious character of the violin and of the strings in general with the mute becomes dry and woody in the pizzicato.

The following are some examples:

I. Stravinsky: *Petrouchka*, p. 140. Ed: Russe de Musique

The following passage in reality is not difficult.

I. Stravinsky: *Jeu de cartes*, p. 12. Ed: Schott

M. Ravel: *Trio*, p. 25. Ed: Durand

Modern polyphonic writing:

K. Szymanowski: *Narcisse*. Ed: Universal

K. Szymanowski: *Driades et Pan,* from *Mythes*. Ed: Universal

Very difficult polyphony that would have made a violinist of the previous century shiver.

A. Berg: *Concerto for violin and orchestra,* II mvt. Ed: Universal

K. Szymanowsky: *Concerto for violin and orchestra*, cadenza by Paul Kochansky. Ed: Universal

I. Stravinsky: *Concerto for violin and orchestra*, "Finale", Ed: Schott's Sohne

THE VIOLA

The roll of the viola [1] has changed in the 19th century from that of simply an instrument in the string quartet to one comparable to the violin. By acquiring a different look and reaching an expressive and autonomous value as an instrument, it has achieved a notable place in the orchestra along with the others in the quartet. In the last quarter of the century the instrument has taken giant steps through such soloists as the English violist, Lionel Tertis, performing the *Chaconne* of Bach and the works of the composers Hindemith, Bloch, and Walton.

Tuning

The normal tuning for the viola is as follows: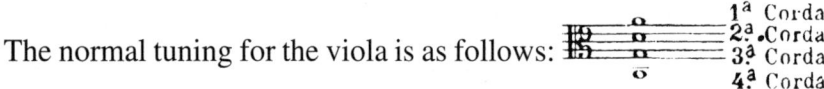

As for the violin and the violoncello, different tunings are possible. Once such tuning had the purpose of changing the color of the instrument, adding brilliance by tightening the strings. Often the purpose was to facilitate technique through the manipulation of the open strings. Today, however, standard intonation is higher and therefore more brilliant than it was in the past. Likewise technique is much more advanced so as to avoid the open strings.

Range:

In orchestral writing it is advised not to supersede the .

The viola is written in the alto clef and, in its highest register, in the treble clef.

Timbre

The viola always displays a somewhat indecisive character that allows it little emotive display. Its delicate and melancholy timbre must be well approached if the composer wishes to take advantage of the instrument. One should also note that not only is the timbre somewhat bland, but also the position of the instrument in the orchestra does not help to augment its character. If, therefore, the instrument is to emerge from the group of strings, its placement and careful balance in the setup of the group must be considered.

On the other hand no other instrument can substitute for the viola in its poetic languor and its penetrating intensity in the upper register. Note that also the fourth string is difficult and produces a breathy sound.

Production of the sound

Everything that was said concerning the violin as regards bowing is the same for the viola. One should consider, however, that simply because of the quiet nature of the instrument that certain bowings are less effective on the viola than on the violin.

---

[1] i. e., the role of the viola in the orchestra. In classical literature, 18th century, there are famous uses of the viola as soloist, e.g., the *Sinfonia Concertante* for violin, viola, and orchestra of Mozart. In the 19th century, however, the viola declined as a soloistic instrument.

Pizzicato

The pizzicato can be effective in the following range:

The higher the use, the dryer and less penetrating the sound. Note that the sounds that are nearest the natural harmonics on the fingerboard are those which are the most vibrant even if they are very high.

Tremolo

The stretch of the hand on the string should be kept at least in the primary positions at the maximum limit of a diminished fifth. The stretch of a perfect fifth is possible, but it presupposes a reach that may make the technique quite uncomfortable. (See tremolo on the violin.)

Fingering and positions

The criteria for fingering and for positions is the same for the viola as it was for the violin. It is necessary to take into consideration, however, that the larger size of the viola imposes a greater stretch in the left hand; therefore, one assumes that the technique would be less agile. There are seven positions normally used. One does not usually play above the seventh position on the same string. The medium positions, therefore, are much more used than on the violin.

Natural harmonics

The sixth harmonic is more easily played on the viola than on the violin, but it is always somewhat dangerous.

Artificial harmonics

For their production one should return to the section on artificial harmonics for the violin. One can obtain the 3rd through 6th on the viola. The 6th is dangerous and the 4th is advised for orchestral playing since it is easier. The 5th and 3rd should not be excluded though from the composer's vocabulary.

Glissando

The portamento is normal on string instruments and can be extremely effective. The abuse or misuse of the technique is certainly in bad taste. In contemporary scores one finds harmonic glissandi. The use is most effective.

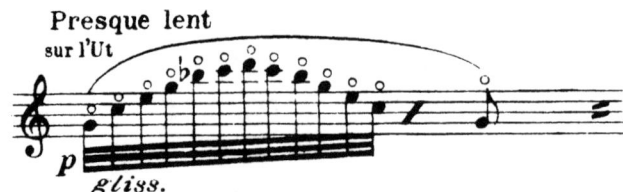

M. Ravel: *L'heure espagnole*, p. 120. Ed: Durand

Below is the complete series of all harmonics obtainable by the movement of the finger on the string. If needed, for certain effects, sounds above the 6th harmonic are given; however, because of their lack of consistency and their uncertain intonation, one should not use them at rapid tempos.

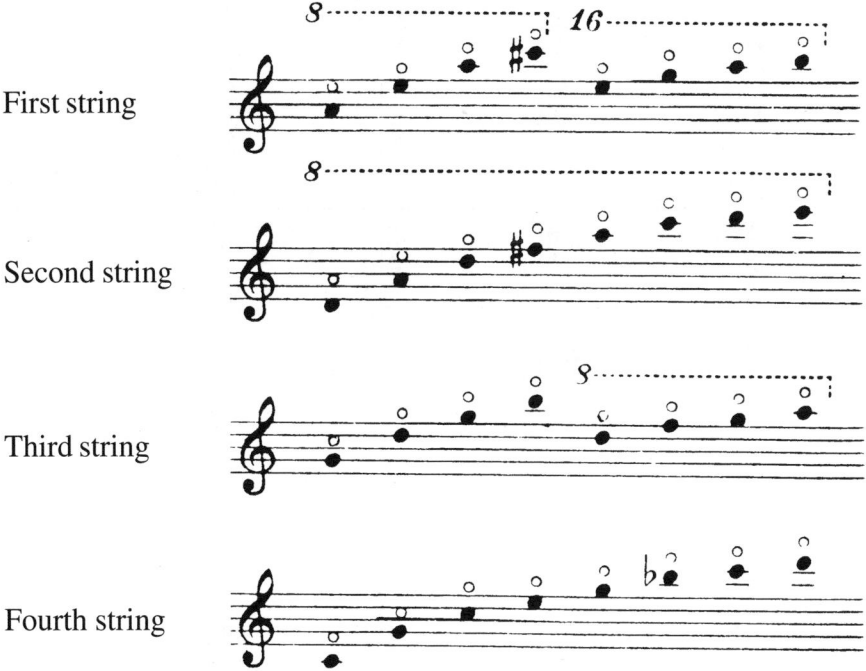

Double, triple, and quadruple chords

One will be able to use the following table indicating double, triple, and quadruple chords in the same way as on the violin. It should be noted, however, that the extension of the finger beyond the limits of one position is considered practically impossible on the viola due simply to the fingerboard's being much larger than that of the violin.

In chords of three and four notes it is necessary that (at least in the first two positions) the stretch between two fingers not go beyond that which comprises two boxes successively on the table. Also the stretch between the first note of a box and the last must be considered due to this stretch.

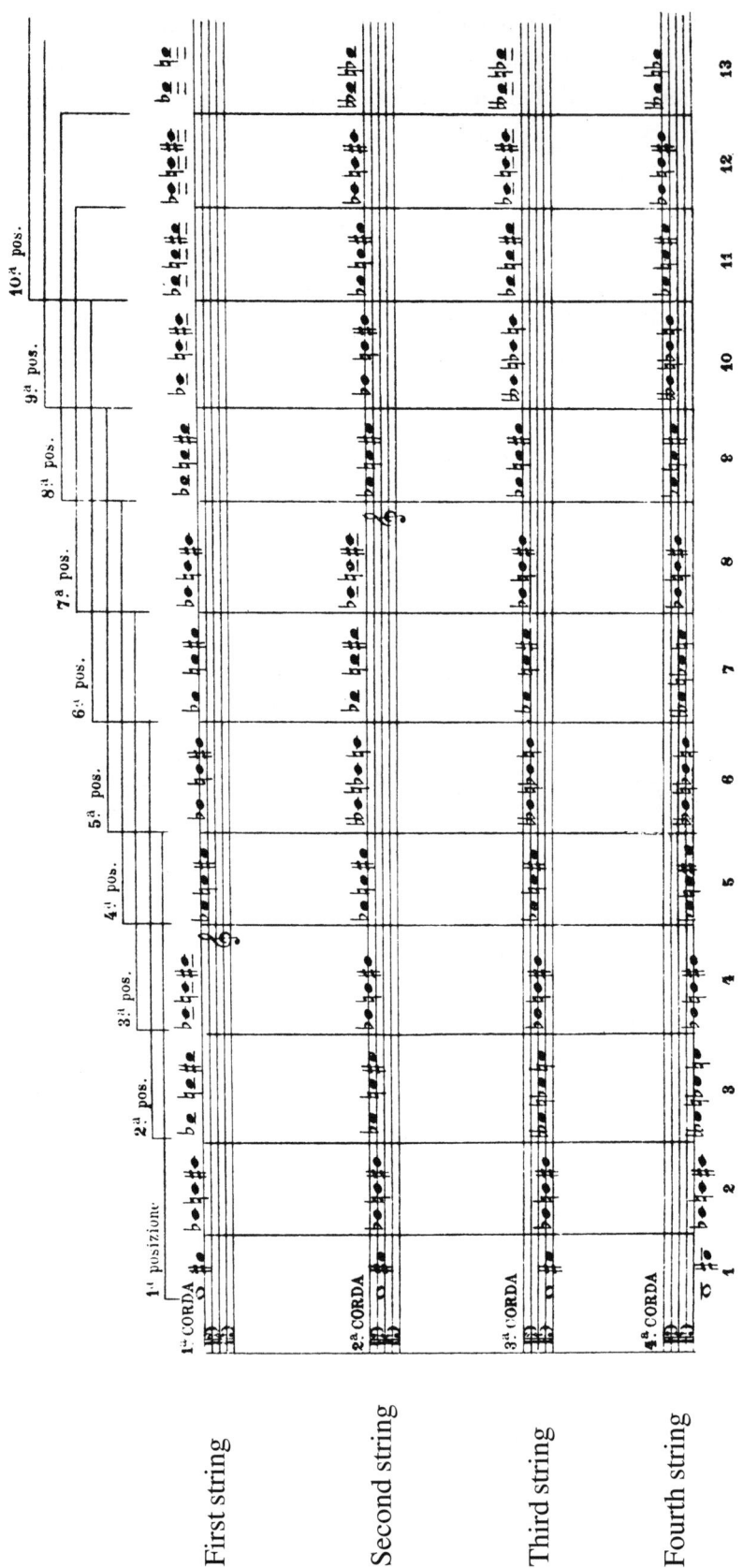

The following are some examples of chords:

(1) Uncomfortable because the enlargement imposed between the first and the second finger stiffens the other fingers and limits their spontaneity.
(2) The third finger has an uncomfortable position.
(3) On the viola, the perfect fifth is more difficult than on the violin because of the larger fingerboard. Its use should be limited and therefore its playing with the third or fourth finger.
(4) The extension of the fourth finger makes the position of the hand uncomfortable.
(5) G♯ interpreted enharmonically as A♭ and played in a more comfortable way with the fourth finger.

All of the chords proposed as examples are determined by the tables. Stravinsky in his *Trois pièces pour quatuor*, p.1, entrusts to the viola an interval of a minor ninth.

Mute

That which was given for the violin should be considered the same for the viola.

Other examples

The following prestissimo passage is quite difficult especially because of the large number of accidentals. The violist of the past (one knows that there was a time when only the worst violinist were violists) would make a terrorized face if he suddenly found a page of this difficulty. Moreover, today, the conductor will have to realize that he will have to settle for only an approximation for that overwhelming Straussian sonority. If one desires precise intonation and absolute neatness of execution, it would be best to accept that the viola will only be capable of less.

R. Strauss: *Elektra*, p. 186. Ed: Furstner

P. Hindemith: *Konzertmusik* for viola and big chamber orchestra, fourth movement. Ed: Schott's Sohne
E.R. 2935

The following is a model phrase that is thought to be in the character of the viola.

P. Hindemith: *Der Schwanendreher*, Concerto per viola e piccola orchestra, p. 23. Ed: Schott's Sohne

The following is an example of the use of the violas in the high register as second violins.

A. Casella: *Scarlattiana*, third part. Ed: Universal

VIOLA D'AMORE

During recent years, the old viola d'amore has received new interest either for a certain humanistic spirit that has oriented many musicians toward studies and research of the past (and therefore toward the curiosity of old timbres) or for the tendency to value sonorities in order to satisfy the curious unusual instincts of those who have lived and are living the great drama of contemporary music. Some violinists have dedicated themselves to the instrument, e.g., in Italy Professor Renzo Sabatini of the Naples Conservatory, a virtuoso and cultivated musician; in Germany, Paul Hindemith who also as composer honored this instrument in his *Sonata, o*p. 25 - II, VI *Kammermusik*, op. 46 - 1.

The viola d'amore has seven gut strings that once were tuned in a different way than now. It was the famous French performer, Chrétien Urban (1790-1845), who established the following tuning:

Under the fingerboard are fixed seven other strings of metal tuned in unison to those that are in the normal position on the instrument, i.e., these are able to vibrate in sympathy with a very effective resonance.

Range

Timbre

Berlioz in his treatise on instrumentation states: "The timbre of the viola d'amore is soft and sweet with a character that I would say is angelic, a combination of the harmonics of the violin and the viola, affording itself more to the legato style, to meditative melodies, and to ecstatic and religious sentiments."

It is important to cite the viola d'amore, since in recent years it has found a resurgence of interest among musicians. Nevertheless it is not expected to have a future in the orchestra. More than the citation that has been made would be useless. It is not worth, either, citing other types of viole (*viola da gamba*, *viola di bordone*, *viola pomposa*, etc.), for they are hardly known today. According to Eugenio Albini [1], the unsuccessful instrument that Zandonai had constructed specifically for *Francesca da Rimini* was not a *viola pomposa*, as he called it, but a small violoncello with five strings.

---

[1] Eugenio Albini: *Gli strumenti musicali moderni*, Ed. Paravia, Torino, 1936, p. 35.

VIOLONCELLO

For a very long time the violoncello remained primarily a means for cantabile passages that were not necessarily of a virtuosic nature. At the end of the eighteenth century its technique, however, was profoundly modified through the work of A. F. Servais who created the *puntale* (peg), the means for anchoring the instrument solidly on the floor. Previously the instrument had been held firm by the knees in such an uncomfortable way that that which could be done by the player was very limited. Also the *capotasto* [1], used for the first time by Boccherini and developed later by Romberg, Servais, Popper, and Piatti, has revolutionized the technique of the instrument and has extended its tessitura to a height to which the musicians of a century ago would have never thought possible.

Around 1910, the virtuoso and formidable Catalonian musician, Pablo Casals, brought the instrument to a dignity and a nobility before unknown. To this aim he developed an extension of the fingers as complement to the use of the *capotasto* to avoid the portamento and to be able to express oneself with greater efficiency. He adapted technical means toward the realization of great stylistic aspirations. To Casals, and many others, one must attribute the revival of the wonderful *Suites* by Bach for solo violoncello that before him were thought to be cold and arid recitations, good for only didactic purposes.

Tuning

The normal tuning of the strings for the instrument is as follows:

First string
Second string
Third string
Fourth string

Experiments exist of different tunings dating back to Bach who for one of his *Suites* for violoncello set this tuning:

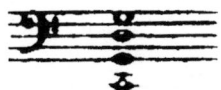

Recently further attempts of this kind have been made; however, performers find it uncomfortable to feel under the fingers an unusual tension of the strings. They prefer to play in the normal tuning even that music that was conceived for a different tuning.

---

(1) The *capotasto* is the high point of the keyboard, to which the strings are attached. This word, however, refers also to the thumb placed across the string at a right angle to press on the string in order to function as a moveable *capotasto*. The word almost always refers to this use. The *capotasto* is indicated by the following sign: ♀

Range

(1) In prudent passages with stepwise motion one can go above the A. This tessitura can give to the phrase a great expressive tension, but, in general, for the violoncelli of the orchestra it is better to not supersede the normal range. If one requests that performers in orchestra play out of the recommended tessitura, surely a loss of precious time in the rehearsal will occur. The A besides being a very good note, played normally, is also a very good easily reachable harmonic.

Clefs

The composer may write for the violoncello in the bass, tenor, and treble clefs depending on the need. However, once a practice existed that required the composer to write the notes an octave above their sounding pitch when the treble clef was followed immediately by the bass clef without the use of the tenor clef. Today, however, this strange anomaly has definitely been abandoned.

Timbre

The low register is secure and mysterious at *piano*, harsh at *forte*. The high register has such a possibility of sonorous penetration that it is often referred to as the tenor of the string section. The sound, masculine and sensual, whose seductive quality cannot be thwarted by lesser composers, is not to be abused, for it quickly reaches a satiable limit. The medium register is the least sonorous although capable of soft and delicate colors.

Production of the sound

The bow of the violoncello has recently made such progress that it is on an even par with the bow of the violin and the viola. It is suitable for all bowings and different ways of producing sounds (staccato, balzato, gettato, etc.).

Pizzicato

The pizzicato is most effective to 𝄢 . Above this note it becomes dryer, more opaque, and less vibrant. Plucking the string on the fingerboard produces a soft vibration with a sweet sonority. As one nears the bridge, the effect becomes more marked, very sonorous, and dry with an almost percussive accent.

For performance in the orchestra it is best not to go beyond 16th notes at a quarter note = 88; however, for brief passages this marking may be superseded. Stravinsky in the *Capriccio for piano and orchestra* hazards this quite daring passage that is most difficult for all of the celli.

I. Stravinsky: *Capriccio* for Piano and orchestra, p. 75. Ed: Schott's Söhne

Also the pizzicato lends itself to guitar effects strummed or arpeggiated, ascending or descending. An arrow "up" indicates that one should strum up, "down" for the opposite way. When there are no indications it should be assumed that one should use an up-stroke.

This passage, either up or down at *forte* or *piano*, should be approached no faster than 16th notes at a quarter = 100.

Tremolo

With regard to the regular execution of the tremolo, there are no different observations to be made than those on the other instruments. As for the movement between two sounds, it is suggested that the maximum stretch of the hand on the same string not be greater than a major third. With the use, however, of the technique previously described, the *capotasto*, other tremolos are possible as follows: for these intervals: major and minor 2nd, minor 3rd, perfect 4th, diminished 5th

N. B. - With the tremolos of a third, and above all with those of a second, one can ascend even more.

for the perfect 5th starting from the 2nd position, not below and not above

for a minor 6th starting from the 4th position, not below and not above

for a major 6th starting from the 5th position, not below and not above

for a minor 7th starting from the 6th position, not below and not above

for a major 7th and octave starting from the 7th position, not below and not above

The following uses all of the above tremolos.

(1) One is advised to use a rapid tremolo with the low C because the 4th open string with its slow vibrations gives the tremolo a quite confused effect.
(2) For the positions see the section on positions and fingerings.

It is obvious that all of the tremolos in the preceding passage must be played on the same string; therefore, one does not have to write any indication when the tremolo is of a certain width. In general, however, it is prudent to indicate the string on which the tremolo must take place in order to avoid the playing of the tremolo on two strings with a poor result.

Of course the virtuoso performer can supersede any of the limits that have been indicated.

Harmonics

The length of the strings of the violoncello are such that the harmonics are easy to play and are more beautiful and sonorous than on the violin. The following is a table of harmonics.

The 6th harmonic is for the most part difficult and inefficient.

Artificial harmonics

With the use of the *capotasto* it is possible to obtain the 3rd, 4th, 5th, and 6th harmonics. As was the case for natural harmonics, the 6th is likewise difficult here; however, on the first and second string it can be played quite easily. The 3rd is possible starting from the intermediate position between the 1st and 2nd position.

Pizzicato harmonics, especially natural ones, are quite sonorous.

Double harmonics are also possible on the violoncello. It is obvious that with natural harmonics the process is easier, but they are also possible with artificial harmonics provided that the two fundamental sounds are not different from those of the *capotasto*, i.e., they are in the relationship of a fifth.

Naturally these virtuoso techniques would be useless in writing for the orchestra, where, by dividing the cellos, there would be a way to achieve the effect with much more security.

Glissando

In general that which was said about the violin can be applied to the violoncello.

Glissando – of a fifth that is executed with the *capotasto* that slides on the strings.

Glissando – of harmonics that provides a wonderful effect.

The complete series of all the harmonics that are obtainable with the gliding of the finger pushing against the string are below. (Avoid fast tempos in the use of the very high harmonics due to their uncertainty and unpredictable intonation.)

First string

Second string

Third string

Fourth string

E.R. 2935

Glissando pizzicato:

M. Ravel: *Duo for violin and violoncello*, part II. Ed: Durand

V. Mortari: "Pizzicato" from the *Piccola Serenata for solo violoncello*. Ed: Carisch

C. Scott: *Pastoral and Reel*, p. 1. Ed: Schott

The following simple example was also used in the orchestra.

M. Ravel: *L'heure espagnole*, p. 41. Ed: Durand

The D with which the lower part begins takes the indication *sur le ré* (on the D), i.e., on the second string. Since, however, a glissando does not begin well on an open string, Ravel added "*Appuyer du bord du sillet de manière à altérer le ré aussi peu que possible tout en permettant à la corde de vibrer.*" (Lean on the side of the nut in a way to alter the D as little as possible so to enable the string to vibrate.)

Fingering and positions

The positions and the fingerings of the violoncello are very different from those of the violin and the viola, for the distance between one finger and another does not normally permit the embracing of more than a half step. The only exception is that of the distance between the first finger and the second that can cover an entire whole step. The position size, therefore, does not go beyond a major third. With the use, however, of the *capotasto*, the position enlarges up to a perfect fourth and, in some exceptions, up to a perfect fifth. As one ascends toward the upper register and the positions of the left hand become tighter, the thumb is used as the *capotasto*. The hand is moved in a way that the fourth finger, the shortest, is sacrificed and, often, not utilized; therefore, only for exceptions, and in the position of the *capotasto*, does one use the notes playable with the fourth finger.

The position of the left hand, therefore, has three aspects: (1) the normal position that covers the minor third; (2) the position with extension that covers a major third; (3) the *capotasto* position that allows the perfect fourth and in exceptional cases the perfect fifth.[1]

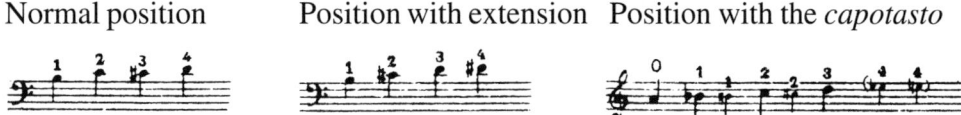

The left hand secures the first of the positions on that part of the finger board that is situated on the "handle" of the violoncello. From the 7th position and higher, the left hand covers positions on the part of the fingerboard that are above the body of the instrument and from this position the *capotasto* is used.

---

(1) In the high positions, as has been said and as will be seen, the possibilities of extensions increases until reaching in the highest, positions at the 2nd octave.

198

The following is a table of the positions:

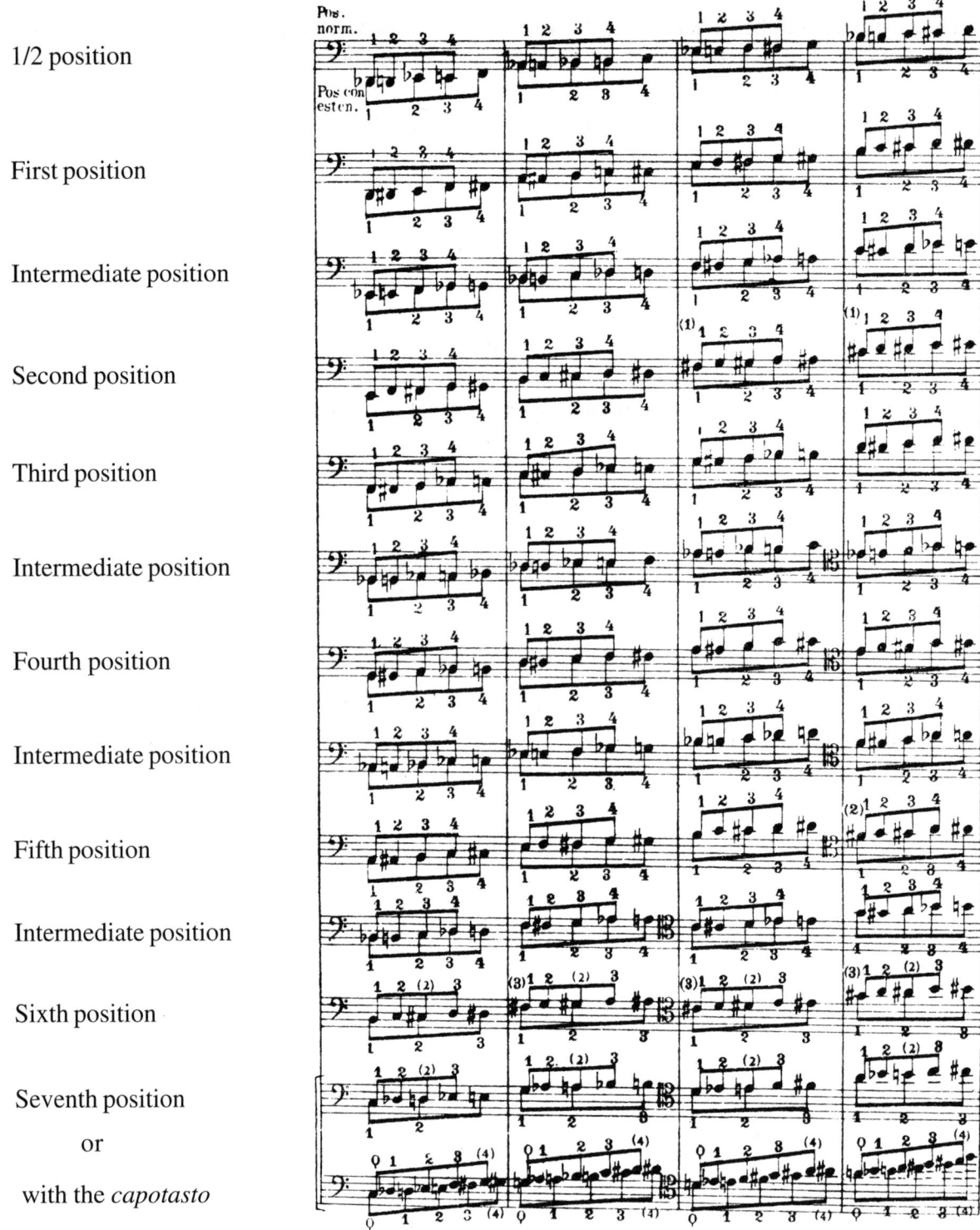

1/2 position

First position

Intermediate position

Second position

Third position

Intermediate position

Fourth position

Intermediate position

Fifth position

Intermediate position

Sixth position

Seventh position
or
with the *capotasto*

(1) The F♯ and not the F natural, and further, the C♯ and not C natural as the strictly diatonic traditional criterion of the positions prefer. Clearly illogical criteria impose the placement of a half step in the left hand thereby rendering a uselessly complicated concept of position.

(2) (3) For analogy that which is pointed to above is valid.

In the sixth and seventh positions normally the left hand is placed so that the fourth finger is most uncomfortable; therefore, in this high register in which the notes on the fingerboard are very close, the extension between the second and third or the third and fourth finger is possible. The stretch between these fingers can easily go the distance of a whole step and can cover a major third without the use of the fourth finger.

One should not go beyond the seventh position on the first string and as a rule, also in the *capotasto* positions. If the phrase remains in the tessitura of the seventh position and if it tends to become higher, one should use the *capotasto*. If, on the other hand, the high position is reached temporarily, then one should retain the lower positions and the *capotasto* should not be used.

From the table that precedes, it is clear that a scale can be played in the same position if the open strings are used in the formation of the scale. Only the first position lends itself well to this statement.

In other cases when there are no open strings, the scale must combine different positions.

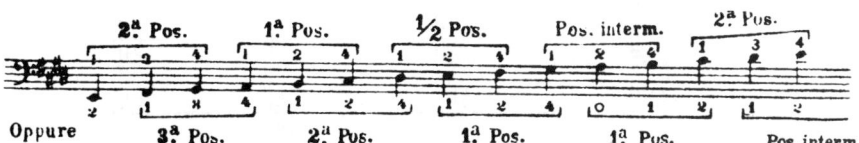

The chromatic scale regardless of its spelling should be played with the following combined positions.

All that is shown above refers to the basic technique used in orchestras today; however, the modern conquests of Casals, Alexanian, Stutschewsky, and others have opened new horizons to an epoch that does not seem near to closing. This spirit is still alive in all of the violoncellists of the world, above all in Casals. The modern cellist, for example, prefers, when and where it is possible, not to use the *capotasto* in cantabile passages simply because it is a technique that sacrifices expression. Therefore, in general, the player tends to prefer the first and the fourth positions that are the most comfortable.

Double, triple, quadruple chords

As for the violin and the viola, the table indicates double, triple, quadruple chords.

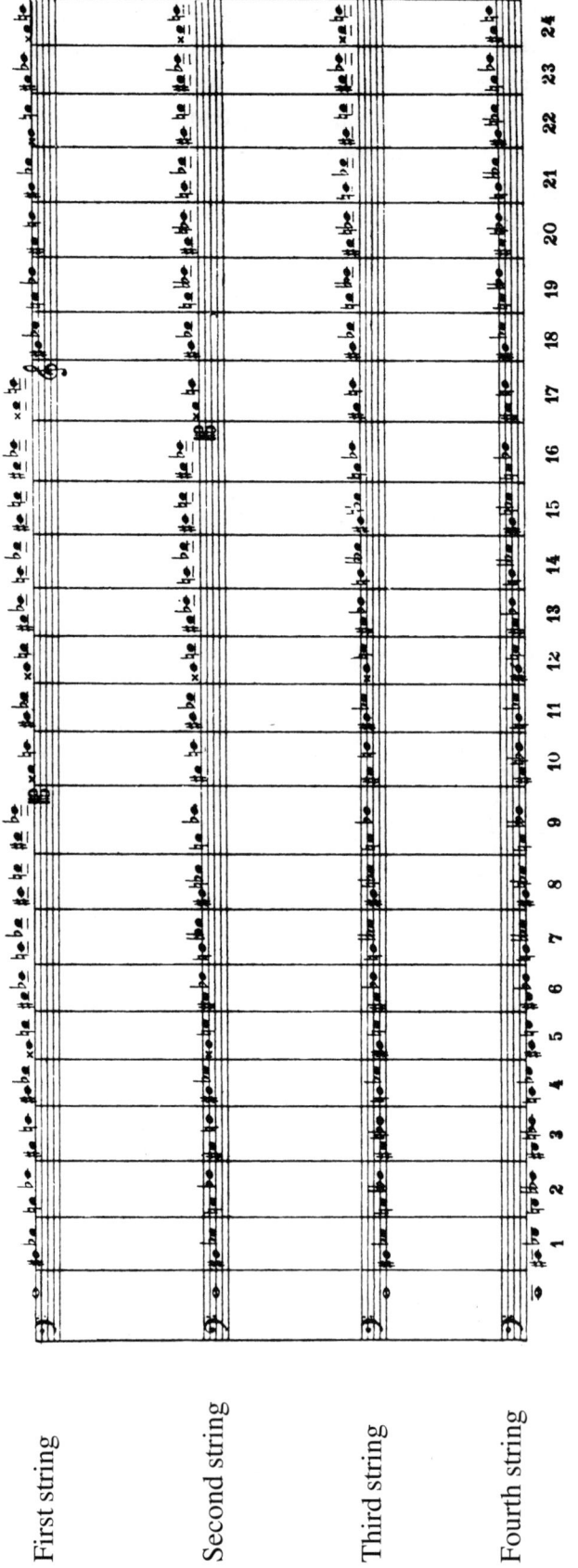

In this table the normal placement of the left hand covers a group of five boxes, in the limit of which the composer may select the notes that he needs for his combinations of two, three, or four sounds, distributed on two, three, or four strings.

By acknowledging any group, for example that which from box four goes to box 8 (inclusive), the following are some combinations of two, three, and four notes:

The note that one finds in the first box of the group considered, must be played as a rule with the first finger. The notes that are in the successive boxes must be played respectively with the second, third, and fourth fingers.

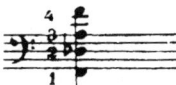

This chord is found in the group that goes from the fifth box to the ninth box. The low F is played with the first finger, because it is found in the first of the five boxes; the D♭ with the second because it is found in the second box, and so fourth.

This chord is found in the second group that goes from the third box to the seventh box. The C that is found in the first box of the group must be played with the first finger; the F that is in the third box, with the second. (Between the first and second finger a greater stretch is possible). The A♭ that is in the fourth box is played with the third finger; the D that is in the fifth box with the fourth.

One may refer to the following other chords on the table:

In the group of five boxes the fourth finger of the left hand can be placed in these two ways:

Boxes		I	II	III	IV	V
Fingers		1, 2	3	4		
	or	1	2	3	4 [1]	

Two notes in the same box may be played with the use of the thumb employing the *capotasto* if they are found on two successive chords (with the use of a small device it is possible for the thumb to cover three chords). Two, three, and also four notes found in the same box can be played with one finger if the finger is placed flat across the string therefore functioning as the *capotasto*. Infinite combinations are possible. The thumb placed on one or two strings allows the other fingers to extend on the fingerboard until reaching notes that in our table stay at the distance of five boxes, if the *capotasto* is in the first or second position; in the distance of seven boxes if the *capotasto* is in the third and fourth position; the distance of eight boxes if the *capotasto* remains above the fifth position.

---

(1) This second combination is obtained with a widening between the 1st and 2nd fingers.

One is advised to be prudent when writing for the violoncello in the orchestra. It is better to maintain the maximum limits indicated below.

(1) When the thumb is used as the *capotasto*, the hand is moved in a way that the fourth finger is sacrificed and often not used. In this case it is substituted with the second or third finger.

It is possible to use double strings throughout the entire range of the instrument on major and minor thirds, perfect, diminished, and augmented fourths and fifths, major and minor sixths, major and minor sevenths, and octaves. Likewise, the minor ninth starting from the second position, the major ninth starting from the third position, the tenth starting from the sixth position, the unison starting from the fourth position, the major second starting from the third position, and the minor second starting from the fourth position are possible.

Some examples of chords are as follows.

(1) When one uses the *capotasto* the hand moves; therefore, the other fingers cannot line up across the string. In this case a perfect fifth is obtained with two fingers held closely together.

(2) These three chords could be played also in fifth position and be therefore fingered as follows:

3	3	3
3	2	1
3	2	1
1	1	1

Of the first of these chords one observes that the double fifth (F, C, G) is uncomfortable played with the fourth finger. In general, the first finger can be comfortably extended flat across all of the four strings: also the second finger with minor discomfort. The third finger placed flat is fine if it does not cover more than three strings and the fourth not more than two strings.

(3) The fourth finger flattened for the fifth seriously threatens the vibration of the open C.

Double notes and chords in the high register or combinations of nonadjacent sounds are fine if they are not reached with a change of position. It is better if they are preceded by a pause or from notes that permit an opportune preparation.

Mute

The discussions pertaining to muting on the other string instruments apply likewise to the violoncello.

Examples of passages for the violoncello

V. Mortari: "Marcia" from the *Piccola Serenata for solo violoncello*. Ed: Carisch

M. Ravel: *Duo for violin and violoncello*, part IV. Ed: Durand

Two passages of pianistic origin and most unidiomatic for the violoncello at the fast tempo requested by the composer.

A. Casella: "Bourrée" from the *Sonata for piano and violoncello*. Ed: Universal

I. Stravinsky: *L'oiseau de feu*, p. 65. Ed: Chester

M. Ravel: *Duo for violin and violoncello*, part II. Ed: Durand

A. Schönberg: *Kammersymphonie*, p. 31. Ed: Universal

A Schönberg: *Erwartung*, p. 15. Ed: Universal

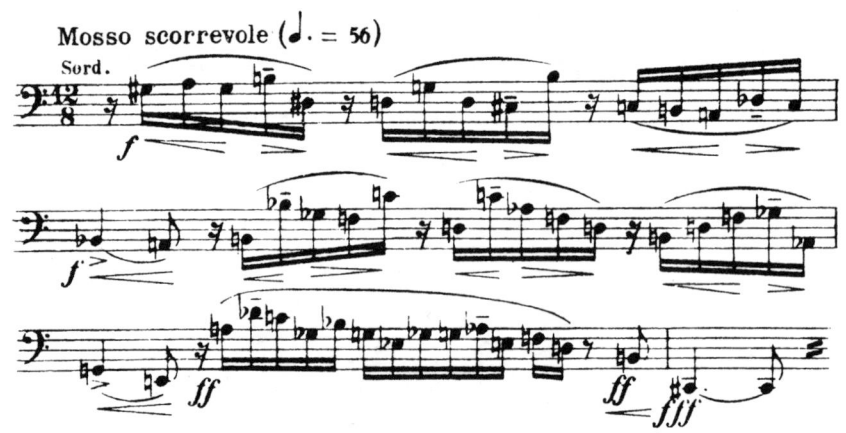

A. Schönberg: *Erwartung*, pp. 60-61. Ed: Universal

A. Schönberg: *Concerto* for violoncello and orchestra, p. 28. Ed: Universal
from a *Concerto for Harpsichord and Orchestra* of G.M. Monn. (1717-1750)

A. Schönberg: *Variazioni per orchestra*, op. 31, p. 50. Ed: Universal

CONTRABASS

The time when the contrabass was considered an unimportant instrument, as Berlioz called it *porteurs d'eau* (water carriers or porters), is quite remote. Its technique, as that on the other strings, has made enormous strides in that today it has proved itself as an instrument capable of an expressiveness heretofore unknown. It should be enough to prove the above to cite the admirable solo that accompanies, in the last act of Verdi's *Otello*, the entrance of the Moor as he approaches Desdemona in order to assassinate her. Certainly Verdi would have never dared write this passages in the days of *Nabucco* or in those of *Rigoletto*. Undoubtedly there will be a continued technical development.

Tuning

The old contrabass with three strings has now long disappeared. The modern instrument has four strings tuned as follows:

The sounding pitches are one octave lower:

On some contrabasses there is a fifth string added that reaches the low C.

In the modern orchestra there are generally at least two contrabasses with five strings.

Range   Sounding

(1) This G was chosen as the lowest extreme because besides its being a good note to rest on, it is, at the same time, an excellent harmonic and as such is easy to reach. The virtuoso, however, can always supersede these limits.

Timbre

While the first string, above all in the highest positions, has singing possibilities of a certain true sweetness, the other strings, especially the fourth, conserve a dark severity. The expressiveness of the contrabass can slide easily into certain effects, e.g., mysterious, dark, and grotesque parodies or, in very lyric passages it can flow easily into a languid, comic quality.

Production of the sound (bowings)

One can assume that all that was said for the violoncello concerning bowings applies to the contrabass; however, the bow is heavier and lends itself less to light and brilliant bowings. As for the other bowings, the nature of the instrument makes it less adaptable for certain effects than the violoncello. Nevertheless some brilliant effects are possible, e.g., the *balzato* and the staccato at half bow.

G. Verdi: *Falstaff*, beginning of act III. Ed: Ricordi

Pizzicato

The pizzicato is quite good to 𝄢 (sounding) 𝄢 . Above this note it becomes dryer and less vibrant. The technique becomes more sonorous when the notes coincide with a natural harmonic especially as one plays higher. Like on the violoncello, the pizzicato that is played on the fingerboard has a sweeter and softer sonority than other pizzicatos. Others become quite hard and marked when played at the place where the bow is normally used. Near the bridge produces an almost percussive effect.

For the normal performer in an orchestra it is best that the maximum tempo of the pizzicato not supersede 16ths at a quarter = 72. As for all instruments of course the virtuoso performer will be capable of executing faster tempos. The following is part of a pizzicato passage that tends to tire the hand simply due to its length and tempo.

P. Tchaikowsky: *Fourth Symphony,* "Scherzo". (pizzicato ostinato)

Tremolos

As for the true tremolo there are few important considerations. As regards the simple trill, it can be executed on the entire range of the instrument. Tremolos of a minor third with the exception of the fourth position are possible on the same string.

Starting from the fifth position, with the *capotasto* one can play tremolos of a major third and a perfect fourth.

Harmonics

The harmonics of the contrabass are most sonorous and beautiful. Their use in simple passages and in chords can be quite effective.

Natural Harmonics

The harmonics above the sixth must be used with great prudence. It is best that the left hand have time to slide on the string until reaching comfortably the position, a reaching that, evidently, presumes a progression that is stepwise. Starting from the ninth harmonic, the overtones are practically unusable. On the fourth string it is best not to go beyond the sixth harmonic. The fourth string, on the contrary, renders true harmonics that can be trusted, i.e., the fourth and fifth. The second and third are at times not secure.

The harmonics played pizzicato are more pleasing and effective than on the violoncello.

Given that which has been said about the stretch of the left hand, it is obvious that the production of artificial harmonics is feasible only in the highest positions where they are not easy.

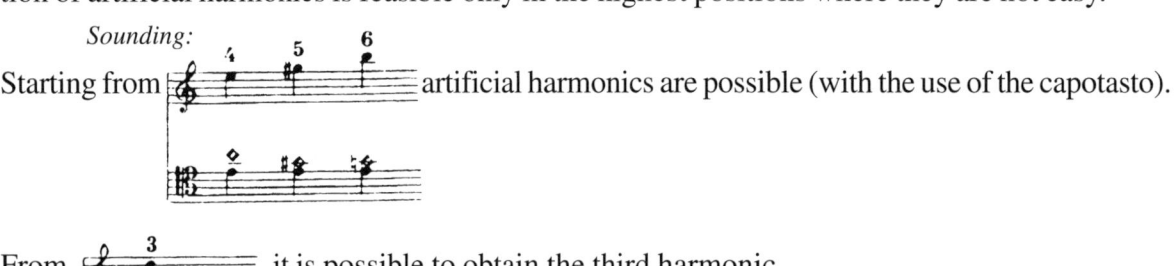

All these artificial harmonics can be played to:

Sounding:

However, it is better to be prudent and avoid the highest notes. They can be quite perilous, above all on the second and third string. The harmonics on the fourth string, natural and artificial, are quite opaque, of an almost cloudy nature, and can be at times difficult to execute.

Glissando

The glissando is an easy effect.

It is also possible to play the glissando pizzicato.

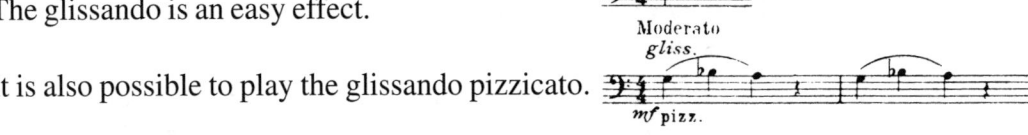

A glissando using harmonics is quite effective on the contrabass. For this effect one can press up to the twelfth harmonic on the first three strings and to the ninth harmonic on the fourth string.

Double strings

The use of double strings is possible in the range indicated below.

a minor and major third

a perfect fourth  — The perfect fourth is an interval that can be of uncertain intonation.

an augmented fourth

a perfect fifth

a minor and major sixth

a minor and major seventh

an octave

These two octaves  are difficult.

(1) This octave can be played with the use of harmonics giving  . The true limit, however, with use of harmonics is  .

In writing for orchestra double notes are of little use. Where used, it is best that they are limited to low positions that are less difficult and perilous in their execution.

Fingering and positions

Only with stretching can the distance between the first and second finger, or between the third and fourth, cover a half step, otherwise the normal reach between one finger and the other of the left hand, at least in the first positions, does not even cover this interval. The width of these intervals, therefore, must not be pushed pass the major second or the diminished third.

As one sees in the example, in order to cover a semitone two fingers are necessary, unless the first and second or third and fourth are used. Also on the contrabass it is possible to use the *capotasto*. The *capotasto* is used generally from the seventh position, i.e., where one finds the first harmonic, for it is easier and tuning is more secure. With the *capotasto* the normal stretch between two fingers is a half step and with the enlargement between the first and second finger, it may also reach a whole step. Starting from the fifth position the normal stretch of the left hand covers a minor third.

The *capotasto* can be used with exceptions in positions lower than the seventh. The high positions of the second and third string on some instruments can be quite perilous because with the natural lowering of the string in use, the bow can also touch the other strings.

A scale can be played in one position if the open strings are used; however, in this case one should take into consideration only the half step.

In the other cases, when open strings cannot be used, a scale is performed by combining different positions.

The chromatic scale, however it is spelled, is played usually with the following regular fingering pattern.

The following pattern, more modern, permits a small movement of the left hand.

Table of positions

	Fourth string	Third string	Second string	First string
1/2 position				
First position				
Intermediate position				
Second position				
Third position				
Intermediate position				
Fourth position				
Intermediate position				
Fifth position				
Sixth position				
Intermediate position				
Seventh position				
or				

Examples of passages for the Contrabass

(*) In the original manuscript Mozart scored *coll'arco roverscio* [sic] (with the bow turned over) that means unequivocally *col dorso dell'arco* (with the back or spine of the bow), i.e., *col legno*. In the Breitkopf edition Mozart's indication was interpreted, not very intelligently, as *f coll'arco cresc.*, a phrase that makes little sense. The passage, followed as Mozart wished it to be, is of singular and great effect.

S. Kussewitzky: *Studio*, Ed: Forberg

I. Stravinsky: "Duetto" from *Pulcinella*, p. 55. Ed: Russe de Musique

214

I. Stravinsky: pp. 52-53 id.

QUARTER TONE INSTRUMENTS

The aspirations of modern composers to stray from the tempered system has encouraged experiments with music using quarter tones. The most important among these can be found in the school founded in Prague in 1923 by Alois Hába and still directed by him today. [Note: Again one must realize that the reference was made in 1946 and that many composers have used quarter tones in their works since the time of Casella.] A piano in quarter tones was constructed at this school. The instrument utilized two keyboards tuned a quarter tone apart. Likewise in Prague wind instruments, a harmonium, and most recently a guitar were constructed.

These instruments are of course not in general use; however, they represent a great temptation for the explorations of a new musical language.

Instruments in quarter tones were also constructed in Italy by Professor Silvestro Baglioni of the University of Rome.

EXAMPLES OF ORCHESTRAL SCORES

V. Tommasini – *Paesaggi toscani* – pp. 39, 40 - Ed: Ricordi
Play of the woodwinds with the trumpets.

218

F. Busoni – *La sposa sorteggiata* – p. 87 - Ed: Breitkopf
Light orchestra

220

A. Honegger – *Rugby* – p. 30 - Ed: Salabert
Bold scoring for the winds: Allegro

V. D'Indy – *Jour d'été à la montagne* – p. 108 - Ed: Durand
The third of the chord is only given to the flutes.

E.R. 2935

G. F. Ghedini – *Maria d'Alessandra* – Act II, scene I – Ed: Ricordi
The piccolo is used in its lowest register.

F. Previtali – *Espressioni sinfoniche* – pp. 14, 15 – Ed: Ricordi
Treatment of the winds in a fugal setting.

E.R. 2935

A. Casella – *Sinfonia op. 63* – pp. 128, 129 – Ed: Universal
Light and mysterious orchestra.

Casella – *Sinfonia, op. 63* continued

V. Mortari – *L'allegra piazzetta* – Ed: Carisch S. A.
Wind soloists with grottesque effects.

D. Milhaud – *Cinq études pour piano et orchestre* – p. 18 – Ed: Universal
Duet between the trombone and the piano

P. Dukas – *Ariane et Barbe-Bleu* – pp. 71, 72 – Ed: Durand
Brilliant scoring of the winds.

Dukas – *Ariane et Barbe-Bleu* – continued

G. Mahler – *III Sinfonia* – p. 46 – Ed: Universal
Sonority of all the winds; note the low D in the timp.

G. F. Malipiero – *Pause del silenzio* – p. 54 – Ed: Chester
An example of a lugubrious sonority.

I. Stravinsky – *Oiseau de feu* – pp. 8, 9 – Ed: Chester
Colorful and fanciful orchestration.

Stravinsky – *Oiseau di feu* – continued

234

V. Mortari – *Fantasia per pianoforte e orchestra* – Ed: Forlivesi
Poetic and mysterious effect.

E.R. 2935

A. Casella – *La giara* – p. 100 – Ed: Universal
Double tongued notes by the tpts in a race with the violins.

A. Schönberg – *Erwartung* – pp. 63, 64 – Ed: Universal
Fluttertonguing by almost all of the winds.

Schönberg – *Erwartung* – continued

A. Casella – *Pagine di guerra* – pp. 36-39 – Ed: Chester
(Italian Battleships on the sea)

Casella – continued

Casella – continued

E.R. 2935

Casella – continued

E.R. 2935

M. Ravel – *Bolero* – p. 35 – Ed: Durand
Strings pizz like a guitar and the use of the piccolo trumpet.

E.R. 2935

A. Casella – *Paganiniana* – pp. 175, 176 – Ed: Universal

244

Casella – continued

E.R. 2935

V. Mortari – *Trittico* – Ed: Carisch S. A. *per soprano, mezzosoprano, coretto femminile e orchestra* – for soprano, mezzo soprano, feminine chorus, and orchestra.

Mortari – continued

F. Alfano – *Eliana* – p. 13 - Ed: Ricordi
Special effect by the bass drum.

G. Puccini – *Turandot* – p. 41 – Ed: Ricordi
Notable use of the percussion section.

O. Respighi – *Feste romane* – p. 60 – Ed: Ricordi
Use of the sleigh bells in a beautiful orchestral mixture.

I. Stravinsky – *Les Noces* – pp. 71, 72 – Ed: Universal
Most effective use of the percussion section.

Stravinsky – continued

G. Petrassi – *Coro di morti* – p. 47 – Ed: Suvini e Zerboni

253

The composer, Edgar Varèse, wrote an entire work, *Ionisation*, (Ed: Ricordi), for the percussion battery. The last section is below and following: pp. 21, 22, 23.

The sign: ![symbol] in the piano part indicates that all the chromatic tones between the two written notes must be played simultaneously by using the entire arm.

E.R. 2935

Ionisation – continued

Ionisation – continued

L. Dallapiccola – *Preghiera di Maria Stuarda* – Ed: Carisch S. A.

Dallapiccola – continued

Range of the instruments in the modern orchestra
The notes given under the bracket are considered to be the most effective area of the instrument's range.

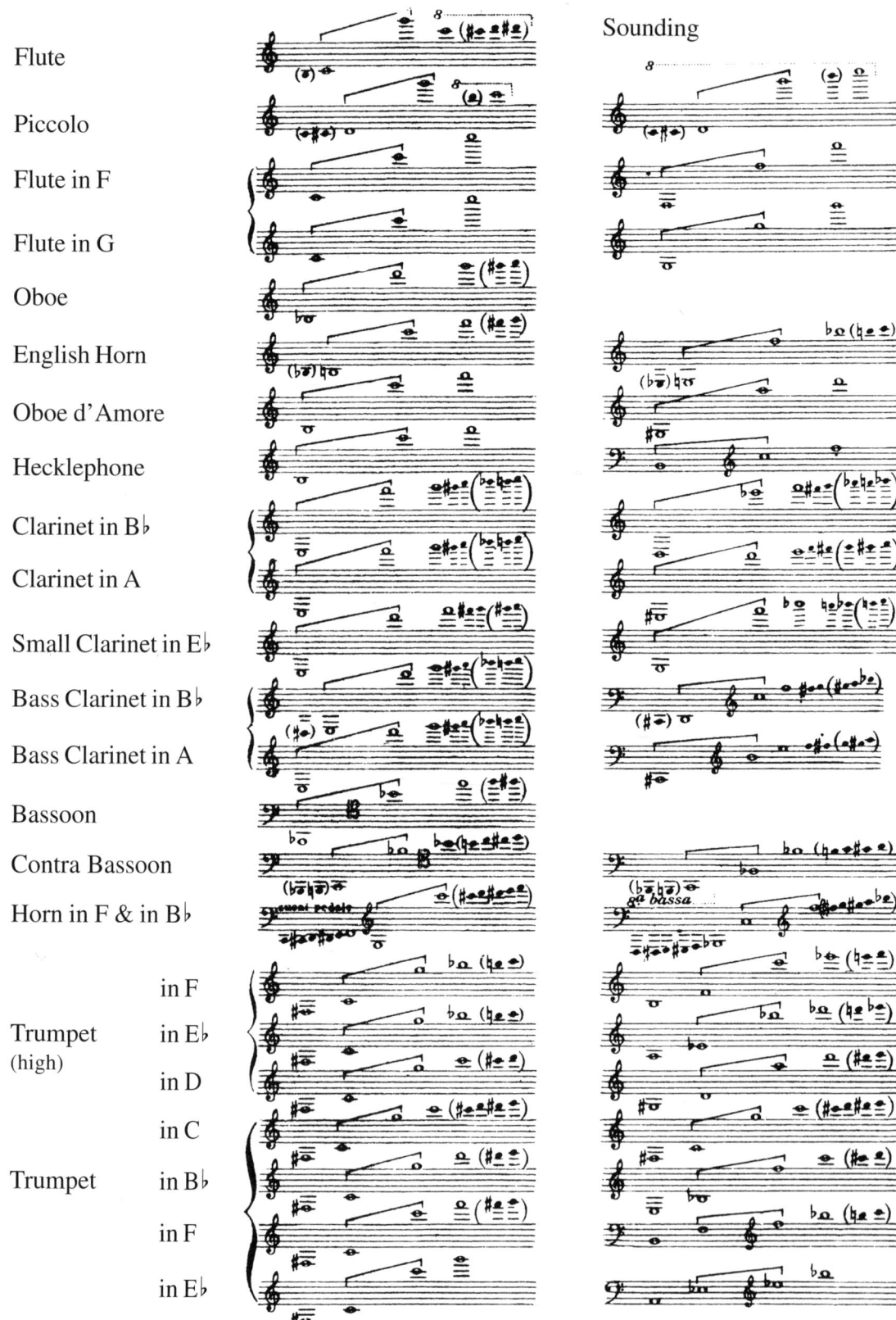

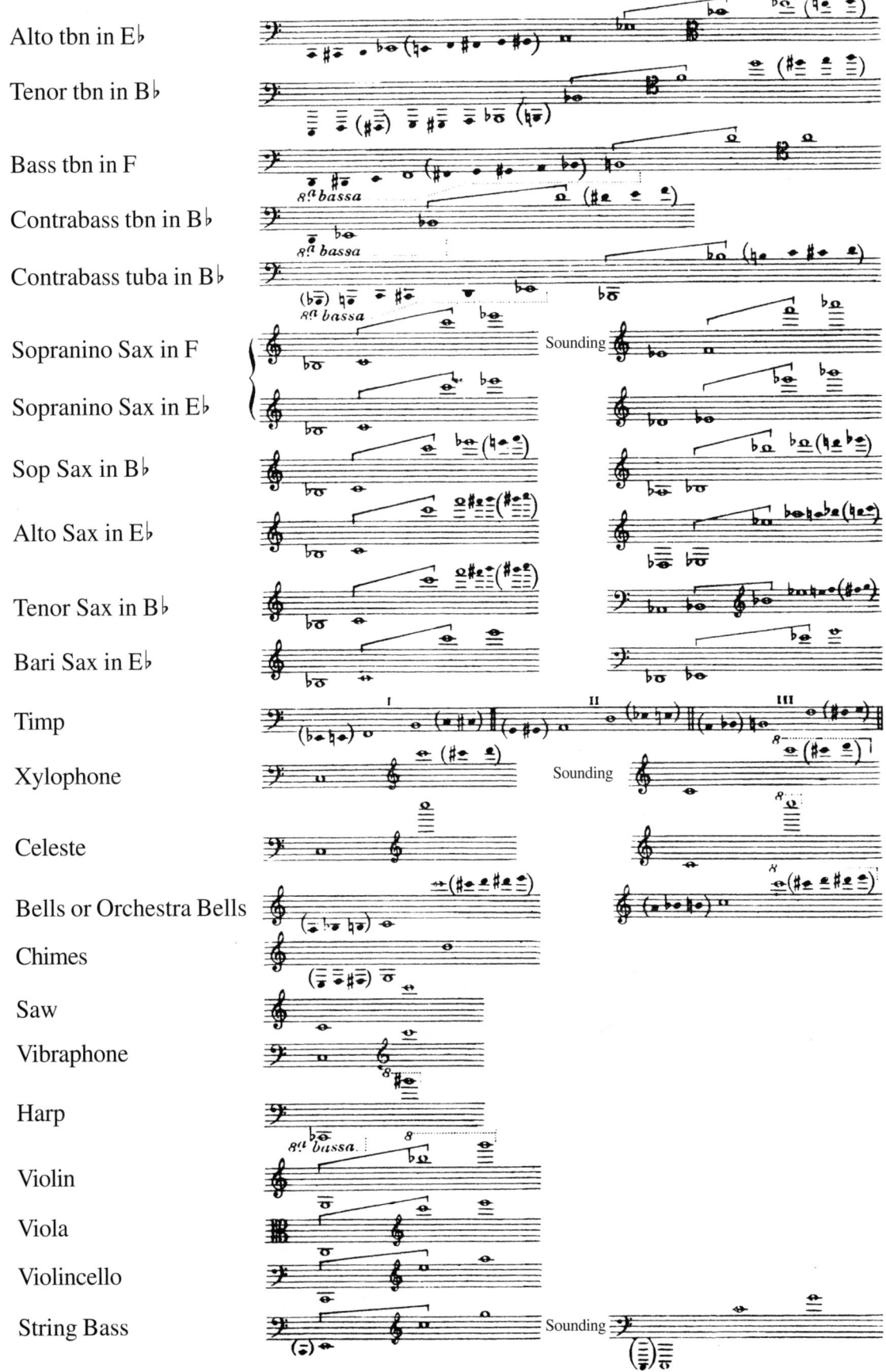

Trills on the wind instruments normally used in orchestra

The best range is that between the open notes, the range between the black notes is exceptional, generally difficult, of little spontaneity, and often defective.

(x) more or less defective or of little difficulty
(xx) difficult and of poor effect
(xxx) impossible, or almost, and very poor
(1) not always possible

Range of the most used tremolos on the wind instruments

(x) more or less diffective or a little difficult
(xx) difficult or of poor effect
(xxx) impossible, or almost, and very poor
(1) good or best or conditionally possible

Natural Harmonics on the String Instruments

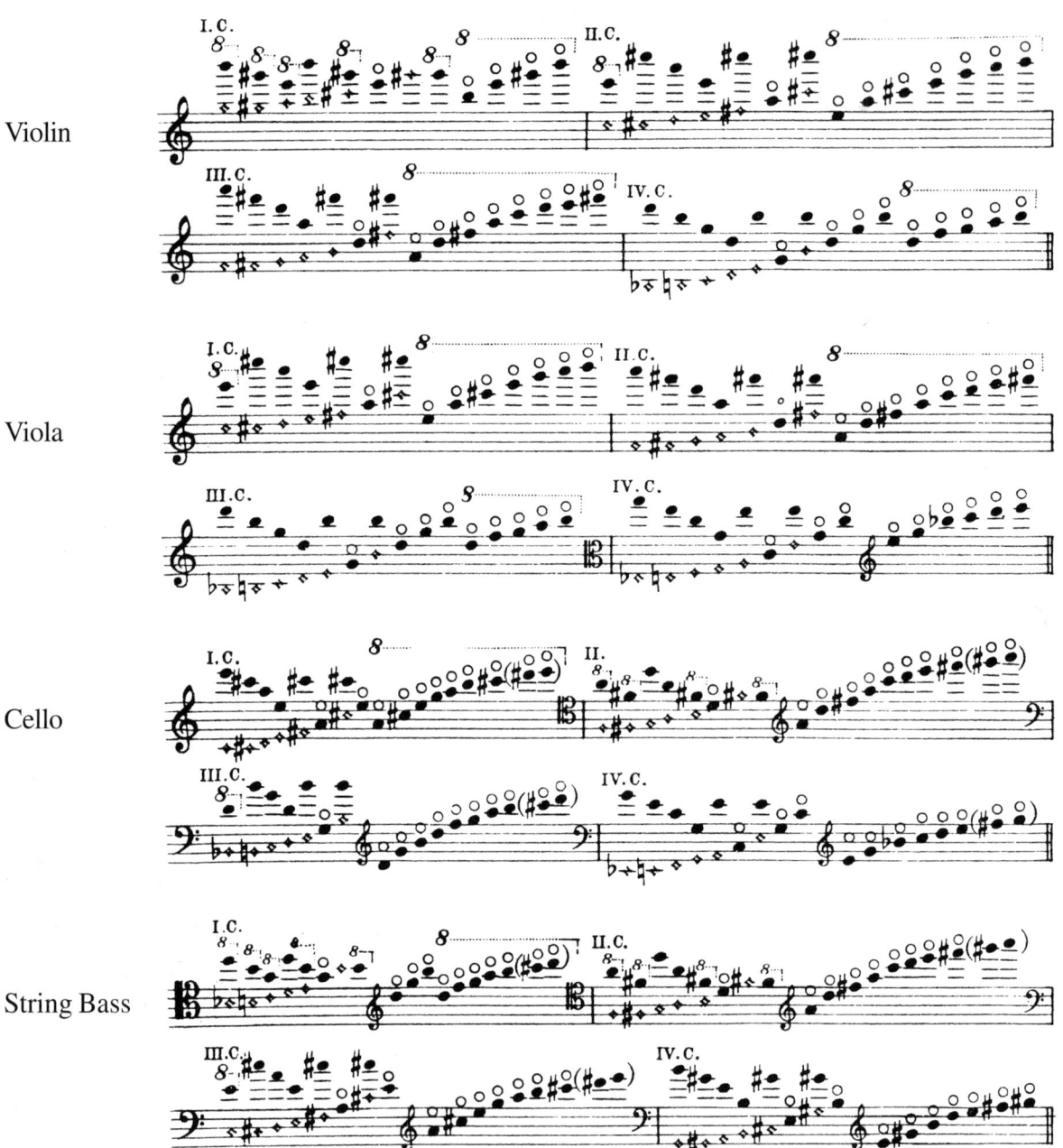

IN CLOSING

Although this treatise was written with care, it is necessary to realize that a work of this kind is always restrained by certain limits and that, as in all art, the contents need daily practice, the sum of the experiences of an entire life, and experiences that often encompass more sweat than art.

To the young composer who begins the difficult study of orchestration, we wanted to offer the most practical ideas possible given by those whom we consulted; however, this could not be enough. It is necessary to keep in continuous contact with the most knowledgeable professors of the orchestra, ask them questions often, learn from their practices, from their specific competencies, and from their ability. All things cannot be contained in one text. In this way usually one can reach a true knowledge of the instruments and hope therefore to be able to face the obscure and dangerous road of the future. So it was with the great composers like Stravinsky and Ravel. For all of their lives they were in close and determined contact with the practices of the performers.

With this advice, dictated by long and lived experience, we close our work and hope that it is useful to the young, who are all set to learn the art of orchestration, a fascinating, very difficult, and complex art. It will not tolerate amateurishness.

A. C. - V. M.

Rome, September 1946

INDEX

Chapter	Page
Preface	5
Consultants	6
The sound	7
Flute	12
Piccolo	26
Alto Flute	29
Bass Flute	30
Oboe	31
English Horn	39
Oboe d'amore	42
Soprano Oboe	42
Heckelphone	42
Clarinet	43
Small Clarinet	51
Alto Clarinet	52
Bassett Horn	53
Bass Clarinet	53
Contrabass Clarinet	55
Bassoon.	56
Contrabassoon	65
Sarrusaphone	67

Positions on the Brasses 69

Trills on the Instruments with Mouthpieces 74

Summary of the Trills for the Instruments with Mouthpieces 75

Horn 78

Trumpet in C, in B♭, in F, in D 89

Bass Trumpet in E♭, in C, in B♭ 94

High Trumpet in E♭, in F 95

Very High Trumpet in B♭ 95

Cornet 96

Tenor/Bass Trombone 99

Alto Trombone 109

Bass Trombone 109

Contrabass Trombone 109

Flicorni and Tubas 110
    Sopracuto Flicorno
    Sopranino Flicorno
    Soprano Flicorno
    Contralto Flicorno
    Tenor Flicorno (Bombardino)
    Bass Flicorno (Euphonium and Bass Tuba)
    Basso Grave Flicorno (Bombardone) and Contrabass Tuba
    Tuba, the Double Contrabass
    Wagnerian Tuba

Saxophone 117

Percussion 124

a) Instruments of determined pitch 124

b) Instruments of indeterminate pitch 127

Summary of the Percussion 132

Various Instruments More or Less in Use in the Orchestra 133

    Bells   Flexatone
    Chimes   Vibraphone
    Mandolin   Harmonica
    Guitar   Harmonium
    Saw   Ondes Martenot

Jazz 137

Harp 141

Piano 150

Harpsichord 153

The String Instruments 160

    Violin (161)
    Viola (182)
    Viola d'amore (189)
    Violoncello(191)
    Contrabass(206)

Quarter Tone Instruments 215

Examples 216

Normally Used Ranges of the Instruments 258

Trills on the Woodwind Instruments 260

Normally Used Tremolos on the Woodwinds 262

Natural Harmonics on the String Instruments 264

In Closing 265

Index 266

Index of Names 269

Additional charts 274
    Trills for the Double Horn
    Trills for All of the Trumpets
    Trills for the Flicorni from the Flicorno in B♭ to the Trombones

Casella / Mortari / Fraschillo 275, 276, 277

INDEX OF NAMES

Albeniz, I. – 108

Albini, E. – 190

Albisi, A. – 23, 30

Alexanian, D. – 199

Alfano, F. – 247

Bach, J. S. – 39, 95, 134, 153, 184, 193

Baglioni, S. – 215

Balakireff, M. – 127

Bartók, B. – 128, 170, 177

Beethoven, L. – 53, 69, 89, 127, 150, 165, 168

Berg, A. – 135, 179

Berlioz, H. – 51, 121, 128, 152

Bizet, G. – 121

Bloch, E. – 184

Boccherini, L. – 191

Böhm, Th. – 12, 26, 43

Buffet L. A. – 43, 56

Busoni, F. – 219

Casals, P. – 191, 199

Casella, A. – 14, 62, 63, 87, 89, 93, 97, 108, 114f, 124, 126f, 130, 132, 133, 135, 143, 152, 153, 161, 189, 203, 215, 224, 235, 238, 243, 275

Caselnuovo–Tedesco, M. – 48, 59, 168

Catalani, A. – 28, 42

Ciaikowsky, P. I. – 60, 207

Colacicchi, L. – 140

D'Indy, V. – 55, 124, 150, 220

Dallapiccola, L. – 129, 132, 135, 256

De Falla, M. – 43, 159

Debussy, C. – 13, 15, 21, 23, 25, 27, 28, 79, 126, 128, 150, 170

Denner, J. Ch. – 43

Dorsey, T. – 138

Dukas, P. – 38, 62, 228

Ehlers, A. – 153

Ellington, D. – 138

Frescobaldi, G. – 153

Gerlin, R. – 153

Gershwin, G. – 115, 121

Ghedini, G. F. – 221

Gounod, C. – 128

Grock, P. – 44

Hába, A. – 215

Hampton, L. – 138

Händel, G. F. – 91, 95

Harich–Schneider, E. – 153

Haydn, J. – 127

Heckel, W. – 56, 57, 58

Hindemith, P. – 107, 149, 182, 188, 189

Honegger, A. – 37, 91, 220

Ibert J. – 101

Incagnoli, S. – 31

James, H. – 138

Kirkpatrick, R. – 153

Kochansky, P. – 181

Kreisler, F. – 165

Krenek, E. – 134

Kussewitzky, S. – 212

Landowska, W. – 153

Liszt, F. – 54

Lorée, F. – 31

Mahler, G. – 50, 56, 79, 80, 115, 130, 131, 132, 133, 134, 150, 161, 162, 230

Malipiero, G. F. – 231

Martenot (Brothers) – 136

Mascagni, P. – 48

Meyerbeer, G. – 53

Milhaud, D. – 89, 227

Miller, G. – 137

Molière, G. B. – 45

Monteverdi, C. – 165

Mortari, V. – 22, 57, 92, 142, 143, 149, 165, 196, 203, 226, 234, 245

Mozart, W. A. – 44, 53, 100, 104, 133, 150, 166, 182, 221

Mussorgski, M. – 39, 84, 113, 123

Muzzi, P. – 72

Paganini, N. – 163, 164

Pelitti, G. – 112

Perrachio, L. – 149

Petrassi, G. – 24, 105, 118, 132, 252

Petrolini, E. – 45

Piatti, A. C. – 191

Pizzetti, I. – 13, 32, 44

Popper, D – 191

Poulenc, F. – 107

Previtali, F. – 222

Puccini, G – 126, 133, 248

Pugnani, G. – 165

Ravel, M. – 20, 22f, 25f, 30, 33, 35, 37f, 42, 46, 53f, 60f, 63, 66, 87, 89, 92f, 94, 101, 107, 113, 118, 123, 124, 127, 130f, 148, 172, 178, 184, 196, 203, 242

Respighi, O. – 12, 88, 89, 110, 130, 250

Rimsky-Korsakov, N. – 36, 41, 47, 57, 59, 127, 166

Romberg, S. – 191

Rossini, G. – 150

Sabatini, R. – 189

Saint–Saëns, C. – 41, 55, 62, 94, 126, 128

Salò (da), G. – 161

Salzedo, C. – 146

Sax, A. – 55

Scarlatti, D. – 153

Schaeffner, A. – 15

Schillings, M. – 42

Schönberg, A. – 12, 19, 22, 27, 47, 50, 54f, 88f, 108, 134, 204, 205, 236

Scott, C. – 196

Scozzi, R. – 31

Segovia, A. – 134

Selmer, H. – 118

Servais, A. F. – 191

Shakespeare, W. – 48, 59, 150

Spivack, Ch. – 138

Stradivari, A. – 161

Strauss, R. – 42, 53, 66, 80, 107, 113f, 121, 129f, 162, 188

Stravinsky, I. – 12, 15, 17f, 22, 29, 33, 37, 40, 49f, 52, 54, 62, 64f, 88f, 94f, 109, 114, 116, 127f, 137, 150, 151, 160, 178, 181, 182, 192, 203, 208, 214, 232, 150

Stutschewsky, J. – 199

Szimanowsky, K. – 163, 178f

Tansman, A. – 14

Tertis, L. – 183

Tocchi, G. L. – 146, 149

Tommasini, V. – 217

Urban, Ch. – 189

Varèse, E. – 127, 129, 131, 253

Verdi, G. – 79, 177, 206f

Veretti, A. – 135

Vignanelli, F. – 153

Vivaldi, A. – 43, 133

Wagner, R. – 12, 51, 53f, 56, 79, 100, 109, 113, 128

Walton, W. – 47, 182

Weber, C. – 44

Whiteman, P. – 140

Widor, Ch. M. – 160

Wieniawski, H. – 165

Zandonai, R. – 30, 38, 190

N. B. – The notable length of the tubing of the horn makes the emission of the sound more difficult, above all in the low register, and those trills that employ the valves will be very defective.

The use of the right hand in the bell can correct the sounds and collaborate with all elements for the excellent production of all trills.

I. Trills for the Double Horn in F/B♭

★ trills obtainable with only the lip * more or less defective
** not advised because of the difficulty or of poor result (horn in B♭) *** impossible, or almost, or very bad

(1) One can trill also with the valve.
(2) The trills on this line employ the seventh partial and therefore are defective.
(3) From ( ) and up all of the large trills are possible with only the use of the lip, and therefore are difficult.

273

II. Trills for all of the Trumpets and the Flicorni from the Sopranino in B♭ to the Baritone Flicorno in B♭

* more or less defective
** not advised because of the difficulty or bad effect
*** impossible, or almost, or very bad

(1) the trills on this line use the seventh partial and therefore are most defective.
The trills in the last three columns produce with different harmonics from those indicated on the top line.

III. Trills for the Flicorni from the Flicorno in B♭ to the Contrabass Flicorno in B♭, the Tubas, and the Trombones with valves

* more or less defective
** not advised because of the difficulty or bad effect
*** impossible, or almost, or very bad

(In this table the old notation is used, i.e., equal for all of the instruments regardless of how they are tuned. The sounding notation has been adopted for the lowest instruments).

(1) the trills on this line use the seventh partial and therefore are most defective.
(2) the use of the treble clef for the writing of high notes imposes a movement at the octave above, according to the so called uniform notation, that in this case is illogical and therefore is not observed in this text. The trills in the last three columns are produced with different harmonics from those indicated on the top line.

Alfredo Casella (1883-1947)

Born in Turin in 1883, Alfredo Casella showed early ability as a pianist. He received his first piano lessons from his mother, and at the age of twelve sought entry into the Paris Conservatory. In 1901, he was admitted into the composition class of Gabriel Fauré. In total, Casella remained in Paris for almost nineteen years, during which time he was closely associated with Ravel and Enescu. His compositions, however, fell more under the influence of Gustav Mahler and Richard Strauss rather than the impressionists.

In those early years in Paris, he enjoyed a career as pianist and harpsichordist, working as an accompanist and in chamber music. This was also the period in which he wrote his first two symphonies. While his music changed directions with the influence of Stravinsky, it received little public acclaim.

In 1915, Casella returned to Italy and settled in Rome, taking up the modest post of piano teacher at the Conservatory of Music of Santa Cecilia. In 1923, he gained the position of presenting piano masterclasses at the conservatory, and became an influential figure to young Italian musicians. In 1923, he organized the *Corporazione delle Nuove Musiche*, affiliated with the International Society for Contemporary Music; the members among whom were Respighi, Malipiero, Castelnuovo-Tedesco, and the conductor/composer Vittorio Gui. Today, considering its membership, the organization would hardly have been thought revolutionary. While the group soon dissolved, Casella remained a leading figure in the crusade to bring a wider awareness of contemporary musical trends to the Italian public and was regarded as a leading figure in Italian music of his time.

A proponent of fascism, he died before international retribution on those who supported this cause could be made. His works encompass every genre: operas, ballets, symphonies, concertos, and a considerable quantity of orchestral, chamber, and instrumental music. This text is one of his final accomplishments.

Virgilio Mortari (1902-1993)

Virgilio Mortari studied at the Conservatory of Milan with C. A. Bossi and I. Pizzetti. By the time he received the diploma in piano and composition, he had already been named the winner of the first competition for composition by the *Società Italiana di Musica Contemporanea* for his *Sonata per pianoforte, violino, e violoncello*. His next great success came in 1927 with performances in Italy and France of his chamber opera, *Secchi e Sberlecchi*. After some activity as a professional pianist, Mortari completely dedicated his efforts to composition and teaching. From 1933 to 1940, he was professor of composition at the B. Marcello Conservatory in Venice and in 1940, he took the same position at the Saint Cecilia Conservatory in Rome. In 1934, he founded in Venice an association for chamber music and following this effort, collaborated with Alessandro Casella in the founding and organization of the *Settimane Musicali Senesi*. From 1944 to 1946, he served as artistic director of the *Accademia Filarmonica Romana,* and from 1955 to 1959, he held the directorship of the *Teatro La Fenice a Venezia*. In 1963, he was appointed vice president of the Saint Cecilia Conservatory in Rome. Winner of many composition prizes, he was the first Italian to be awarded the *Montaigne* in 1980.

The position of Mortari among Italian composers of the twentieth century is quite singular. Although neither isolated, an imitator, or the head of a school, he was always a part of Italian musical life and was undecidedly a member of the Casella revolution, having been a disciple of Pizzetti. He was responsible for the solid academic formation of many young Italian musicians.

Thomas V. Fraschillo, DMA

Thomas V. Fraschillo has served as catalyst and mentor for the music profession in the area of Wind Music for 35 years. His influence on extremely high standards of performance has been felt by virtually every wind music organization in the Southeast and his performances serve as models throughout the world whether in the professional or academic arena. Through his recent recordings, *The Music of Luigi Zaninelli* and *L'Orchestra di fiati-University of Southern Mississippi Wind Ensemble* (recorded in Italy with the USM Wind Ensemble), and his publishing, conducting, and lecturing in the United States and Italy, he is considered an international musician/scholar. His most recent publication, a translation from the original Italian of Alessandro Vessella's *Studi di strumentazione (Instrumentation Studies)* published by BMG Ricordi, Milan, and distributed in the United States by Shawnee Press, has put his name in music libraries of the English speaking world. As a result of this effort BMG Ricordi has contracted Dr. Fraschillo to complete a translation of probably the most significant music publication on writing for orchestra in Europe after the second world war, *La Tecnica dell'orchestra*, by A. Casella. Publication of this text will take place in the spring of 2004. Further Dr. Fraschillo serves as a frequent conductor and lecturer in Italy as an American scholar. It should be noted that he lectures in Italy in the Italian language. His most recent conducting in Italy has been with *La banda dell'esercito*/The Italian Army Band from Rome in November 2002. His engagement with them in the summer of 2002 also signaled a very important first for the Italian Army in that Dr. Fraschillo was the first American born conductor to have been invited to appear in a public performance by what is considered Italy's most prestigious wind ensemble. The concert with Dr. Fraschillo conducting was the opening concert of the International Festival in Spoleto, "The Festival of Two Worlds, *Festival dei due mondi*." His appearance was enormously significant for Conductors of Bands in that the opening performance featured such international artists as Gian Carlo Menotti, the renowned composer who organized and began the event some 25 years ago, the Orchestra and Giuseppe Verdi Chorus of Milan with Riccardo Chailly conducting, and the famous Italian actress, Claudia Cardinale whose work was being displayed in a film retrospective.

Dr. Fraschillo has devoted a significant amount of his career to the education of young people in both Mississippi's urban and rural environments. For example his ten-year tenure at Meridian High School was highlighted by an invitation to perform at the Midwest International Band and Orchestra Clinic in Chicago, the nation's oldest and most prestigious music event for wind and string educators. The invitation was only the second to have ever been given to a band from Mississippi until now. In December, 2001, a former USM student of Dr. Fraschillo, Mohamad Schuman of Stone County High School, was the third conductor to take a group from Mississippi to perform for this international audience. Further Dr. Fraschillo's students have broken barriers not before reached, for he taught and helped place the first two African-American female students from Meridian, Vanessa Cox and Melanie Thomas, in the Mississippi Lions All-State Band. Not only were they the first to be minority female members, but also they were the first African-American young women to be in the very highest positions in the group.

Dr. Fraschillo has attained a level of international leadership that has significantly raised the awareness of bands by professional musicians from throughout the USA, Europe, Asia, and Canada in that he has served as President of the world's largest organization for band directors, the National Band Association, and now serves as its Executive Secretary. As the recently elected Vice President of the prestigious American Bandmasters Association, Dr. Fraschillo will proceed through the sequence to the president's position following a long line of distinguishedpast presidents. Further he serves as secretary and member of the Board of Directors of the Chicago based Sudler Foundation, a foundation that enhances the music education and experiences of young people through the John Philip Sousa Honor Bands and various competitions for young conductors, e.g., the Sir Georg Solti International Young Conductors Competition in honor of the late Sir Georg Solti, conductor of the Chicago Symphony Orchestra.

Under his leadership the University of Southern Mississippi's Wind Ensemble has been featured on frequent public radio broadcasts in Mississippi, on *Performance Today*, a program of PRI (Public Radio International), and has performed for many regional and national conventions including those of the American Bandmasters Association and the College Band Director's National Association. In 1998, he brought the national convention of the American Bandmasters Association to the Mississippi Gulf Coast for its annual meeting.

As a result of all of the above he is constantly in demand as a conductor and lecturer throughout the world and attracts a steady stream of graduate students to USM to study in its Doctor of Musical Arts in Conducting degree program.

INGRAF s.r.l. - Via Monte S. Genesio 7 - Milano
Stampato in Italia - Printed in Italy - Imprimé en Italie 2004